BARBARA GRAY, CFA

Secrets of the Amazon III

A strategic map for investors & CEOs to survive & conquer the new disruptive era

First published by Brady Capital Research Inc. 2019

First edition

ISBN: 978-1-9994884-2-0

This book was professionally typeset on Reedsy.
Find out more at reedsy.com

Contents

Advance Praise for Secrets of the Amazon III

Barbara takes you into a disorienting new world, one of fascinating innovation and peril, where traditional organization and business models are being shredded. Sixty-five million years ago, out of the darkness of space, a meteorite smashed into earth and wiped out the dinosaurs. Today, entrepreneurs are harnessing the power of instantaneous communication, e-commerce, Al, machine learning, and quantum computing to deliver an annihilating hit to established organizations and businesses of all sizes. Within these pages you will find out what you must do to not only survive, but prosper!

— *Rob McEwen, Chief Owner, McEwen Mining Inc. & Founder, Goldcorp Inc.*

Barbara reminds me of storm chasers who model and predict where the tornado is going to fall next. Although trained as a sharp financial analyst, in writing *Secrets of the Amazon III*, Barbara masterfully intertwines her unique macro observations on human behaviour (or as she calls it Emotional Capital) and its impact at the micro level within a company or sector. If you pay attention, you may even be able to avoid the proverbial tornado.

— *Deepak Chopra, Former CEO, Canada Post Corporation*

Barbara constantly explores disruption and the possibilities of where financial markets want or could go. Her works are essential reading, if you mentally want to "*understand and stay a step ahead of the market*".

— *J. Lorne Braithwaite, Founder, Cambridge Shopping Centers Ltd. (Ivanhoe Cambridge)*

Barbara is uniquely gifted in distilling complicated, fast-changing business dynamics into an investment framework that can provide much welcomed clarity and insight. In *Secrets of the Amazon III*, she has once again delivered in making the complex far more comprehensible. I am grateful to her for doing so.

— *Gregg M. Schoenberg, Founder, Wescott Capital & Co-Founder, The Financial Revolutionist*

Disruptive innovation remains a powerful force upending the status quo everywhere from Main Street to Wall Street. Barbara knows the roadmap between those two waypoints extremely well and always finds the shortest, most efficient distance between them.

— *Nicolas Colas, Co-Founder, DataTrek Research*

We live in a time of significant transformational change within and across industries as technological advancement, coupled with changes in societal values and norms, creates huge winners and losers in the marketplace. The buzzwords of the day are "*creating an emotional connection with customers*", "*building a tribe-like following*" and "*creating a social purpose that resonates with customers*". In many cases we know what is happening but we lack a roadmap to tell us why it is happening. Fortunately Barbara Gray has done some incredibly thoughtful work to consider the root causes of these changes. In particular, her advancement of the Customer Capital Pyramid (and the other Pyramids) concept is a tremendously useful visual depiction of how successful firms are advancing beyond offering functional value (price versus quality) to build market share.

— *Paul Taylor, Former Chief Investment Officer, BMO Harris Investment Management Inc.*

In a world where disruption of comfortable business practices has become a main theme, Barbara Gray is leading the way in disrupting the analytical community by actually reporting events — both positive and negative — and their implications in the world of retail. She never hesitates or softens her disdain for those companies who are failing to understand the violence of the changes occurring in the retail channels. If she makes no friends among those companies that fail to adapt to the new realities, she should be making many friends among investors, both private and institutional, whose success depends on better insights into the rapidly changing environment.

Given how fast-paced those changes are taking place, there is little time to savour even recent success because there is more coming every day. As Barbara's third book in as many years should alert you, if investors do not stay abreast of these ever-changing developments, they risk investing for yesterday's battles, not today's. If nothing else, you should understand the mindset behind the new disruptive reality, and to do that, the fastest and easiest way is to read her books (her latest in particular, of course).

But her book goes beyond the investing community. There are important insights for the managements of those companies in the new retail milieu — to understand the new value pyramid, and be prepared for the battle for retail supremacy that is being waged right now.

As they say at the ballgame, you can't tell the players without a programme and every investor and manager needs this guide to the future players, both winners and losers.

— *C. Ross Healy, Chairman, Strategic Analysis Corporation*

The Rules of the Game are Changing

The collision of tectonic shifts in technological, economical and societal forces is leading to an acceleration in structural disruption, creating an increasingly VUCA (volatile, uncertain, complex, ambiguous) environment for companies:

- **Technological Change Is Accelerating:** According to The Future Today Institute's *2019 Tech Trends Report*, the number of observed tech trends increased by 40% last year, from 225 to 315, as a result of the convergence of different technologies and inflections across the board.
- **Industry Boundaries Are Not Just Blurring, They Are Being Decimated**: As Sanjiv Yajnik, President of Capital One Financial, warned in March 2018 during his SXSW presentation *Leading Transformation at Scale*: "*The breadth and depth of the change coming towards us is unprecedented*".
- **Bricks-and-Mortar Foundations Are Eroding**: As Travis Kalanick, the founder of Uber, tweeted in March 2018: "*Over $10 trillion in real estate assets will need to be repurposed for the digital era in the coming years*".
- **Companies Are Facing an Existential Threat**: As Sean Sullivan, an angel investor who helped coin the term "cloud computing" back in 1996, warned in December 2018: "*There is an existential threat to Fortune 500 companies before the end of this decade*" (wsj.com).

This rapid transformation in the corporate landscape is creating chaos and uncertainty, changing the rules of the game, both for corporate executives and investors.

Why This Is Important for You — The Corporate Executive:

To avoid the fate of once iconic companies like Sears Holdings, you need to realize your company can no longer function as a non-tech company. More importantly, in order to strategically position your company to capitalize on opportunities resulting from shifting societal, technological and economic forces, you need to stay on top of the latest and emerging structural disruption trends — not just in your industry, but in all industries.

Why This Is important for You — The Investor:

To avoid being seduced by value traps like Sears Holdings, you need to be wary about analyzing companies on a siloed basis through the rear-view mirror. You also have to be careful about relying on traditional quantitative valuation metrics like P/E and P/BV ratios as you might miss out on investing in companies that are building defensive moats by playing the long game. For example, back on June 4, 2018, the WSJ published a fascinating article, *Value Investors Face Existential Crisis After Long Market Rally: Shares of fast-growing companies such as Apple and Netflix find a spot in value portfolios. Our approach to value has evolved.* Nearly a year later, in May 2019, Warren Buffett disclosed that Berkshire Hathaway has been buying shares in Amazon. And on June 1, CNBC published a fascinating article, *Everyone still relies on a stock's P-E ratio to invest, but a study shows it's bunk*, discussing the quant study by Bank of America

Merrill Lynch which found that nearly 80% of investors rely on a company's P/E ratio, making it the most popular metric for the 14th consecutive year. However, this metric is not working as low P/E stocks have underperformed the market since 2010 while high P/E stocks, like the FANGs (Facebook, Amazon, Netflix, Google), have contributed to the majority of the market's gains. And according to an analysis published on June 6 by JP Morgan's U.S. chief equity strategist, value stocks are trading at the deepest discount to the market in the past 30 years on both a P/E and P/BV basis (marketwatch.com).

How Can I Help You?

My driving passion in my two-decade career as a sell-side equity analyst is to come up with new ways to look at and value companies. I've never been your typical follow-the-herd, sell-side equity analyst. Back in September 2006, I incurred the wrath of a few corporate clients that I classified as "*straw houses at risk of collapsing*" in my controversial Three Little Piggies-themed research report, *If the Economic Wolf Comes Knocking, Is Your Trust Built of Bricks or Straw?* And in January 2008, I went against the Street and committed career suicide with my research report, *Yellow Pages No Longer a Conservative Investment: Downgrading to SELL*, in which I warned investors that the accelerating shift to online and emergence of the then new online disruptors like Facebook and Craigslist would increase its business risk profile.

One of my favourite artists is Georges Seurat, a French post-Impressionist painter and the father of pointillism. If you think about it, pointillism, a technique in which small dots of colour are applied to a canvas to form an image, is analogous to the mosaic theory in investing. Like Georges Seurat, each week I start with a blank canvas and piece together emerging structural disruption trends across industries, creating a 3–6-page research note, providing unique, thought-provoking and forward-looking insights to my institutional investment and corporate clients. And every three months, I bring my completed canvases together to create a collage of emerging structural disruption themes in the form of a 50+ page in-depth research report.

In this book, we travel to the land of unicorns and castles, where you will discover how quickly the rules of the game are changing. But before we start out, I will equip you with my proprietary Value Pyramid which will provide you with a valuable strategic framework to navigate the new disruptive era.

The Value Pyramid

Figure 1: The Value Pyramid

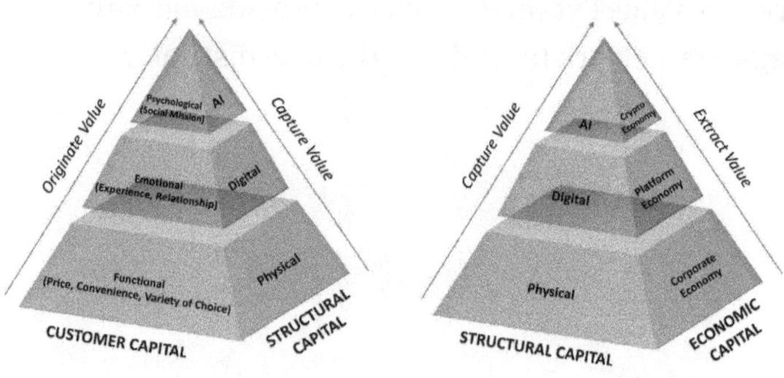

Source: Brady Capital Research Inc. (March 2019)

The Value Pyramid illustrates how the value equation is changing for companies. The three sides of the Value Pyramid are:

- **Customer Capital (*Value origination through customer value proposition*)**: In the age of Amazon, companies can no longer compete on a FUNCTIONAL customer value proposition basis (i.e., price, convenience, variety of choice), so they need to create EMOTIONAL connections and PSYCHOLOGICAL attachments with their customers.

- **Structural Capital (*Value capture through capital investments*)**: Companies that operate on only the PHYSICAL layer need to invest in moving up to the DIGITAL and AI (artificial intelligent) layers.
- **Economic Capital (*Value extraction through economic system*)**: Although most companies operate in the traditional CORPORATE ECONOMY, we are seeing the rise of a new class of disruptors that operate in the PLATFORM ECONOMY, which are ideally positioned to advance in the future to the emerging CRYPTO-ECONOMY.

How to Use the Value Pyramid – For Corporate Executives

My strategic thesis is that companies need to re-think how they originate, capture and extract value. I recommend using the Value Pyramid as a strategic framework to assess where your company currently is positioned on each side of the Value Pyramid and then determine where your competitors (both incumbent and emerging disruptors) are positioned. This will enable you to determine whether you face a high level of structural risk (i.e., radical industry transformation could create obsolescence in your company's core activities and assets), a moderate level of structural risk (i.e., to survive, you need to evolve your business model and make significant strategic moves) or if you have an opportunity to expand your total addressable market (i.e., you operate at the peak of the Value Pyramid).

How to Use the Value Pyramid — For Investors

My investment thesis is that value is flowing up the three capital sides of the Value Pyramid, so in terms of your investment portfolio you want to avoid the value traps of companies still operating at the base layer of the Value Pyramid, especially the customer and structural capital sides. And you want to look for companies that are building defensive moats by playing the long game — sacrificing short-term profits by investing in intangibles higher up the capital pyramid like customer relationships, R&D and platform ecosystems.

The real magic of the Value Pyramid comes from the concept of convergence. For example, the conductor of an orchestra brings together individual music instruments to create a symphony, in which the whole is more than the sum of the parts. Likewise, companies that operate at the peak of the Value Pyramid have the opportunity to capitalize on the higher forms of capital to expand their total addressable market and achieve exponential valuation growth. I call this new valuation thesis the Convergence Multiple.

Although the Value Pyramid seems simple, as you will discover in the next two sections, it is the product of my nearly decade-long intellectual journey into researching the convergence of emerging societal, technological and economic forces.

The Evolution of The Value Pyramid

February 2, 2010—So, I am at a crossroads trying to figure out what to do. I feel the need or desire to create something. Add real value to the world rather than just work for a firm. I need to find something I can be totally passionate about that would fulfill my talents and strengths so I can get back in the flow. But the question is, what? When people ask me what I am doing and I tell them I resigned from my position as an equity analyst at an investment firm, I think they are confused as to why. But in my mind, I need to create this gap so I can come up with the next big thing to carry my career/life forward in a meaningful way.

My decision to take a break in order to find meaning in my life — including my career — would lead me, one month after writing that journal entry, to embark on a two-and-a-half-month road trip across the United States with Greg, my then fiancé. During that trip we attended the SXSW conference in Austin, which is what opened my eyes to the exposing disruptive force of social media and, using Joseph Campbell's terms, "*summoned my call to adventure*". It was the starting point of my "*Hero's Journey*" into the emerging land of abundance economics that was being shaped in real time by the convergence of rapid structural shifts in societal, technological and economic forces.

Customer Capital: The Shifts in Societal Forces

On January 6, 2011, just weeks after my baby, Brady, was born, I published my first research report as an independent analyst, *Social Media: An Exposing Disruptive Force — Look for Companies with 'Heart' and 'Soul' But Beware of 'Empty Shells'.* As you'll discover from the following excerpt from that report, it was my new "shell, heart and soul" thesis that formed the foundation of the first side of the Value Pyramid — customer capital:

I believe customer relationships will be the new driver of firm value. As the power shifts from the company to the consumer, I believe investors will start to focus less on a company's brand and more on its customer relationships. As evidenced by the recent high-profile bankruptcies of Fortune 500 companies such as Lehman Brothers and Washington Mutual, a company's brand equity is a reflection of its past accomplishments and reflects current, not future, value.

I believe the transparent nature of social media will peel away the layers of a company, exposing the true authenticity and depth of its customer relationships...for example, many investors dismissed lululemon, stating the company was a fad and nobody would pay $90 for a pair of yoga pants, no matter how good they were, especially in a recession. But if we peel back the company's layers, we gain a much deeper insight into the company, as shown in Figure 2:

- **First Layer: The Shell.** I believe lululemon has a very solid "shell". Although its apparel is premium-priced, this is more than offset by its long economic life and the high quality of both the company's product and service.

- **Second Layer: The Heart.** I believe lululemon has "heart" as it has created a strong emotional attachment by offering its customers the promise of a more active, happy and healthy lifestyle, and the brand symbolizes being fit and active and looking good while doing it.
- **Third Layer: The Soul.** I believe what differentiates lululemon from most companies is its "soul" as its mission statement is "*creating components for people to live longer, healthier, more fun lives*", and its vision is "*elevating the world from mediocrity to greatness*". The company's culture was born from a group of yogis, dancers, runners and customers who follow the brand like a religion and act as volunteer evangelists.

Figure 2: My Original Customer Capital Thesis: Shell, Heart & Soul

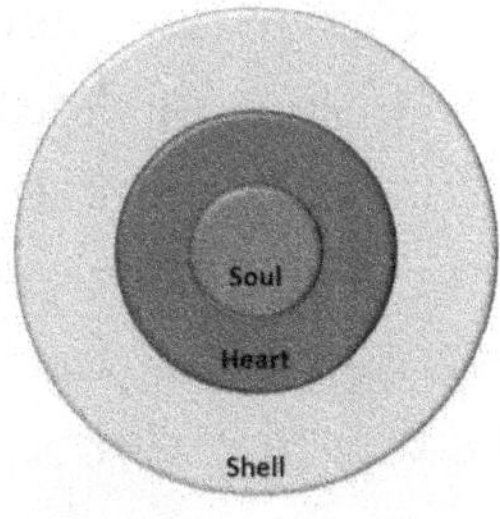

Source: Brady Capital Research Inc. (January 2011)

On the other end of the customer engagement spectrum is

Yellow Pages (which recently changed its name to Yellow Media), which I believe exemplifies what happens to a company with an "empty shell" that starts to crack. On January 12, 2008, I went against the Street and downgraded the stock to SELL based on my investment thesis that Yellow Pages' formerly strong economic moat was narrowing as we would start to see customer attrition as the traditional yellow pages directory business model was disrupted. However, many on the Street remained in denial of these structural changes and maintained their conviction in the company's strong brand name and customer relationships.

Structural Capital: The Shifts in Technological Forces

It's interesting how you can spend so much time working on something and it's not until the last second that you get a revelation that brings everything together. This is what happened to me. I'd just finished the final draft of my research report on LinkedIn and was sharing with my husband, Greg, how LinkedIn's new Talent Pipeline platform allowed companies to keep their applicant data current. I did not think much of it until he explained to me that this was one of the biggest challenges facing companies, and that he actually struggled with this same problem back in the mid-1990s when he created Vision2Hire, one of the first web-based applicant tracking systems. And the next morning it dawned on me: through the "power of we," LinkedIn had discovered the holy grail of business relationship management: how to transform candidate pools, business prospect leads and business customer bases from depreciating into appreciating assets.

It was this revelation that led to the foundation of my structural capital thesis, which I introduced in my May 2012 research report, *LinkedIn: Disrupting by the 'Power of We'*. My thesis was that LinkedIn had developed a structural asset with data on then over 160-million professionals and over 2-million companies with a built-in powerful incentive mechanism for members to keep their Professional Profile current, continue to expand their professional network, join new Groups and actively engage with other members by sharing expertise or content. Thus, the data on its members appreciates in value over time instead of depreciating.

Connecting the Dots...

Ironically, although I had been on an intellectual journey for the previous four years, it was only when I undertook a physical journey to New York City (I had traveled east to speak at the CFA Society Toronto event, *Social Media's Impact to the Investment Process*) and used Airbnb and Uber for the first time that the dots finally connected. This inspired me to write the article, *Social Capital: The Secret behind Airbnb and Uber*, which I published on LinkedIn in June 2014. It ended up going viral, and has been viewed by over 400,000 professionals. I think what really resonated with people was my concept of the Social Economy Pyramid, which actually represents the three peak levels of the Value Pyramid.

When I was thirty and single and living in New York City, I had a dream: to return one day with my husband and push our baby in a stroller through Central Park. A few weeks ago, albeit more than a decade later, my dream came true. But we didn't stay in a hotel and travel by yellow cab, instead we used Airbnb to book a guy's condo on the Upper East Side and we travelled by Uber to the airport.

How is it that Airbnb and Uber have been able to build thriving ecosystems in just over five years with such significant scale and influence that they are now valued at $10 billion and $12 billion, respectively? And how have these companies become such a disruptive force that they are the target of deafening protests from the highly ensconced hotel and taxi industries in cities around the world? Two words: Social Capital.

As shown in Figure 3, there are three levels of companies that operate in the Social Economy. And the higher a company moves up the Social Economy Pyramid, the faster the rate of value acceleration as they are able to achieve a higher level of disruption and access multiple social value drivers.

Figure 3: The Social Economy Pyramid: Years to Reach $10-Billion Valuation Mark

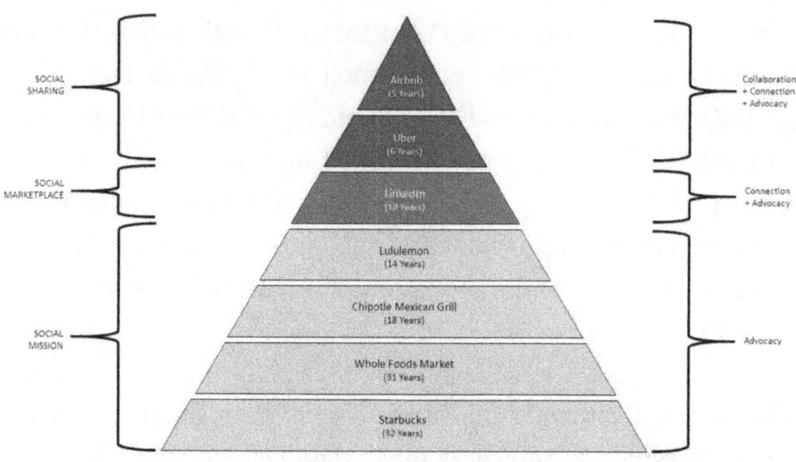

Source: Brady Capital Research Inc., Bloomberg (June 2014)

Social Mission Companies such as Starbucks, Whole Foods, Chipotle Mexican Grill and lululemon are able to access the first social value driver: Advocacy. As discussed in my November 2011 thematic research report, *Social Capital: A New Strategic Play for Investors: Look for Companies with Heart and Soul*, by creating Positive Social Capital (i.e., shared values and positive externalities) for their stakeholders, these companies are able to attract people looking to align their values with whom they buy from, work for and work with. This leads to the creation of a thriving stakeholder ecosystem. As Social Mission companies are founded on movements and follow a blue ocean strategy, they are on the low end of the disruption scale as they create new uncontested marketplaces.

Social Marketplace Companies such as LinkedIn and Zillow, which are also on a social mission, are able to access the first two social value drivers: Advocacy and Connection. As I discussed in my May 2012 report, *LinkedIn: Disrupting by the 'Power of We'* and in my recent April 2014 report, *Zillow: Disrupting the $75 Billion Realtor-Centric Machine,* LinkedIn and Zillow empower professionals by enabling them to connect with one another and build Bridging and Linking Social Capital through their platforms which foster transparency, authenticity and engagement. Social Marketplace companies, such as LinkedIn and Zillow, appear unthreatening with nascent business lines but they are both starting to gain footholds in the low-end markets and the revolutionary power of their consumer-centric marketplace platforms make them ubiquitous disruptive forces to be reckoned with.

Social Sharing Companies such as Airbnb and Uber, which have a social mission and are also Social Marketplaces, are able to access all three social value drivers: Advocacy, Connection and

Collaboration. The revolutionary power of Airbnb and Uber comes from their ability to harness technology to create a social sharing platform that facilitates trust by creating transparency and dual accountability. This enables individuals to form weak ties (i.e., Bridging Social Capital) with one another, leading to the personal sharing of goods and/or services (i.e., Linking Social Capital).

Airbnb, which has now processed a total of 11-million reservations, creates a compelling accommodation alternative for its guests by offering them a fun way to discover and book unique accommodations with its current base of over 350,000 hosts offering 600,000 home listings in 34,000 cities in 192 countries around the world. And Uber now operates in over 70 cities in 36 countries around the world. These rapidly expanding social sharing companies are directly attacking the incumbent hotel and taxi industries on both the supply and demand side and are threatening to erode their following traditional economic moats:

1. **Low-Cost Producer:** The incumbents' high fixed cost structure (which provides them with process and scale cost advantages) is becoming a competitive disadvantage as many travelers have grown tired of the impersonal experience of staying in cookie-cutter hotels and the inefficient and impersonal experience of traveling in taxis. In comparison, Social Sharing companies such as Airbnb and Uber are the ultimate low-cost producers as they have the potential to create infinite supply by empowering individuals to generate income from underutilized personal assets (i.e., Property, Plant, & Equipment such as a house or car and Human Capital such as property

management or chauffeuring services).

2. **High-Switching Costs:** Customers are no longer held captive to the incumbents as Airbnb and Uber now present more attractive and personal alternatives.
3. **Intangible Assets:** The value of a brand name is depreciating as Airbnb and Uber are creating long tails in travel by replacing artificial institutional trust with Social Capital by democratizing the tools of production and distribution and connecting supply and demand by capitalizing on the filtering efficiency of social network reviews and facilitating trust through dual accountability systems (i.e., both the hosts and the guests rate each other).
4. **Network Effect:** Unlike hotel and taxi companies that seek to constrain supply to keep prices high, Airbnb and Uber are creating structural assets that appreciate in value as they attract more and more new hosts/drivers (i.e., supply) and travellers (i.e., demand) to their platform, leading to the ultimate network effect.

I have no doubt that the Social Economy will transform how we travel, live, work, play and consume. And just as the democratization of content led to structural disruption in media-related sectors over the past decade, the emerging democratization of goods and services by Social Sharing companies will lead to structural disruption over a much wider range of sectors. And the secret to understanding this accelerating tectonic shift starts with Social Capital.

Economic Capital: The Shifts in Economic Forces

After my article went viral, I became obsessed with researching the emerging sharing/on-demand economy as I was fascinated with this new form of commerce that was surfacing below the depths of the blue ocean. And as you will discover, this formed the foundation of my economic capital thesis. As I wrote in my September 2014 research report, *A Deep Dive into the Sharing Economy: Where the Long Tail Meets the Blue Ocean*:

We started off surfing the Internet in the early 1990s with the advent of the World Wide Web. In 1995, we climbed aboard the rising dotcom wave, dipping our toes into the new ocean of corporate e-commerce, until the wave came crashing down in March 2000. But out of the corporate dotcom wreckage emerged the next generation of companies that brought us user-generated content (Blogger in 1999, TripAdvisor in 2000, Yelp in 2004, YouTube in 2005) and social networking (LinkedIn in 2003, Facebook in 2004 and Twitter in 2006). These companies went beyond the depths of corporate e-commerce to create a new undersea social world of transparency, authenticity and engagement promoting individual empowerment, community and collaboration.

The Web 2.0 companies created online networks of people. And over the past decade, their membership base grew, new social exchanges emerged and the density of connections within and between members of the different social networks increased. This led to the creation of a massive global network of highly connected individuals, which continuing our ocean theme, is like the coral reef, which is known as the "*rainforest of the sea*". And this coral reef laid the foundation for the emergence of one of the most diverse and self-sustaining ecosystems on Earth, which would enable people to transact beyond the depths of the corporate ocean: the Sharing Economy. While the first ripples of the Sharing Economy appeared over a decade ago, the Sharing Economy movement started to gain momentum in the aftermath of the recession as a result of structural shifts in the following three forces:

- **Technological:** Through leveraging technology (i.e., smartphones, apps, social networks, user-generated reviews, online marketplaces, cashless payment systems), Sharing Economy companies are able to offer a superior functional value proposition to sellers and buyers of their products and or/services.
- **Economic:** As individuals awaken from the hangover caused by their excessive debt-fueled individualistic and materialistic consumerism binge, they are starting to seek a more meaningful life and alternative means to earn an income. Sharing Economy companies meet this demand as they create a unique, authentic and personal experience for sellers and buyers, building a strong emotional connection to their product and/or service. And from an economic perspective, they enable sellers to earn passive income (i.e., by renting out their assets or selling their used goods) and active income (i.e., through monetizing their own human capital) while enabling buyers to achieve access without ownership.
- **Societal:** Through their social missions focused around accessibility, sustainability and community, Sharing Economy companies are able to create a psychological attachment among their stakeholders (sellers, buyers, partners, employees) to what their companies stand for. As Robert J. Shiller

> wrote in *Finance and the Good Society: "capitalism has to be expanded and democratized and humanized"*. This is what the Sharing Economy is about.

Sharing Economy companies are so attractive from an investment perspective because, in addition to accessing non-consumption on the demand side, they access non-provision on the supply side. Put another way, Sharing Economy companies are where the "*long tail meets the blue ocean*".

In the book, *Blue Ocean Strategy: How to Create Uncontested Marketplaces and Make Competition Irrelevant*, W. Chan Kim and Renee Mauborgne advise "*instead of focusing on the competition, you focus on making the competition irrelevant by creating a leap in value for buyers and your company, thereby opening up new and uncontested market space.*" This is the strategy being pursued by many of the companies as they create a leap in value for their buyers through leveraging leading-edge technology to offer a unique, authentic and personal experience focused around their social mission. In doing so, the companies gain access to new tiers of non-customers which opens up a new market of non-consumption, leading to an abundance of demand.

In Chris Anderson's book, *The Long Tail*, he discusses how the democratization of content will lead to a reversal in the economics of the mass market era. This captures the basic essence of the supply side of the Sharing Economy. But as the Sharing Economy revolves around the democratization of assets, goods and services, we are dealing with not just falling distribution costs, but falling structural and customer capital costs. And the under-utilized personal assets, goods and talent that were "*previously dismissed as beneath the economic fringe*" can now be exchanged between people below the depths of the corporate ocean. And as the Sharing Economy movement, which began with the idealistic and socially conscious Millennial generation, shifts inter-cohort to Baby Boomers and Generation X, we are seeing the emergence of a long tail in personal assets, goods and talent, leading to abundance of supply.

Exploring the Secrets of the Amazon

Ubernomics: Returning Home to My Tribe

When I decided to leave the corporate world in 2010, I was the proud owner of a BlackBerry, I had never tweeted or blogged, and I dressed in Armani suits. I really had no strategic plan or idea of where my research would take me, but I was driven by a strong intellectual curiosity and a passion for reading business strategy books. I launched Brady Capital Research with the lofty aspiration to create an investment research firm "*for the next generation of investors*" by focusing on innovative and high-growth companies that are making a positive difference in the world. At the time, I had no clue that I was embarking on a six-year journey of pioneering research into the emerging field of abundance economics (i.e., Ubernomics). At the start of 2016, I decided to re-read the 30-plus research reports and articles I had written during the previous six years, realizing they basically tracked the evolution of my discovery of my Ubernomics theory, which inspired me to create my first book, *Ubernomics*, which I published in October 2016.

It was actually when I was in the final stages of writing *Ubernomics* that I had a serendipitous encounter with Ed Pennock, a Bay Street veteran who I had worked with over a decade ago at Blackmont Capital. As fate would have it, Ed was also in the home stretch of his own Hero's Journey and had recently launched Pennock Idea Hub with the mission to "Reinvent Research". When we embarked on our first marketing trip in September 2016, it truly felt like I was returning to my tribe as it felt so good to be back in the boardroom sharing insights from my *Ubernomics* research.

In January 2017, I published my first research report, *Where Do the Ubernomics Fault Lines Lie in Your Portfolio?: An Assessment of Structural Risk.* My overall investment thesis was that the Ubernomics Quake had started — if the Content Quake last decade measured a four to five on the Richter scale, the Ubernomics Quake would be a nine. For the shift in content from scarcity to abundance led to structural disruption last decade in a number of publishing and media-related industries. Now we have now gone from yellow pages to yellow taxis as the shift from scarcity to abundance has advanced from the democratization of content to the democratization of physical and human capital. Whereas the Content Quake resulted from a tectonic shift in only one force (i.e., technology), the Ubernomics Quake was resulting from the collision of tectonic shifts in societal, technological and economic forces.

I still remember sitting across the boardroom table from the president of one of Canada's largest institutional investment firms, warning him of the rising structural disruption risk for retail REITs. My thesis, which was controversial at the time, was based on my research back in the summer on the intersection of the traditional corporate world with the sharing/on-demand economy. I was so fascinated by the topic that I created a database and strategic classification framework, identifying over 150 publicly traded companies that entered into strategic partnerships with sharing/on-demand start-ups. And one of the start-ups was Deliv, a goods delivery company, which had brought aboard retail REITs such as General Growth Properties, Macerich, Simon Property Group, Taubman Centers and Westfield as strategic investors in February 2014 and February 2016. On the surface, this appeared to be a win-win for both parties — the valuable customer capital would allow Deliv to scale its business and the structural capital would provide retailers in malls with a cost-effective way to deliver their merchandise to their customers. However, digging deeper, I realized this was further evidence of the acceleration toward online shopping, which would ultimately threaten to render both the core activities (leasing space to retailers) and core assets (the shopping malls) of retail REITs with obsolescence.

A month later, I rang the alarm bell on rental car companies with the publication of my radical research report, *Driving into the Abyss: How the Auto Fault Line is Creating Deep Structural Cracks for Avis Budget & Hertz.* My basic thesis was that most investors weren't aware the extent to which the rental car companies were losing share to Uber. And I turned out to be right — over the next three months, the share price of Hertz plummeted by two-thirds and Avis by one-third.

Secrets of the Amazon: Amazon's Invasion of the Retail Shoreline Is Just Beginning...

In *Secrets of the Amazon,* which I published in November 2017, I navigate readers down the raging river where we witness the unfolding of the retail apocalypse. In my June 13, 2017 research note, *The Flywheel,* I commented: "*I'm thinking we should change the name of our research from "Ubernomics Fault Lines" to "Amazonomics Fault Lines" as every week we learn of new disruptive developments from Amazon."* Unbeknownst to me, three days later, the Amazonomics Quake hit, sending tremors down the retail fault line with Amazon's surprise announcement that it would be acquiring Whole Foods for $13.7 billion. For ten days after Amazon's announcement, I published an in-depth research report, *The Unstoppable Amazon: An Assessment of the Rising Structural Risk Along the Retail Shoreline*, warning that the dam which had been protecting the retail shores of the structural and supplier channels was now blown open with Amazon's acquisition of Whole Foods.

By piecing together emerging structural developments, I was able to uncover valuable and timely insights for investors. For example, in April 2017, I warned about the rising obsolescence risk of the department stores and how Amazon's CPG (consumer packaged goods) summit to re-think how to design, package and ship for DTC (direct-to-consumer) foreshadowed its disruption to the CPG ecosystem. In May, I cautioned how casual dining restaurants could lose their high-margin booze profits with the shift to restaurant delivery and how the quiet moves that Amazon was making into the pharmacy market could spell trouble for the drug retailers. And, in September, I warned about the threat of disruptive new DTC entrants such as Casper to Sleep Country Canada.

I also reveal the secrets of the Amazon, including the truth about Alexa, who is not just Bezos' secret weapon, but the Amazonian warrior hiding in his growing line-up of Echo devices. Just like the Greeks used the Trojan Horse to enter the city of Troy, Bezos is using the Alexa-enabled Echo devices to gain a stronghold in households. And I connect the dots from my *Ubernomics* research and propose a new thesis that the companies best positioned to differentiate themselves from

Amazon are luxury brands that can dig into their roots to create authentic experiences to enhance the emotional connection with their customers. For the experience moat is the secret for companies to escape the coming reckoning as Amazon begins its invasion of the retail shoreline.

Secrets of the Amazon 2.0: Avoid Value Traps and Play the Long Game

In *Secrets of the Amazon 2.0*, which I published in October 2018, I trek deeper into the Amazon and uncover the secrets of the three pyramids. I still remember sketching out my concept of the three capital pyramids on my flight back from SXSW.

Figure 4: The New Value Flow Framework

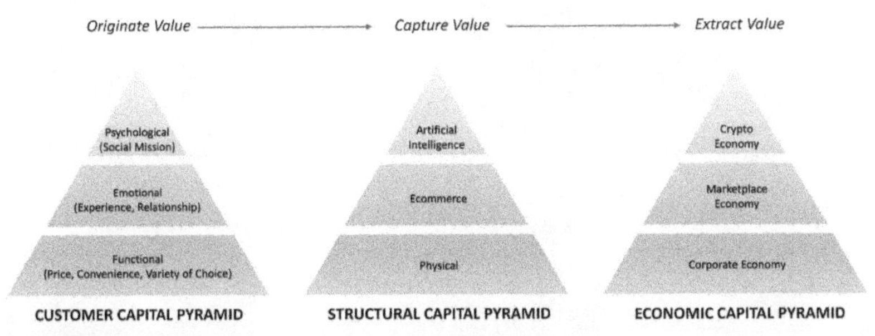

Source: Brady Capital Research Inc. (March 2018)

As I discussed in my April 16, 2018 research report, *The Next Frontiers: A New Perspective on How Companies Originate, Capture and Extract Value*, the unprecedented breadth and depth of change is disrupting the value equation for companies. My strategic thesis, as shown in the New Value Flow Framework (Figure 4), is that companies need to re-think how they originate value in terms of their customer value proposition, capture value through their capital investments and extract value through their economic system. My basic investment thesis is that value is flowing up the pyramids, so in terms of your investment portfolio you want to avoid the value traps of companies still operating at the base layer of the customer and structural capital pyramids.

I also watch the drama unfold as Bezos, with Alexa by his side, started to invade new frontiers such as healthcare and banking. As I voyage to these next frontiers, I discover that industry boundaries aren't just blurring, they are being decimated. Most importantly, I learn how the acceleration in structural disruption is changing the game for investors.

Welcome to the Land of Unicorns and Castles

In this finale to the *Secrets of the Amazon* trilogy, we travel to the land of unicorns and castles. The term "unicorn" is defined as a start-up that reaches a valuation of over $1 billion. The term was coined in November 2013, by Aileen Lee, the founder of Cowboy Ventures, in her TechCrunch article, *Welcome to the Unicorn Club: Learning from Billion-Dollar Start-ups.* In the article, she discussed how only 39, or 0.07%, of the 60,000 U.S. consumer and enterprise software start-ups funded in the past decade had been able to reach a $1-billion valuation. She classified this elite herd of companies, led at the time by Facebook, LinkedIn, Workday, Twitter and Service Now, as unicorns (techcrunch.com). But over the next five years, the flood of venture capital led to a unicorn baby boom, increasing the size of the herd in the U.S. by nearly four-fold to 145 (techcrunch.com).

These unicorns, many of which were born during the economic downturn a decade ago, have been carefully nurtured in the bountiful flower-filled meadow of Silicon Valley. But they are now looking for greener pastures as they yearn to break free of their reins and prance into the public arena. The heavyweight of the unicorn herd is Uber, which I wrote about bullishly in my June 2014 *LinkedIn* article, *Social Capital: The Secret Behind Airbnb and Uber*, back when it was a mere six-year-old filly weighing in at only $10 billion. And Uber, the UBERcorn, is gazing in admiration at the Amazon castle sitting atop the peak of its kingdom and stretching as far as the eye can see. For Uber, like many of the unicorns, understands the secrets of the Amazon: playing the long game by investing at the peak of the Value Pyramid in customer relationships, R&D and platform ecosystems.

Although the Amazon castle is illuminated by a rainbow that stretches across the pink-coloured sky over its kingdom, the hard truth is that not every unicorn deserves a rainbow valuation, especially those that are not yet self-sufficient (i.e., profitable). As I shared in my April 2 research note, *The Two Flavours of Kool-Aid*, I'm excited about the upcoming stampede of unicorns as my mindset is what Heidi Grant Halvorson and E. Tory Higgins call "promotion focus", as they describe in their book, *Focus: Use Different Ways of Seeing the World for Success and Influence*: "*Promotion focus is about maximizing gains and avoiding missed opportunities. Prevention focus, on the other hand, is about minimizing losses*". Just like we saw with the dotcoms nearly two decades ago, promotion-focused investors are now in danger of getting caught up in the "*cult-like following*" of these unicorns and drinking what I call the "pink Kool-Aid".

At the base of the hill, the waves crash violently against the shore as the ocean rages and turns a toxic shade of gray-blue as structural disruption forces build below the surface. For prevention-focused investors are also at risk of drinking the Kool-Aid. But the Kool-Aid in this case is blue, not pink, and the danger is the toxicity of "blue Kool-Aid" increases as the rate of structural disruption increases. For example, back in January 2008, I warned investors to stop drinking Yellow Pages' "blue Kool-Aid" as I was worried the accelerating shift to online and emergence of the then new online disruptors like Facebook and

Craigslist would increase its business risk profile.

And I continue to caution investors against drinking the "blue Kool-Aid" of companies that still operate mainly at the base of the Value Pyramid. The accelerating waves of structural disruption are crashing over the sides of traditional sailing ships, eroding their foundation. And as we've witnessed with the recent capsizing of once iconic companies like Toys 'R' Us and Sears Holdings, those weighed down by heavy debt burdens are particularly vulnerable.

In the next fifteen chapters, you will discover structural disruption developments for hundreds of publicly traded companies, operating in over half of the GICS sub-industries. To make this book more user-friendly, I have highlighted companies that are publicly traded in bold.

In Chapter 1, I discuss how Amazon goes on ***The Offense***, raising the minimum wage for its U.S. employees to $15 per hour, opening its new Amazon 4-star curated long tail marketplace store and launching its accelerator program for manufacturers. And in light of Facebook's Cambridge Analytica data scandal, I remind readers of the saying "*if you're not paying for the product, you are the product*".

In Chapter 2, I talk about how Amazon is bringing back ***The Amazon Man*** — the next generation of the milkman — by enabling Prime members to designate one day of the week to receive all their packages. And a week after I enthuse about the upcoming unicorn stampede, the narrative changes for the FANGs, which have declined 13–25% since peaking on October 1.

In Chapter 3, I share how I'm shell-shocked by the toxic red tide that has washed over the markets since the beginning of October, but I advise that we have to avoid being blinded by the red glare as structural disruption forces continue to build ***Below the Red Tide***. In light of the rise of new forms of payment, packaging, marketplaces and delivery as the world shifts to e-commerce, I pose the thought-provoking question: *Could the future of retail see the disappearance of the middleman?*

In Chapter 4, I warn of ***The Existential Threat*** facing Fortune 500 companies as the market continues to plummet. As Christmas approaches, my mood lightens as I share how visionary Santa Claus' business model is and I joke about how Kohler just introduced a smart toilet.

In Chapter 5, I explore the concept of ***The Community*** as I share how the founders of Starbucks, lululemon and WeWork planted seeds for their community-driven social missions eleven years apart. I also discuss how the Minecraft obsession of my 8-year-old underlines why tech giants are racing to create the "Netflix of Games" to capitalize on the shift in media consumption.

In Chapter 6, I discuss ***The Empowerment*** arising from innovations like Google's Live Transcribe for the deaf, Uber Freight's Yelp-like app for drivers and Amazon's Live Creator app for sellers. We are also seeing the introduction of smart devices like LG's new line of washers, dryers and dishwashers, Eight Sleep's mattress, and MSC Cruises' virtual cruise assistant.

In Chapter 7, I reflect upon the explosion in population of a new invasive and disruptive form of transportation species I just witnessed while attending the SXSW conference in Austin — ***The Scooters***. I also discuss how the value of sustainability is shining through with the roll out of Amazon Day, the long-awaited launch of Telsa's Model 3 and Lyft filing to IPO.

In Chapter 8, I share how there have been five major strategic developments since I was interviewed on Yahoo! Finance's morning show about my March 25 research report, *Why I'm Not Drinking the LYFT Kool-Aid & New Insights from SXSW*, which have added to the toxicity of ***The Kool-Aid***. And guess what? Alexa, who has not yet turned five, just earned her MD — she is now HIPPA-compliant.

In Chapter 9, after an initial review of Uber's S-1, I pose the question: *Could Uber be **A Different Species** of unicorn than Lyft?* which led to my April 29 research report, *Take A Once-In-A-Lifetime Ride On An UBERcorn*. I also share how one of the red flags in my Lyft report is playing out as Lyft is facing two class-action lawsuits from investors claiming it exaggerated its U.S. market share at 39% in its prospectus. And I confide how disillusioned I felt walking though the new Hudson Yards mall and share my thoughts on how the retail apocalypse has worsened since I was in NYC in September as it seemed like every block I walked down had at least one to two vacant retail spaces.

In Chapter 10, I talk about how the rules of the game are changing — fast — just days after Warren Buffett discloses that Berkshire Hathaway has been buying shares in Amazon, we are about to witness the IPO of Uber — one of the largest tech IPOs in history. I also question whether Lyft is ***The Naked Unicorn*** as I confide how I felt a bit like the child who innocently cried out, "*But* *he isn't wearing anything at all"* in the book, *The Emperor's New Clothes.* And I advise the key to corporate survival these days is the willingness for management to innovate and colour outside industry lines.

In Chapter 11, I explore how companies are embracing the membership economy as a means to deepen the emotional connection with their customers, increase loyalty and increase switching costs. The chaos and uncertainty deepens as Amazon rolls out next-day delivery just days after the retail apocalypse wreaks havoc on the stock prices of mall-based retailers while Merrill Lynch reveals that the mighty P/E ratio no longer works. And at this moment, I realize my Value Pyramid – the product of my nearly decade-long intellectual journey down "***The Road Not Taken***" researching the convergence of emerging societal, technological and economic trends – could serve as a strategic map for investors and CEOs looking to survive and conquer the new disruptive era.

In Chapter 12, I propose that Bezos' secret weapon for invading the $3.5-trillion healthcare space is a little girl not yet five years old — ***Dr. Alexa.***

In Chapter 13, I discuss how value in the auto space is flowing to the peak of the Value Pyramid and warn that we are starting to see the upending of the century-old automobile business model as we enter ***A New Automotive Era.***

In Chapter 14, I reflect on the excitement I felt taking my first Uber ride while visiting NYC with my husband and baby (who is now in kindergarten). And you'll discover why I'm not drinking the LYFT Kool-Aid but I am excited to take a once-in-a-lifetime ride on ***The UBERcorn***.

In Chapter 15, ***Secrets of WeWork***, I share how I had no clue that when I joined the WeWork tribe back in October 2017 that I was becoming part of a fast-growing cult that would grow from 168 to over 650 locations in its bid for global domination. And I discuss how WeWork's rebranding to The We Company in January proves my long-held thesis that it has always been more of a human capital than a real estate play.

Chapter One: The Offense

As I read about how Netflix is moving into interactive TV, it made me think about the first book I ever wrote (which I typed on a typewriter!) back when I was in primary school: a choose-your-own-adventure book. Now, decades later, I'm putting the final touches on my third book — Secrets of the Amazon 2.0. To maintain its exclusivity and scarcity value, I plan to once again price it at Amazon's stock price the date of publication — which given Amazon's current stock price of over $2,000 per share, implies the book will cost over 70% more than Secrets of the Amazon! Speaking of books, it seems like my premonition that I shared in my September 19 "New York, New York" research note that Amazon Books "points to the future of bricks-and-mortar retail as this highly curated boutique leverages Amazon's user-generated ratings to showcase a constantly changing selection of the best-rated book" was prescient, as Amazon just opened a new concept store in Soho called "Amazon 4-star". And on a final note, I can't wait to read Chip Wilson's upcoming book "Little Black Stretchy Pants: The Unauthorized Story of lululemon".

The Curator: October 2, 2018

Amazon 4-star points to future of bricks-and-mortar retail

Amazon just opened a new concept store in Soho very similar to Amazon Books called "Amazon 4-star". The 4,000-square-foot store is essentially a physical curation of the long tail of Amazon's marketplace, with a weekly rotating stock of 2,000 products, rated 4 stars and above, top sellers or new and trending. The store is divided into similar sections as Amazon's website, with the biggest section being electronics to showcase Alexa devices and a section promoting AmazonBasics. To enhance the discovery experience, the store also has tables featuring the "most wished for" and "locally trending" products. Like with Whole Foods, Amazon is using the stores to attract people to become Prime members, offering lower prices for Prime members on its digital price tags and the ability for them to easily pay with their Prime app rather than a credit card (techcrunch.com). **Harley-Davidson**, which is struggling with its fourth year of declining sales, is turning to Amazon to help it attract younger customers. As part of its new digital strategy, Harley-Davidson will start selling its apparel and riding gear, which was previously only available on its own website or from licensed dealerships, on Amazon (cnbc.com).

Space, the final frontier

If you recall, I opened my April 16 research report *The Next Frontiers* with the lyrics to *Star Trek*. It turns out that "*Space is the final frontier*" for Bezos. Amazon has partnered with **Iridium Communications** to bring Internet connectivity to the "whole planet". Iridium Communications is working with AWS to develop a satellite-based network called CloudConnect for Internet of Things (IoT) applications. CloudConnect, which is set to launch in 2019, will reach beyond the 10–20% of the planet covered by cellular networks to bring the rest of the world within the reach of AWS (cnbc.com). Interestingly, according to recently deleted job postings, AWS is hiring a software engineer and a product manager "*to help innovate and disrupt the launch,* *satellite and space world with new AWS products, services and features...for a new AWS service that will have a historic impact*" (geekwire.com).

Amazon Music comes to Canada

After launching Amazon Music Unlimited to 28 countries back in December, Amazon is finally bringing the subscription music streaming service to Canada. It will be available to Prime members for C$7.99 per month or C$79 per year, to non-Prime members for C$9.99 per month. In addition, those with an Echo device can subscribe for only C$3.99 per month but this is limited to a single device (venturebeat.com). You can now watch TV through your Echo Show as Hulu will soon provide its live-streaming TV service to the device (techcrunch.com). Hulu is a joint venture with **Disney, Century 21st Fox** and **Comcast** each owning 30%, and **AT&T** the remaining 10%. Amazon has named the first ever female duo to broadcast the coming season of Thursday Night Football on Prime Video, bringing aboard Andrea Kremer, the chief correspondent for NFL network, and Hannah Storm, a veteran ESPN (**Disney**) Sports Center anchor. Amazon is paying $130 million to the NFL to livestream football games for the next two seasons, a 30% premium to the $50 million it paid last season. As further evidence of the power of Amazon's flywheel, its NFL streams will be powered by AWS and available to over 100 million Prime members in over 200 countries (geekwire.com). After releasing a handful of "choose your own adventure" animated kids programs, **Netflix** is pushing further into interactive TV, developing specials that let adults engage with the plot. For example, it will be using this interactive format for the first time for its upcoming *Black Mirror* episode (techcrunch.com).

Consumer confidence hits an 18-year high

Consumer spending is expected to remain strong with consumer confidence hitting an 18-year high in September. The Conference Board reported consumer confidence reached 138.4 in September, up from 134.7 in August (cnbc.com).

Home Depot starts to offer same-day delivery

Home Depot is enhancing the convenience value proposition for its customers, partnering with goods delivery platforms Roadie and Deliv to offer same-day delivery. The same-day delivery service, which starts at a cost of $8.99, is available for over 20,000 products in the top 35 metro areas across the U.S. (bloomberg.com). Roadie, which utilizes unused capacity in passenger vehicles, has raised $25 million since it launched in Atlanta in 2015 while Deliv, a crowdsourced same-day delivery service for multinational retailers, has raised $40 million since it launched in Menlo Park in 2012. Interestingly, **UPS** is a strategic investor in both start-ups, while Deliv also raised capital back in 2014 and 2016 from Class A retail REITS such as GGP (acquired by **Brookfield Property Partners** in August 2018), **Macerich**, **Simon Property Group**, **Taubman Centers** and Westfield (**Unibail-Rodamco-Westfield** as of June 2018). Interestingly, in our first research report back in January 2017, *Where Do the Ubernomics Fault Lines Lie in Your Portfolio*?, we cautioned investors how the retail fault line was creating a high level of structural risk for retail REITs, citing this as evidence of the shifting consumer dynamic toward the acceleration of online shopping that threatened to render both the core activities (leasing space to retailers) and core assets (shopping malls) obsolete.

GrubHub acquires Tapingo for $150 million while Cargo raises $30 million

Amazon has expanded its two-hour free grocery delivery

service from Whole Foods via Prime Now to 10 additional cities, bringing the total to 48 cities across the U.S. (cnbc.com). **Grub-Hub** is paying $150 million to acquire Tapingo, a mobile app for advance ordering for food delivery or pick-up available at over 150 college campuses. We note Tapingo had raised $36 million since launching in San Francisco in 2012 (media.grubhub.com). Cargo, which enables rideshare drivers to open their own convenience store in their car, just raised a $22 million Series A round. Since Cargo launched in NYC in 2016, it has generated over 2 million transactions and has expanded its distribution salesforce to 12,000 drivers across 10 cities (techcrunch.com). We note this follows closely after Cargo's $5.5 million seed round in January led by **Kellogg Company**'s VC fund, eighteen94 capital, which also participated in this round. Farmer's Fridge, which sells chef-curated healthy meals and snacks through its automated smart refrigerated vending machines, just raised a $30 million Series C round. Since Farmer's Fridge launched in Chicago in 2013, it has built a network of 200 vending machines throughout Chicago and Milwaukee (techcrunch.com).

Amazon building new distribution warehouse – 3rd in metro Vancouver & 10th in Canada

Amazon is building a new distribution warehouse in Tsawwassen, its 10th in Canada and its third in metro Vancouver. The new 450,000-square-foot warehouse will create 700 full-time jobs and is set to open next year (vancouversun.com).

lululemon advancing athleisure beyond product fit to feel fit

Over the past two years, **lululemon** has developed a way to identify and measure each person's unique pattern of movement. To capitalize on this, lululemon has created a "Signature Movement Experience" treadmill for its stores that will enable customers to learn more about their unique pattern of movement and allow its educators to provide highly customized product recommendations. In essence, lululemon is looking to advance high-performance clothing beyond objective factors (i.e., size, activity, compression, moisture-wicking properties, breathability) to more subjective factors (i.e., how it feels by tailoring it to each person's movement patterns and personal preferences) (fastcompany.com). This is totally aligned with Chip Wilson's original community-based social mission for lululemon "*to create components for people to live a longer, healthier, and more fun life*". On this note, I can't wait to read Chip Wilson's upcoming book, *Little Black Stretchy Pants: The Unauthorized Story of lululemon*, which is set to be released on October 16. As I wrote on page 63 of *Ubernomics* in the section titled *Social Capital: The Secret to lululemon's Success*: "*I have a strong personal affinity to both the stock and the company. In addition to being one of the first analysts to initiate coverage on it shortly after its IPO in September 2007, I used to live at 3rd and Arbutus, just around the corner from lululemon's original store in Kitsilano, Vancouver. And as a professional female who lives an active and healthy lifestyle, I am its picture-perfect target customer*".

Last week, Amazon raised the alarm bell on wage inflation as it went on the offense with the announcement that it will be raising the minimum wage for its U.S. employees to $15. Amazon is also taking the offense in bricks and mortar as it experiments with a number of concepts as it looks to enhance the emotional connection with its Prime members. This week, we learned it is preparing to open its new Amazon 4-star curated long tail marketplace concept store in Berkley and that it is looking for retail space for Amazon Go in the U.K. But the biggest revelation I gained into the future of retail is from its new "powered by Amazon" pop-up showroom.

Amazon is also being opportunistic in launching its own private-label brands, debuting its bed-in-a-box mattress as the largest mattress retailer in the U.S. files for bankruptcy. And Amazon is looking to further ramp up its private brand portfolio with the launch of its "Our Brands" accelerator program for manufacturers. To attract younger customers, retailers are playing defense — Target is partnering with an oral care subscription start-up while Walgreens is doing a mini-store pilot with beauty box subscription start-up Birchbox.

The Offense: October 10, 2018

Amazon goes on the offense – raises minimum wage for its U.S. employees to $15

Facing a record low national jobless rate of 3.9%, and the need to hire over 100,000 warehouse workers in the U.S. for the holiday season, **Amazon** is wise to go on the offense on the labour front. Last week, Bezos announced he is raising the minimum wage for Amazon's 250,000+ employees in the U.S., or 40% of its global workforce, to $15 per hour effective November 1, and he called for Congress to raise the federal minimum wage, which is less than half this level at $7.25. Given the tight labour market, Amazon's bold move will impact every other companies' ability to attract and retain workers and put pressure on them to raise their wages, increasing overall inflation. For example, **Walmart**, which employees 1.5 million workers in the U.S., just raised its minimum wage to $11 in February while **Target** raised its minimum wage to $12 in September with plans to raise it to $15 by 2020. To partly offset the cost and increase wage standardization, Amazon is eliminating certain incentive pay and stock compensation for hourly warehouse and customer service employees (wsj.com). The increase in wages is likely to push companies toward automation. For example, **Fast Retailing**, the parent of Uniqlo, is expanding its partnership with logistics firm **Daifuku** and investing $885 million to automate its warehouse and distribution system (retailtouchpoints.com).

Some advertisers moving over half of search budget from Google to Amazon

Some advertisers are moving over half of their search budget from Google to Amazon, representing hundreds of millions of dollars. This is not yet quantitatively material to **Alphabet**, which generated $94.5 billion in advertising revenue last year, but it foreshadows Amazon's rising threat to Alphabet's cash-cow advertising business, which generates 86% of its total revenue. According to Havas Media, 20–30% of its clients, mostly CPG companies, are shifting 50–70% of their total search budgets to Amazon (cnbc.com). Currently there seems to be little defection from the huge and highly lucrative auto, travel and entertainment clients, but we believe the auto industry could be its next target given Amazon has been driving faster into the auto space.

"Powered by Amazon": The future of retail?

Amazon's New Mall Of America Installation Is Absolutely Fabulous. It is rare to see an article expressing such enthusiasm as this *Forbes* article written by Chris Walton, a 20-year retailing veteran who was most recently Target's VP Store of the Future. In the article, he expresses his view on how *Good Housekeeping* magazine's new GH Lab pop-up store at the Mall of America, designed in partnership with Amazon, could be the next generation of 21st century retailing. The pop-up enables you to touch and feel products and further research and order products by scanning their SmileCode tag using your Amazon app. Essentially, this concept of a "powered by Amazon" showroom leverages Amazon's POS and fulfillment capabilities, reducing the barriers to entry by eliminating the need for inventory, reducing theft, minimizing labour requirements, and even lessening the need for retail know-how (forbes.com).

Mattress Firm files for bankruptcy as Amazon starts selling its own mattresses

Mattress Firm (**Steinhoff International**), the largest U.S. mattress retailer with 3,500 locations across the country, filed for bankruptcy on October 5. It will be begin to close 200 locations over the next few days and plans to exit to 700 stores, or one-fifth of its current store base, in certain markets where it has too many locations in close proximity to one another (cnbc.com). Ironically, Amazon has starting selling its own bed-in-a-box foam mattresses under its AmazonBasics line, with a twin size mattress starting at $130 (businessinsider.com).

Amazon launches "Our Brands" accelerator program to ramp up private brands

Amazon, which is up to 120 private brands, is looking to further ramp up its private-label business with the launch of its "Our Brands" accelerator program. Amazon is looking to attract manufacturers to make products over a wide range of categories for its collection of private brands, offering onboarding support, marketing services and tools that track performance and customer feedback (cnbc.com). Speaking of private label, household products companies face a rising threat of substitutes as Target is launching Smartly, its private-label value-focused household essentials brand that features over 70 items, most costing less than $2 (supermarketnews.com).

Target and Walgreens partner with DTC start-ups; Walgreens forms alliance with Kroger

Target is partnering with quip, the first to-market DTC oral care subscription company. quip will be providing Target with valuable supplier capital in the form its electric toothbrush starter kits. In return, Target will provide quip with valuable structural capital as it will be selling quip's starter kits for $25 at all of its 1,800 Target stores and on Target.com. However, quip seems to be the beneficiary as it will have the opportunity to build a direct relationship with customers that buy its toothbrush as refills will only be available from its website (digiday.com). We note that quip, which has sold 1 million toothbrushes since it launched in Brooklyn in 2014, has raised $22 million to date.

To transform its beauty aisle and attract younger customers, **Walgreens** is taking a strategic minority stake in Birchbox and launching a pilot program to open mini Birchbox stores in 11 of its Walgreens locations. The stores will feature full-sized skin care, make-up and hair products from over 40 brands, curated from customer data from its beauty box subscription service. To make beauty discovery a fun experience, the stores will be staffed by Birchbox-trained beauty consultants and offer customers the opportunity to build their own Birchbox by selecting from jars of product samples (fastcompany.com). Interestingly, the majority stake in Birchbox was sold for only $15 million to its existing investor, Viking Global Investors, in a fire sale back in May. In addition to retailers partnering with start-ups, we are starting to see alliances form between grocery and drug retailers, such as the new pilot program between **Kroger** and Walgreens. Walgreens will provide valuable structural capital by enabling Kroger's customers to pick up their online grocery orders at its pharmacy locations while Kroger will provide Walgreens with valuable supplier capital in the form of some of its private-label brands (cnbc.com).

FAO Schwartz partnering with department stores to expand internationally

The iconic toy retailer FAO Schwartz will be opening its new 20,000-square-foot flagship store in Rockefeller Plaza on November 16. In addition, to capitalize on the upcoming holiday season, FAO Schwartz is strategically partnering with department stores to quickly expand internationally, providing them with valuable supplier capital in the form of an experiential brand to attract customers in return for structural capital in the form of space to open up a pop-up boutique store. For example, FAO Schwartz is opening pop-up shops in two Selfridges stores in London, in two Myer (**Myer Holdings**) Australia stores in Sydney and Melbourne, and in El Cortes Ingles stores in Madrid. In addition, FAO Schwartz will be opening permanent boutique shops inside nearly 90 **Hudson's Bay Company** stores in Canada and is partnering with Kidsland China (**Kidsland International Holdings**), a major toy retailer in China, to open two massive stores in Beijing and Shanghai next year and as many as 20 smaller-format toy stores across China over the next few years (cnbc.com). It seems like Toys 'R' Us is not dead yet. The hedge fund debtors of Toys 'R' Us have decided to cancel the bankruptcy auction of its brand name and other IP assets (i.e., registry lists, website domains, Geoffrey the Giraffe) and try to revive the company (financialpost.com).

Walmart acquires women's plus-sized online retailer for $100 million

Walmart is acquiring Eloquii, a women's plus-sized online retailer, for $100 million. Eloquii, which was started by The Limited and shut down in 2013, has raised $42 million since it re-emerged as an online retailer in 2014. According to NPD Group, half of American women aged 18–65 wear plus-size clothing and spent $21.4 billion on it in 2016 (techcrunch.com). Walmart is embracing in-store technology, deploying Auto-C self-driving machines to clean and polish its store floors. It is using Auto-C machines in 78 of its stores and plans to introduce them soon to another 360 locations (mediapost.com). Walmart is also moving further into the video-streaming space. It is partnering with MGM to exclusively license family-friendly original series to enhance the content for its free, ad-supported streaming service operated by Vudu. The first short-form original will debut in Q119 on Vudu's "Movies On Us" service, which was launched two years ago and currently features 7,000 movies (techcrunch.com). We note Walmart acquired Vudu in 2010 for $100 million.

Tencent Music looking to IPO in U.S. at $25–$30 billion valuation

Tencent Holdings is spinning off Tencent Music Entertainment Group, filing to list shares in the U.S.. At a proposed valuation of $25–$30 billion, this would be the biggest U.S. IPO by a Chinese company to date. Last year, Tencent Music's revenue doubled to $1.66 billion and it generated a profit of $199 million. Although Tencent is the leading music streaming service in China with 800 million users, it only has 23 million paying subscribers versus **Spotify**'s base of 83 million paying subscribers. However, Tencent Music is more of an interactive media company as 70% of its revenue came from the 4.2% of its users that paid for social entertainment services such as online karaoke, live streaming and merchandise sales (techcrunch.com). Speaking of Spotify, it has launched the beta of its Spotify for Podcasters platform, opening podcast submissions to everyone and offering listener metrics such as daily stats and engagement (techcrunch.com).

Facebook launches Portal while Google unveils Home Hub

Facebook is venturing deeper into consumer hardware with the launch of its long-awaited Facebook Portal video chat device. The tablet-like device, which is integrated with Alexa, features a wide-angle camera which uses AI facial recognition to track you as you move around the room to make chatting more natural. To address privacy and trust concerns resulting from its Cambridge Analytica data breach, the device has a physical privacy shield to cover the camera and also allows you to turn the audio off. The $199 Portal and $349 Portal+ devices are now available for pre-order from Facebook, Amazon and **Best Buy** (wsj.com). At its Made by Google event in NYC on October 9, Google unveiled Home Hub, a competitor to the Echo Show. However, unlike the Echo Show and the new Facebook Portal, you can't use it to video chat as Google decided to exclude a camera for privacy reasons. The Home Hub allows you to see responses from Google Assistant and features Home View, a one-stop dashboard for controlling and managing all the smart devices in your home. The Home Hub, which includes six months of free access to YouTube Premium, is available for pre-orders in the U.S., the U.K. and Australia for $149 (theverge.com). Similar to Google's new Home View, to help users better set up and control their smart home, Amazon has done a major visual redesign to its Alexa app (techcrunch.com).

Boundaries blurring between home appliance makers and food retailers

The June Intelligence Oven, a Wi-Fi connected countertop oven with a built-in camera that recognizes your food, will now automatically cook select dishes from Whole Foods. June is collaborating with Whole Foods, adding cook settings to the control menu for its June Intelligence Oven for over 30 of Whole Foods' 365 Everyday Value products. In return, Whole Foods will sell June's ovens at select Whole Foods' stores and start selling its second-generation oven on Amazon in early 2019 (cnet.com). We note that June is a modern appliance company that has raised $30 million since launching in San Francisco in 2013. This could foreshadow the further blurring of boundaries between home appliance makers and food retailers and CPG companies as we note that Amazon itself just entered the home appliance space with the debut of its AmazonBasics Alexa-enabled microwave.

Amazon opening second 4-star store in California as it looks to bring Amazon Go to the U.K.

Just a few weeks after Amazon opened its first curated long tail marketplace concept store, Amazon 4-star, in Soho, it is now preparing to launch a second Amazon 4-star store in Berkley, California (mercurynews.com). In addition, Amazon could be looking to bring Amazon Go to the U.K, as it is apparently looking for retail space of 4,000–5,000 square feet (thenextweb.com).

IBM opens its Food Trust blockchain platform to all players in food supply chain

IBM just announced its Food Trust platform is now available for commercial use to all players in the food supply chain and that **Carrefour** has joined its growing ecosystem (forbes.com). We note that in our August 25, 2017 research note, *Boom!*, we discussed how IBM had formed a consortium of ten leading CPG companies (Dole, **McCormick & Company**, **Nestle**, **Tyson Foods** and **Unilever**) and food retailers (Kroger and Walmart) to work together with its IBM Blockchain Platform to identify the most urgent areas across the complex global food supply chain that could benefit from the transparency and traceability provided by blockchain technology.

SoulCycle brings live music concerts to its spinning classes

The fitness industry is starting to embrace experiential events.

SoulCycle is bringing live music concerts to its spinning sessions. SoulCycle, which operates 88 studios in 15 markets across the U.S. and Canada, will hold the first event in NYC this month, and then expand to Las Vegas next month, followed by several U.S. cities next year (fastcompany.com). Interestingly, the amount of space leased by fitness centres and gyms in malls and lifestyle centres has increased by 70% since 2013, according to CoStar (footwearnews.com). Despite this, the mall vacancy rate hit a seven-year high of 9.1% in Q3, up from 8.6% in Q2 and 8.4% in Q1, according to real estate research firm Reis. In addition, the average rent for malls declined 0.3% from $43.36 in Q2 to $43.25 in Q3, marking the first quarter-to-quarter decline since 2011 (wsj.com).

"Siri, buy me Transformers" ordered by 5-year old dictator to his iPad. It's ironic as whereas I grew up being inundated by commercials on TV, companies like Hasbro aren't able to reach my boys through traditional ads as they only watch Netflix. But it seems like they've still been able to brainwash them by disguising ads in the form of shows like Transformers. Amazon looks poised to take this one step further as Amazon Studios is in talks with Blake Lively to develop a scripted fashion-themed series with an Amazon Fashion merchandising component and it just became the official retail partner for Shark Tank. Amazon is also looking to revolutionize the way we watch content as it has started livestreaming interactive Thursday Night Football on Twitch. And I'm thinking that Alexa will play a starring role in all of this, especially when it comes to ad targeting, as Amazon was just granted a patent for a "voice-based determination of physical and emotional characteristics of users". Scary... I don't know about you, but between this and Facebook's latest data privacy scandal, I can't help but think more and more

about the saying, "if you're not paying for the product, you are the product".

The Product: October 16, 2018

Amazon livestreams interactive Thursday Night Football on Twitch

Amazon will be livestreaming Thursday Night Football this season for the first time on its video game live streaming platform Twitch, transforming the way we watch live sports. In addition to enabling Twitch users to chat with each other during the game, Amazon provides interactive video player overlays called Extensions which enable users to pull up a widget that shows scores, standings and statistics, as well as compete on a live leaderboard with predictions for each quarter. Amazon is also apparently testing other interactive elements such as the ability to buy merchandise directly from the site (geekwire.com). We note Amazon acquired Twitch for $970 million in August 2016. On the content front, Apple is apparently planning to offer its original TV and movie content for free to Mac, iPhone and iPad owners (cnbc.com). And have we reached peak streaming? Even **Costco** has apparently been in talks with existing providers of video streaming services to potentially offer this service for free to its executive-level members (theinformation.com).

Lines blurring between retail and entertainment

As further evidence of Amazon's unique potential to leverage Amazon Studios to promote its marketplace, it is in talks with Blake Lively to develop a scripted series with a fashion theme and an Amazon Fashion merchandising component (hollywoodreporter.com). Could Amazon be looking to develop its own Shark Tank-like reality show with an accompanying retail site? Amazon is partnering with Shark Tank, becoming its official retail partner and providing $15,000 in complimentary AWS credits to each entrepreneur. Amazon has created a retail site for Shark Tank products which will feature over seventy past Shark Tank-funded products from the past nine seasons as well as products from its future seasons (techcrunch.com). Justice (**Ascena Retail**), the largest tween specialty retailer in the world with over 1,000 tween girls' apparel stores across the U.S. and Canada, is following Amazon's lead and entering the entertainment space. To advance its mission to empower girls and enhance its emotional connection with them, it is launching Justice Studios. Justice Studios will focus on creating original content, starting with *Ultra Squad*, a graphic novel series that will be available in its stores and online on November 3, as well as a documentary titled *Finding Clara* (businessinsider.com)

Walmart Canada spending $175 million to renovate 23 stores as Amazon Air launches in Miami

Walmart Canada is spending $175 million to renovate 23 of its stores, or just over 5% of its base of 400+ stores, by February 2019. To improve its e-commerce operations, Walmart will be creating new areas in the store for online orders and dedicated parking spaces for online grocery pick-up (financialpost.com). On the logistics front, Amazon is expanding its Amazon Air cargo service. It is launching a twice-daily flight out of Miami International Airport to ship packages to destinations across the U.S. from its four warehouses located within 12 miles of the airport. The service, which will be operated by **Atlas Air Worldwide**, will use Prime Air-branded **Boeing** 676-300F airplanes (aircargonews.com). And we now have evidence that Amazon is looking to reduce its reliance on **UPS** and **FedEx**, not just in the U.S., but also on a global basis. Just over three months after launching Amazon Delivery Services Partners in the U.S., it is introducing Project Armada to India to allow entrepreneurs there to manage a fleet of delivery trucks (entrepreneur.com).

Walmart intensifies its efforts to attract lower income consumers

Walmart is partnering with **PayPal Holdings** to enable customers to deposit and withdraw money from their accounts at all its stores by early November (cnbc.com). We note this comes six months after it partnered with **MoneyGram International** to launch Walmart2World, a global money transfer service to serve the two billion unbanked individuals, Interestingly, in May, Amazon made a similar strategic move, partnering with Coinstar to roll out Amazon Cash deposit capability to select grocery stores in the U.S. northeast with plans to have it in 5,000 of its cash-counting kiosks in the U.S. by the end of the year. According to a 2015 FDIC study, there were 9 million unbanked households and 24.5 million under-banked households in the U.S., accounting for a total of over one-quarter of households (fdic.gov). Meanwhile, Oxxo (**FEMSA**), the largest Mexican convenience chain with over 17,000 locations, is leveraging its structural capital to capitalize on the rise in e-commerce in a country where over 60% of the population is unbanked. Oxxo enables people to transact with over 1,000 online merchants by enabling them to make a cash payment at their local corner store. Oxxo also offers a pick-up program in partnership with Amazon at nearly 3,000 locations which enables them to load cash onto their Amazon account and pick up small items valued under $79 (uk.reuters.com). We note that back in March, Amazon launched its first-ever debit card in partnership with **MasterCard** and **Grupo Financiero Banorte** to increase online payment convenience.

Sears Holdings finally files for Chapter 11

U.S. retail sales remain sluggish, rising only 0.1% in September. Department store sales were down 0.8% while restaurant and bar sales fell 1.8%, the largest decline since December 2016 (wsj.com). Speaking of department stores, on October 15, **Sears Holdings** filed for Chapter 11 bankruptcy protection. As part of the bankruptcy, Sears Holdings will be closing 142 money-losing stores near the end of the year, in addition to the 46 it will be closing by next month, leaving it with 687 remaining stores (wsj.com). This bankruptcy has been a long time coming, as in its 2016 10-K, the company warned: "*Our historical operating results indicate substantial doubt exists related to the Company's ability to continue as a going concern*". Meanwhile, **L Brands** is looking at alternatives for La Senza, its struggling Canadian luxury lingerie retailer which is expected to report $250 million in sales and a loss of $40 million this year. La Senza, which L Brands acquired for $700 million in 2007, operates 119 corporate-owned stores in Canada, 5 in the U.S. and 188 non-corporate-owned international stores (financialpost.com). We note this strategic move comes less than a month after L Brands announced it will be closing Henri Bendel, its iconic luxury women's specialty store. Speaking of lingerie, Walmart has just added it to its growing portfolio of e-commerce brands. Just over a week after paying $100 million for women's apparel plus-sized online retailer Eloquii, Walmart is buying Bare Necessities, the largest online specialty retailer of intimate apparel that sells 100,000+ units from over 160 brands (forbes.com).

Wayfair moves both up and down the structural capital pyramid

On the AI layer, **Wayfair** has partnered with Magic Leap to create an immersive mixed reality interior design experience.

Although the Wayfair Spaces app sounds amazing as it allows you to virtually explore professionally designed rooms and then drag and drop items into your actual physical room at their actual size, you can only use it with the Magic Leap headset, which just went on sale in August for $2,300 (venturebeat.com). On the physical layer, to deepen its emotional connection with consumers, Wayfair is opening two holiday pop-up stores. The 400-square-foot pop-up stores will feature a highly curated selection of over 300 SKUs, representing a miniscule fraction of its online inventory of 8 million SKUs. The stores will be staffed by its customer service and home design employees who will be available to recommend products and show customers how to use its online design services marketplace (digitalcommerce360.com). Allbirds, the ecofriendly wool sneaker DTC start-up, will use the proceeds of its new $50 million Series C round to double down on its bricks-and-mortar expansion. Allbirds, which launched in San Francisco in 2015 and recently opened a 4,800-square-foot flagship store in Soho, and plans to open eight more stores across the U.S. over the next year, just opened its first store in the U.K. in London's Convent Garden and is also planning to open stores in Asia (techcrunch.com).

Chapter Two: The Amazon Man

According to the WSJ, 2019 could be a record-breaking year for IPOs, with a number of heavyweight tech unicorns breaking free of their reins as they make their debut in the public arena. When I think about Uber, which is expected to weigh in up to $120 billion, I can't help but remember how bullish I was on Uber in my June 2014 LinkedIn article, "Social Capital: The Secret Behind Airbnb and Uber" back when it was a mere six-year old filly weighing in at only $10 billion. Airbnb, which also weighed $10 billion back then, is looking to join Uber in the ring as is Lyft, which has since increased its weight more than fifteen-fold, from under $1 billion over $15 billion.

A number of unicorns I write about in this week's research note are also joining the stampede. WeWork, which was born in 2010 and weighed in at $20 billion last summer but is in discussions with SoftBank that could value it at up to twice that, is expanding in Japan and NYC and just partnered with Rent the Runway, providing further evidence to our human capital play thesis. Postmates, which is only seven years old, just launched in 134 new cities, expanding its grocery delivery service to 550 cities. And Pinterest, which is on track to nearly double its revenue this year to $1 billion as it approaches its 10th birthday, just added new features to become more shoppable for its 250 million monthly active users.

The Unicorn Stampede: October 23, 2018

Amazon's U.S. Prime membership growth slows as it reaches 97 million

Amazon's U.S. Prime membership growth is slowing. According to *Consumer Intelligence Research Partners* (CIRP), Amazon's Prime membership base reached 97 million in Q318, up 9% from 90 million in Q317 and up only 3% from Q2. At the same time, the gap in spending between Prime and non-Prime members seems to be widening, with Prime members spending $1,400 per year (up from $1,300 a year ago) and non-Prime members spending $600 (down from $700 a year ago) (businessinsider.com).

P&G brings mass customization to consumer products

Procter & Gamble is running a pilot program to allow customers to order personalized 3D printed razors from Gillette. The razor handles, which are available in 48 designs and 7 colours, are printed using stereolithography, a type of 3D printing technology from Formlabs. The razors cost between $19 and $45 and will take 2–3 weeks to ship (cnbc.com). We note Formlabs has raised $104 million since launching in Boston in 2011.

Amazon collaborates with Jonathan Adler as it dives deeper into home furnishings

Amazon is moving deeper into the home furnishings space with the release of Now House by Jonathan Adler, its first exclusive designer collaboration for the home featuring a full line of gorgeous luxury but affordable furniture, décor and bedding. On the Now House Amazon page, you can shop not just functionally by product category, but more emotionally by curated looks and by room (businessinsider.com). We note Jonathan Adler is an American potter, designer and author with over 20 stores worldwide. It's interesting as Amazon's collaboration with Jonathan Adler to create curated online collections is quite parallel to its collaboration with *Good Housekeeping* to create a curated physical pop-up store. And Amazon seems to be embracing the pop-up concept — this week, Amazon Fashion is opening a pop-up boutique in London. The 3,000-square-foot pop-up will sell clothing from its brand partners (i.e., **PVH**'s Calvin Klein and Tommy Hilfiger) as well as its own private-label fashion brands. The pop-up will offer different themes each day to highlight Amazon's range of fashion categories and will be staffed by on-site personal stylists (fashionunited.uk).

USPS proposes 9–12% price hike; JD.com launches its own parcel delivery service in China

The United States Postal Service (USPS) is looking to increase the delivery cost by 9.3% for packages weighing over one pound and by 12.3% for lighter packages. This isn't a direct attack on Amazon though, as the USPS is also looking to raise postal rates across the board to remain competitive, proposing the following hikes: 3.9% on priority mail express, 5.9% on priority mail and 10% on first-class stamps (cnbc.com). Given its recent launch of Amazon Delivery Services Partners in the U.S. and India and Amazon Air cargo service out of Miami, we believe Amazon is looking to not just reduce its reliance on the USPS in the future, but to compete with it. For example, in China, **JD.com** is leveraging its national logistics network and supply chain management technology to launch a **FedEx**-style parcel delivery service. Although JD.com stated that it "*aims to eventually make residential and business deliveries for shippers from anywhere to anywhere within mainland China in the future*", the service is currently only available for businesses and individuals in Beijing, Shanghai and Guangzhou (reuters.com). In the U.S., JD.com, which received a $550 million strategic investment from Google (**Alphabet**) in June, will launch a flagship online store on Google Shopping by year-end. Although JD.com already indirectly sells in the U.S. via Walmart, under its agreement with Google it will ship directly to U.S. consumers from fulfillment centres in the U.S. while Google will handle the payment and order processing (wsj.com).

Target joins the toy wars

With the holidays approaching, the battlefield is becoming more crowded as **Target** joins the toy wars. On the functional level, Target is increasing its variety of choice in toys (doubling its new and exclusive toys to 2,500) and devoting more aisles to toys (500 square feet to 500 stores). On the emotional level, Target is hosting 25,000 "hours of joy" play dates across its stores, allowing kids to test the latest toys and to meet fictional characters (cnbc.com).

Sam's Clubs partners with Instacart which just raised $600 million

Walmart's Sam's Clubs, which partnered with Instacart on a pilot program to offer same-day grocery delivery service in February, is now rolling the service out to over half of its stores by the end of this month (techcrunch.com). We note that last month Walmart partnered with Instacart in Canada in a pilot program but it has yet to partner with Instacart for its own Walmart stores in the U.S. This comes as Instacart, which is now available to 70% of U.S. households, raises $600 million. I'm thinking Instacart might be looking to make an acquisition as it still has $600 million in cash left from its $350 million Series E in April and its $400 million Series D round in March 2017 (techcrunch.com). Meanwhile, Postmates, which just raised a $300 million Series E round, is launching in 134 new cities, expanding its footprint to 550 cities in the U.S. and extending its reach to 60% of U.S. households (techcrunch.com).

Pinterest becomes more shoppable; caveat emptor on the new Facebook Portal

Pinterest, which attracts 250 million monthly active users and is on track to nearly double its revenue to $1 billion this year, has rebuilt its infrastructure to make its app and website more shoppable. Pinterest has added three new features: 1) up-to-date pricing and stock info on all product pins with links to take you to the retailer's website; 2) a new "Products like this" category under each fashion and home décor pin; and 3) a new shopping shortcut that connects users to similar products to a given pin (techcrunch.com). Caveat emptor... Although **Facebook**'s new Portal video chat device comes with an optional privacy shield and does not run ads itself, apparently because it is built on Messenger infrastructure, the data about who you call and data on which apps you use in Portal can be used to target you with ads on other Facebook-owned properties (recode.net).

Walmart and Amazon advance sustainability effort

Walmart is buying 233 megawatts of power from three Midwest U.S. windfarms under development by the North American unit of **EDP Renovaveis SA** (bloomberg.com). Amazon is also advancing its own sustainability efforts. It invested $10 million in the Closed Loop Fund, a social impact fund launched in 2014 that aims to invest $100 million by 2020 to finance the creation of recycling infrastructure and services in U.S. cities (techcrunch.com). Not surprisingly, previous investors include other big generators of packaging waste: beverage companies (**Coca-Cola**, **PepsiCo**, Keurig Dr. Pepper), household products companies (**Colgate-Palmolive**, **Johnson & Johnson**, Procter & Gamble, **Unilever**), packaged foods and meats companies

(**Nestle**) and even Walmart. Amazon will also be installing solar panels at 10 of its 16 fulfillment centres across the U.K. over the next 18 months and has signed a deal to guarantee all of its U.K. buildings are powered by 100% renewable electricity (cnbc.com). In the U.K., Amazon is adding 1,000 highly skilled 'Silicon Valley' R&D jobs, hiring 600 employees for its new office in Manchester, adding 250 to its development centre in Edinburgh and 180 at its Cambridge facility (cnbc.com).

The narrative is changing – both for the market, FANG stocks, and even individual companies like Amazon and Walmart. Since peaking on September 20, the S&P 500 has tumbled 10.3% on escalating investor fears over rising interest rates, higher production and material costs, a slowing Chinese economy and new tariffs. Although growth stocks have been hammered, with the Vanguard Growth ETF down 11.6%, value stocks haven't fared much better as evidenced by the 9.1% decline in the Vanguard Value ETF. The narrative has also changed on the former high-flying FANG stocks which have been dealt the hardest blow, with Netflix, Amazon, Google and Facebook plummeting 25%, 23%, 15% and 13%, respectively, since October 1. With the exception of Amazon, which has declined 25% since peaking at $2,040/share in early September, all the other FANG stocks peaked at around the time of their Q2 earnings in July, with Facebook, Netflix and Google now down 35%, 32% and 19%, respectively, from their peaks.

The narrative on Amazon has turned negative since it reported disappointing Q3 results on October 25. The company seems to be transitioning from a hyper-growth story to more of a growth story as its sales growth momentum decelerated to 28% in Q3 from 38%, 43% and 39% in the last three quarters. However, on the positive side, it is becoming more of a margin expansion story as it grows its *high-margin businesses (AWS, subscription services, advertising) and achieves cost efficiencies. We continue to remain positive on Amazon's ability to achieve long-term value creation. For example, it is actively lobbying for AWS to win the $10 billion Pentagon contract, it just opened its sixth Amazon Go store, it just partnered with Qualcomm to bring Alexa directly to our ears, it has added new perks for Amazon Business Prime members and it just launched a new exclusive brand of home health products. Although we remain concerned about the new risk of wage inflation and the longer-term risk of the absence of a v-commerce platform for Walmart, it seems to be changing its narrative by re-strategizing how it originates value by starting to transform its under-utilized parking lots into town centres and how it captures value by introducing its Sam's Club Now concept store and empowering sales floor employees to use their phone for work.*

The Narrative: October 30, 2018

Amazon transitions from hyper-growth to margin expansion story

On October 25, **Amazon** disappointed the Street. Although the company beat on the bottom line, reporting a record quarterly EPS of $5.25 versus $0.52 a year ago, its sales momentum seems to have slowed. Amazon's net sales rose 28% in Q318 to $56.5 billion, well below its sales growth of 38%, 43% and 39% in the last three quarters. Excluding Whole Foods, which continues to comprise 8% of its top line, Amazon's net sales were up 22%, below the pace of 28%, 31% and 28% in the last three quarters. The big driver continues to be its high-margin AWS division, where net sales rose 46% to $6.7 billion and operating margin rose 560 bp to reach a record high of 31.1%. The company's overall operating margin increased 580 bp to a record 6.6% as its operating margin in North America, which accounts for 61% of its net sales, rose 550 bp to a record 5.9% and its International operating margin improved by 430 bp to -2.5%. Interestingly, Amazon's "Other" revenue, which is mainly advertising revenue, rose 122% to $2.5 billion, implying its advertising business has hit an annual run rate of $10 billion (cnbc.com).

Amazon's lobbying spending hits a record in Q3

Amazon's lobbying spending hit a record in the third quarter as it competed for the $10 billion Department of Defense cloud services contract and dealt with the taxation of online sales. Amazon spent $3.63 million, more than **Facebook** ($2.82 million) but less than **Alphabet**'s Google ($5.46 million). As Amazon was dealing with the taxation of online sales, as well as many other issues, it spent more than the three other companies competing for the cloud services contract: **Microsoft** ($2.24 million), **Oracle** ($1.44 million) and **IBM** ($0.9 million) (fortune.com).

Walmart transforming under-utilized parking lots into Walmart Town Centers

As evidence of how technology is changing the way real estate firms originate, capture and extract value, the new hot jobs in real estate are data scientists. Real estate firms are uniquely positioned to use the digital and AI layers to leverage their existing physical assets and enhance the customer experience. For example, by leveraging the data they capture from their properties, firms can unlock value in their real estate portfolio (pionline.com). Although **Walmart** is not a real estate company per se, it is looking to unlock the value of its under-utilized real estate by adding open-air lifestyle centres to its business portfolio. Walmart is transforming the parking lots at Walmart

Supercentres, which are 6–8 acres in size, into town centres in several states. Its Walmart Town Center concept is designed to create a community feel around its store by curating a mix of local, regional and national retail tenants, including restaurants, daycares, healthcare clinics, food trucks and mobility hubs (businessinsider.com).

Retail REITs view Sears Holdings' bankruptcy as an opportunity to diversify tenant mix

Retail REITs are viewing the bankruptcy of **Sears Holdings** as an opportunity to repurpose the real estate (i.e., hotels, co-working spaces, apartments, fitness spaces, medical facilities), add traffic drivers (i.e., food halls, play spaces) and bring in emerging DTC retail brands like UNTUCKit and Casper. For example, **Simon Property Group** is planning to spend over $1 billion to redevelop the 33 Sears stores in its portfolio while **Washington Prime Group** is planning to spend $325 million to renovate its 28 Sears stores. Other retail REITs with exposure to the closures include **Macerich**, **CBL Properties**, **Urban Edge Properties** and **Kimco Realty** (cnbc.com). However, as we cautioned back in our July 11, 2017 research note *D-Day*: "*this re-invention will result in rising capex costs for the retail REITs in the form of repairs, remodeling and leasing costs. This will lead to a reduction in free cash flow, which combined with the eroding competitive position and reduced cash flow stability from declining lease durations, will increase the risk of a dividend cut for many retail REITs.*" Retail REITs in the U.K. will soon need to look at how to repurpose their real estate as **Debenhams**, which just posted the biggest loss in its 240-year history, is closing 50, or nearly one-third, of its 166 department stores in the U.K. This is much deeper than its original plan to close 10 department stores (cnbc.com) and comes less than two weeks after the bankruptcy of Sears Holdings.

Amazon opens sixth Amazon Go as Walmart debuts Sam's Club Now

Amazon just opened its sixth Amazon Go store in San Francisco at 300 California Street (cnet.com). Amazon Go will soon also be coming to NYC at Brookfield Place (**Brookfield Property Partners**) across from the World Trade Center (recode.net). Walmart's new Sam's Club Now concept store will open next week in Dallas. The store is 32,000 square feet, one-quarter the size of an average Sam's Club store, and will be staffed with "Member Hosts" instead of cashiers and shoppers will pay with the "Scan & Go" mobile app instead of at the cashier stand. In addition, the store will feature an Amazon Go-like camera system for inventory management, electronic shelf labels, wayfinding technology for in-store navigation and AI-infused shopping (techcrunch.com).

Walmart and Target offer free, two-day shipping

To compete with Fulfillment by Amazon, Walmart is expanding its free, two-day shipping service to millions of products offered by third-party sellers on its marketplace. More importantly, Walmart is leveraging its structural capital (i.e., its 4,700 stores) to add convenience as customers will now be able to return these items at the service desk at any of its stores (techcrunch.com). To compete with Amazon and Walmart, **Target** is offering free two-day shipping with no minimum purchase on hundreds of thousands of items this holiday season, effective November 1. It will also have "Drive Up" service available at nearly 1,000 stores and will offer same-day delivery nationwide via Shipt. Target is looking to hire 120,000 seasonal workers, up 20% from last Christmas, and is doubling the number of positions for fulfilling online orders in its stores and distribution centres. Importantly, Target is leveraging its structural capital (i.e., its 1,800 stores) as last holiday season, it fulfilled 70% of all online orders through its stores and this is expected to increase this year (cnbc.com).

Amazon partners with Qualcomm to bring Alexa directly to our ears

According to *How We Will Pay 2018 Edition*, a new study by **Visa** and PYMNTS, the number of consumers owning a smart speaker has nearly doubled to 27% from 14% a year ago. More significantly, 28% of these consumers engaged in v-commerce within the past week, with the most common purchases being groceries and food delivery (www.pymnts.com). Amazon is strategically partnering with **Qualcomm** to bring Alexa functionality directly to our ears. Qualcomm is offering a pre-made chip integrated with Alexa that headphone manufacturers can drop into their headsets. This will reduce the costs for headphone manufacturers, leading to an increased supply of Alexa-enabled headphones (fortune.com). Alexa is also coming to our eyes. North is introducing Focals, $1,000 smart glasses with Alexa functionality that will ship later next year. Focals, which look like normal glasses, connect to your phone via Bluetooth and have a small projector that beams data to your eyes (cnbc.com). Interestingly, the Amazon Alexa Fund participated in North's $120 million Series B round in September 2016. North, which was formerly called Thalmic Labs, was launched in Kitchener, Ontario in 2012. On the smart home front, Amazon is a strategic investor in the $50 million Series F round for Tado, which makes Alexa-enabled smart thermostats and AC controls for private homes and small businesses (techcrunch.com). We note Tado has raised $109 million since launching in Munich in 2011.

Amazon adds new perks for Amazon Business Prime mem-

bers

Amazon is enhancing the functional value proposition for Amazon Business Prime members in terms of convenience (offering free same-day and one-day shipping for orders over $35 on 1 million items, as well as new analytics tools to better track spending) and pricing (its new corporate **American Express** card offers either 5% back or 90 days' interest-free purchases on purchases at Amazon.com and Amazon-owned businesses). Its new analytics tools include Spend Visibility, which allows members to visualize their spending and Guided Buying, which provides companies with greater control other their employees' corporate spending (businessinsider.com).

Richemont partners with Alibaba's Tmall Luxury Pavilion

Richemont has formed a joint venture with **Alibaba** to launch its Net-a-Porter and Mr Porter on Alibaba's Tmall Luxury Pavilion. As Johann Rupert, the Chairman of Richemont, stated: "*Our digital offering in China is in its infancy and we believe that partnering with Alibaba will enable us to become a significant and sustainable online player in this market.*" Under the agreement, which covers Chinese consumers shopping both at home and abroad, Alibaba will provide the technology, logistics, payment and marketing support (ft.com).

Starbucks opens its first sign language branch in D.C.

Starbucks has opened its first sign language branch in Washington D.C., a deaf-centric space with no ambient music where all the employees are fluent in ASL (American Sign Language). This is a brilliant move as it will deepen the emotional connection the deaf community has with Starbucks as well as help it build community in the local neighbourhood, which is home to both Gallaudet University, the only liberal arts university in the world for the deaf and hard of hearing, and Model Secondary School for the Deaf (cnn.com).

VCs have invested $3.5 billion year-to-date in food and grocery delivery services

According to *Pitchbook*, VC firms have invested $3.5 billion in food and grocery delivery services year-to-date, more than triple the amount they invested all of last year. As foot traffic declines, delivery is becoming an important driver of sales growth. For example, delivery now represents 10% of sales in some markets for **McDonald's** (wsj.com). **Blue Apron**, which expanded its in-store pilot program with **Costco** in August, is now partnering with Walmart's Jet.com to offer same or next-day delivery in NYC for a selection of four Blue Apron meal kits (cnbc.com). Although this adds another distribution channel, we question the demand for meal kits in a city that already offers the ultimate in terms of convenience and variety of choice of food. It's interesting as Blue Apron also partnered with **GrubHub** a few weeks to offer on-demand delivery of its meal kits in NYC, which totally didn't make sense as meal kits don't fit the convenience model as they require preparation time (cnbc.com).

Walmart empowers sales floor employees and embraces sustainability

In another smart move, Walmart is empowering employees on the sales floor, giving them access to intelligence only previously available to managers, such as historical sales data and product delivery schedules. Under its new BYOD program, employees are able to download a suite of Walmart apps onto their own phone and then use it to clock in, check inventory and prices, scan products and review sales data. To incentivize employees, Walmart is giving them a discount on their phone bills and promising their personal info on their phones will remain private (hrdive.com). Walmart is also taking steps toward reaching its sustainability goal of having half of its operations powered by renewable energy by 2025. It has entered into an agreement with **SunPower** who will install solar power at 19 of its stores and two of its distribution centres in Illinois, starting in the first half of next year (cnbc.com).

Amazon seems to be stepping back in time into a Norman Rockwell painting, shipping its first physical holiday toy catalogue to millions of kids as it looks to bring back the next generation of the milkman — the Amazon Man — by enabling Prime members to designate one day of the week to receive all their packages. I'm surprised we haven't seen much press on this as I believe the impact on shipping and packaging costs could be materially beneficial to Amazon while materially negative to UPS and FedEx, as well as the packaging-related companies. More big news: WeWork just raised $3 billion in the form of a warrant from SoftBank, valuing it at $42 billion, over twice its $20 billion valuation from last summer. Also on the real estate front, we have evidence of the structural shift to flexible space with CBRE entering the flex office market and Macerich launching a new flex retail space concept, but the bottom line is lease duration is declining which implies higher DCF discount rates. And Starbucks, which I discussed with many of you that I met last week as one of our rare green circles, continues to capitalize on structural disruption opportunities, now partnering with Uber Eats and Line in Japan.

The Amazon Man: November 14, 2018

Amazon Day could solve Amazon's material shipping cost delta

As a brilliant step in moving its Prime members towards a subscription model through promoting sustainability, **Amazon** is testing a new delivery option to enable them to set a specific day of the week for their Amazon shipments to arrive. By designating one day a week as "Amazon Day" this will enhance the convenience proposition for customers by making deliveries more predictable and cutting down on porch thefts. Although it is increasingly convenient to order through Amazon, especially now with Alexa, the reality is that not everyone needs everything all the time. By eliminating multiple deliveries, this could have a material positive impact on Amazon's bottom line by reducing its packaging and shipping costs (cnet.com). For example, this could help solve Amazon's negative shipping cost delta, which was over $8 billion alone for the first nine months of this year as Amazon generated $10.2 billion in subscription services revenue yet spent $18.6 billion in shipping costs. Connecting the dots, we believe that Amazon Delivery Services Partners could be a critical piece of this puzzle as Amazon could basically assign these drivers to the mapped out Amazon Day delivery route. Although e-commerce growth will continue to drive B2C deliveries, we believe the insourcing of delivery of Amazon's heavier packages, which are the most costly for it, could materially negative impact the USPS as well as logistics companies such as **UPS, FedEx** and DHL (**Deutsche Post**). In addition to the consolidation of package delivery, this could consolidate the number of packages, which could have a negative impact on e-commerce-driven expected demand growth for packaging and packaging-related companies. And last, we question whether any other retailer could even create their own "Day", providing Amazon with an even greater competitive advantage.

Macerich launches new flexible retail space concept

To fill the increasing vacant spaces, **Macerich** is formalizing the pop-up concept with the launch of BrandBox, its new flexible retail space concept for online brands. With BrandBox, Macerich is hoping to expand its total addressable market to online brands by offering them an attractive functional value proposition in terms of convenience (i.e., its "plug-and-play" model enables them to open as in short as three weeks), variety of choice (i.e., its flexible modular wall system enables them to choose their opitimal design and size) and pricing (i.e., it offers a lease duration of 6–12 months, a fraction of the traditional 3–10-year commitment) (forbes.com). This comes as **Macy's** applies its radical new downsized "neighbourhood store" format to four of its locations. Ironically, Macy's is hoping to save costs at its underperforming department stores by lowering the functional value proposition as it reduces the variety of choice (reducing its in-store selection as it shrinks its physical footprint by as much as 20%) and decreases convenience (cutting the number of employees by 40% but adding mobile checkout options and installing a desk for picking up online orders and handling returns). At the same time, Macy's is looking to upgrade its "magnet stores", its most productive department stores, spending $200 million this year to renovate 50 stores with plans to renovate another 100 next year. In addition to remodeling the dressing rooms and adding a Starbucks, Macy's is adding 15% more staff and will feature AR and VR on the store floor (wsj.com).

Starbucks partners with Uber Eats and Line in Japan

Starbucks is now moving up the structural capital pyramid to the e-commerce layer in Japan. Starbucks will start offering delivery through Uber Eats from five locations and then scale up over the next two years and it is partnering with **Line** for promotions and on mobile order and payment technology next year (seattletimes.com). Starbucks also plans to leverage the valuable delivery practices it is learning in China, such as re-engineering the packaging for the cup (so the drink stays hot) and the lids (so the drink doesn't spill), and apply them to the U.S. and the rest of the world (cnbc.com). Delivery is also driving growth for **Denny's** as Denny's on Demand now represents 11% of its total sales, with 71% of its locations having at least one delivery partner. Not surprisingly, its on-demand ordering service is most popular during the evening daypart for 18–34-year olds. Denny's launched an Alexa skill in the spring and partnered with Amazon Restaurants in June (skift.com).

Could cubic feet replace square feet as the new metric for warehouse capacity?

As a sign that Amazon is looking to increase the space utilization in its warehouses through vertical expansion as it builds in more densely populated areas, it is looking at shifting the way it measures warehouse capacity from square feet to cubic feet. This is material as, although Amazon is forecasting its warehouse square footage to grow 15% this year, half the rate of the prior two years, its growth in volume could be much higher (cnbc.com).

Amazon releases its first-ever printed toy catalogue

Amazon has started to ship its first-ever printed toy catalogue to millions of customers. Although the 70-page catalogue is designed to look retro, it is high-tech as you can easily obtain more information on the products and add them to your shopping cart just by scanning them with your Amazon app. Amazon is also leveraging its structural capital as the catalogue will be available at its 17 Amazon Book stores and its new 4-Star stores in NYC, Denver and Berkley (cnbc.com). Speaking of kids, **Disney** just announced its new video-streaming service will be called Disney+ and will be available in late 2019 (techcrunch.com).

Amazon offers free two-day holiday shipping for all

Amazon just upped the stakes in the Christmas shopping battle, offering free two-day shipping and free same-day delivery in the U.S. for over 3 million items, including some of the best gifts like toys, electronics, home and fashion (techcrunch.com). To meet the high volume of package deliveries during the holidays, Amazon is hiring seasonal delivery drivers (fortune.com). To facilitate cross-border shopping, Amazon is partnering with **The Western Union Company**. International Amazon shoppers in select countries will now have the option to pay in their local currency at Western Union locations (chainstorage.com). Speaking of delivery, Deliv has raised a $40 million Series C round, bringing its total funding since it launched in 2012 in Menlo Park to $80 million. Although Deliv's past strategic investors include retail REITs and UPS, this time it brought in Google (**Alphabet**) and rental car firm Enterprise Holdings as strategic investors (wsj.com).

Amazon splits new headquarters between NYC and DC

Amazon just announced it will split its new headquarters between the two largest cities on the East Coast: NYC and D.C. Amazon has picked Long Island City and Arlington County's Crystal City neighbourhoods as the locations for its new headquarters (cnbc.com). Speaking of D.C., AWS just opened GovCloud, a new region of interconnected data centres on the East Coast specifically for the U.S. government and contractors. In addition to enabling government agencies and third-party contractors to maintain duplicate copies of their data and apps, having a second data centre region will reduce latency (fortune.com). To inspire over 10 million kids each year to explore computer science, Amazon is launching Amazon Future Engineer. Amazon has committed to fund computer science programs for over

100,000 underprivileged young people in 2,000 low-income high schools across the U.S. In addition, Amazon will award 100 students with four-year $10,000 annual scholarships and internships at Amazon (amazonfutureengineer.com).

Kroger and Albertsons innovate on the AI layer

Kroger has partnered with Google to offer voice shopping for its Kroger Grocery Pickup cart via Google Assistant (progressivegrocer.com). And Albertsons is doing a trial partnership with Takeoff Technologies to automate the process of picking groceries for online orders. Albertsons will portion off areas in selected locations to store a number of items that are popular with online ordering and use robots and conveyers to bring the goods to Albertsons employees to manually compile the order (cnbc.com). We note Takeoff Technologies has raised $15 million since it launched in the Boston area in 2016. Meanwhile, to adapt to the increasing convenience expectations of consumers, 7-Eleven (**Seven & I Holdings**) is piloting a new mobile checkout process called "Scan & Go". Customers just need to scan the product's QR code with their 7-Eleven rewards mobile app and then pay using **Apple** Pay, Google Pay, credit card or debit card. However, hot foods, lottery tickets, alcohol and tobacco are excluded (techcrunch.com).

Amazon brings Alexa and Amazon Music to Mexico

On the music front, Amazon has just brought Alexa and Amazon Music to Mexico (venturebeat.com) and just made its Music Skills API publicly available, enabling developers to stream songs from online services (venturebeat.com). We are also starting to see alliances form between music content providers and hardware providers. For example, just a few weeks after **Sirius XM Holdings** offered a free Echo Dot to its new subscribers, **Spotify** is offering a free Google Home Mini to its existing and new Premium for Family subscribers in the U.S. (engadget.com). We're wondering if this could be the first step for a deeper alliance for Spotify and Google, just like how Amazon stated it is looking to integrate Sirius XM with Alexa later this year. Spotify is also allying with Apple, officially launching its long-awaited app for the Apple Watch (techcrunch.com). **Samsung** is opening up its voice-assistant, Bixby, to third-party developers to build "capsules" (i.e., skills) for the company (wsj.com). However, Samsung has a lot of catching up to do as Alexa already features 50,000 skills. And one of these is to help Americans cook their Thanksgiving turkey as the Butterball Turkey-Talk Line, which has been used by 50 million consumers since it was first launched in 1981, has added an Alexa skill (mediapost.com).

Could The Amazon Hotel be next?

If you remember, back in June, Amazon partnered with **Marriott International** on its "Alexa for Hospitality" initiative. **Alibaba** is taking this one step further, directly entering the hospitality space with the debut of the Flyzoo Hotel, in Hangzhou, China. By leveraging its AI assistant, Tmall Genie, Alibaba is able to cut labour costs in half as well as provide a superior guest experience by enabling guests to use their voice to control the temperature, lights and household appliances in their room as well as buy groceries (chinaplus.cri.cn). Speaking of Alibaba, it just set a new record for Singles' Day, generating $30.8 billion in sales, up 27% from $25.3 billion, but down from the 39% growth it experienced last year (cnbc.com).

Alexa ventures deeper out of bounds into new terrains

Alexa is looking to gain a stronghold in the office. The Alexa app is now available for download from the **Microsoft** Store for Windows 10 PCs in the U.S, U.K. and Germany (techcrunch.com).

Alexa has also arrived on Main Street. **TD Ameritrade**'s retail clients will now be able to buy or sell stocks and ETFs, with a maximum transaction value of $10,000 per trade, through Alexa (businessinsider.com).

Walmart to host its first Black Friday cookie party

Walmart continues to advance up the customer and structural capital pyramids. Walmart is looking to enhance the emotional connection with customers by hosting in-store events such as its first-ever Light Up Black Friday cookie and coffee party. The event will be held at stores across the U.S. from 4 to 6pm on Thanksgiving to kick off the launch of Black Friday (fortune.com). On the AI layer, Walmart has added an AR scanning tool to its iPhone app to enable customers to compare products by pointing the scanner at multiple products on the store shelf (techcrunch.com). To test both associate and customer experiences inside a real store, Walmart is building an Intelligent Retail Lab inside one of its Walmart stores in New York (techcrunch.com). **Office Depot** has realized it can no longer compete against Amazon on a functional value proposition basis (price, convenience, variety of choice). Instead, it is moving up the customer capital pyramid through leveraging its structural capital (i.e., 60% of its 10 million small business customers are located within a 3-mile radius of one of its 1,400 retail stores) and its supplier capital (i.e., its 50,000+ staff) to offer personalized business services such as business strategy, marketing and staffing, as well as subscription services for ink, toner and software (digiday.com).

U.K. suffers over 4,000 net store closures in first half of this year

The retail apocalypse is deepening in the U.K. According to PwC, the top 500 retail streets in Britain experienced a net decline of 1,123 stores (2,692 stores closed while only 1,569 opened) in the first half of this year versus a net decline of only 222 stores in the first half of last year. The categories with the most closures included fashion shops and pubs. The situation is even more dire across the U.K., which saw over 4,000 net store closures in the first half of this year versus a slight increase in the first half of last year (qz.com). Fashion shops could be in deeper trouble as Amazon is bringing its Prime Wardrobe "try before you buy service" to the U.K., just weeks after launching it in Japan (theguardian.com). Meanwhile, across the pond, **Sears Holdings** announced it will be closing 40 stores in addition to the 142 it previously announced that it will be shutting down by the end of the year as part of its bankruptcy proceeding. However, in a new filing, unsecured creditors are demanding that it shut down all its remaining stores, claiming that its plan to survive bankruptcy is "*nothing more than wishful thinking*" and "*an unjustified and foolhardy gamble with other people's money*" (businessinsider.com). And **Lowe's** is closing 20 underperforming Lowe's stores across 13 states in the U.S and 31 locations across five provinces in Canada, including 24 Rona stores. Although the closures only represent 2% of Lowe's overall base of 2,355 stores, they represent over 5% of its base of 430 Rona stores in Canada (businessinsider.com). We note Lowe's announced the $3.2 billion acquisition of Rona in February 2016.

One King's Lane and Glossier open flagship stores in Soho

We are seeing new bricks rise from the rubble in Soho. One King's Lane's new flagship store in Soho is designed to make you feel like you're at home. In addition to featuring a number of different rooms, it offers a home interior design studio staffed by professionals and an upholstery furniture customized service (housebeautiful.com). Glossier is opening its first flagship store in Soho in NYC. The two-storey 3,000-square foot Glossier Flagship store offers the experience of "*conversation, story-telling and community building*". This embraces the idea that retail is still about discovery and art – what Glossier's founder Emily Weiss terms "emotional commerce" (forbes.com). We note that Glossier, a DTC beauty company, has raised $86 million since it launched in NYC in 2014.

Apple finally embraces Amazon

In time for the holiday season, Apple is embracing Amazon as an e-commerce distribution channel. Amazon will start selling the latest editions of Apple's iPhone, iPad, Watch and other devices in the U.S., Europe, Japan and India. And starting in the New Year, Amazon will eliminate Apple products on its platform sold by unauthorized merchants. Not surprisingly, the one Apple device that Amazon will not be selling on its platform is the new HomePod as it is a rival to Alexa (reuters.com).

Chapter Three: Below the Red Tide

As the world shifts to e-commerce, we continue to see the rise of new forms of payment, packaging, marketplaces and delivery. For example, Chinese consumers are embracing biometric payments while Standard Cognition just raised $40 million to advance its cashierless platform. On the packaging front, CPG companies are starting to re-design products for e-commerce as P&G introduced its new "Tide Eco-Box". We are also seeing the emergence of new forms of marketplaces as Neighborhood Goods re-thinks the department store while Rent the Runway opens its online apparel subscription rental platform to brands. And on the delivery side, Instacart is rolling out curbside pick-up while Ford is partnering with Walmart and Postmates to test autonomous grocery delivery.

The New Forms: November 20, 2018

Procter & Gamble rolls out "Tide Eco-Box" as it adapts to new world of e-commerce

Back in May 2017, **Amazon** invited executives from the world's largest CPG companies to a three-day gathering at its Seattle headquarters to convince executives to re-think how their products could be designed, packaged and shipped for direct-to-consumer sales. Over a year later, **Procter & Gamble** is starting to re-design its products for e-commerce, as evidenced by the rollout of its new "Tide Eco-Box". The eco-box, which resembles a wine-box, is environmentally friendly as it has 60% less plastic and it will save on shipping costs as it is lighter and takes up less space in a delivery truck. It will be available on Amazon and Walmart.com in January (cnn.com).

Canada Goose's DTC sales soar 150% in Q3 as it leverages its cult-like following

Our thesis that vertically integrated, high-margin apparel, accessories & luxury goods companies with social missions are uniquely positioned to originate value by leveraging their cult-like following to build DTC distribution channels is playing out. **Canada Goose**'s revenue rose 33.7% in Q3 to $230 million, but, more importantly, its DTC sales soared by 150% to $50 million, accounting for 21.9% of total sales, nearly double the 11.7% level a year ago. As the gross margin for Canada's Goose DTC distribution channel is much higher than its wholesale channel (75.2% versus 50.4%), this led to positive mix shift, resulting in its overall gross margin rising 520 bp to 55.8% (businessinsider.com).

Ford partners with Walmart and Postmates on autonomous grocery delivery pilot

Ford, which partnered with Postmates back in January to test autonomous grocery delivery, is now doing a pilot with both **Walmart** and Postmates. Ford will work closely with Walmart over the next few months to understand its operations, to identify what goods can be transported, and to solve logistical problems (techcrunch.com). This is important as e-commerce is becoming a major growth driver for Walmart. For example, Walmart reported stronger-than-expected 3.4% comparable sales growth in Q319, with 140 bp coming from the 43% growth in e-commerce sales (wsj.com). To further increase the convenience value proposition, Instacart is adding the option of curbside pick-up. Interestingly, Instacart has now partnered with over 300 grocery retailers and offers its one-hour delivery service from 15,000 stores in over 4,000 cities in North America (forbes.com). Just as Instacart has become the go-to on-demand delivery platform, Standard Cognition is seeking become the go-to cashierless checkout platform. Standard Cognition just raised a $40 million Series A round as it seeks to help retailers compete with Amazon Go. In September, Standard Cognition opened a 1,900-square-foot flagship test store in San Francisco and it has partnered with four retailers, including Japanese pharmacy chain **Yakuodo** and three unnamed U.S. grocery, pharmacy and convenience retailers (techcrunch.com). Chinese consumers are embracing biometric payments. According to Alipay, during **Alibaba**'s recent Singles' Day event, 60.3% of customers paid by either scanning their fingerprint or by taking a selfie (techcrunch.com).

David's Bridal files for bankruptcy

David's Bridal, which operates over 300 stores across the U.S., Canada, U.K. and Mexico, filed for bankruptcy on November 19 (cnbc.com). We note Alfred Angelo Bridal filed for bankruptcy back in July 2017. Apparel retailers face rising structural risk from new entrants such as Rent the Runway, which is embracing new ways to extract value by moving up the economic capital pyramid to the marketplace economy layer. Rent the Runway, which has up until now owned the designer apparel inventory it rents out, is increasing its supply by providing access to its platform to 39 lower-end brands such as J. Crew, Levi's and Club Monaco (**Ralph Lauren**) to rent out their inventory. In addition to providing brands with valuable customer capital (i.e., access to Rent the Runway's 10 million members), it provides them with access to valuable data such as the wear rate, style preference and product feedback (fastcompany.com).

Blue Apron cuts jobs as its customer attrition continues

In the meal kit space, **Blue Apron** is cutting 100 salaried jobs as it continues to lose customers, with its customer base declining to 646,000 at the end of September, down 10% from the prior quarter and down 25% from a year ago (wsj.com). Chick-Fil-A, which started to sell "Mealtime Kits" in July, is partnering with DoorDash to offer delivery within a 10-mile radius from 1,100 restaurants, or just under half, of its 2,300 locations (fortune.com).

Microsoft starts to sell Echo devices at its retail stores

Alexa is invading the turf of her new friend, Cortana, as **Microsoft** has started to sell Amazon's Echo devices at its retail stores (theverge.com). Alexa's allure continues to grow as Tidal, Jay-Z's music subscription streaming service, is now available as an Alexa skill on the Amazon Echo. This is the first music streaming service to make use of Amazon's Music Skills API which enables developers to build in support for Alexa rather than having to rely on Amazon (theverge.com). Huawei Technologies, which has developed its Xiaoyi voice assistant for the Chinese market, is working on creating its own voice assistant for markets outside of China (cnbc.com). Interestingly, at the IFA 2018 consumer electronics show in Berlin, Huawei debuted its AI Cube smart speaker, featuring Alexa integration, which it planned to launch in Europe for the Christmas season.

Nordstrom's full-price comp sales only rise 0.4% in Q3

Nordstrom reported disappointing Q318 results with its full-price store comparable sales up only 0.4%, far below the 5.8% growth at Nordstrom Rack. Its digital sales growth also slowed to 20% from 23% last quarter, with digital sales declining from 34% to 30% of total sales. In addition, Nordstrom's net income was hurt by a $72 million charge to repay its credit card holders with delinquent accounts which had been improperly charged with higher interest rates starting in 2010 (cnbc.com). Although Nordstrom is trying to innovate with concepts such as Nordstrom Local, it is still stuck with its legacy department store model and could face the threat of new entrants such as Rent the Runway and Neighborhood Goods. For example, Neighborhood Goods, which raised a $5.8 million seed round in May to re-think the traditional department store, just launched its first 13,000-square-foot store in Plano, Texas. On the customer capital level, the store seeks to create an emotional connection with customers through fun gathering spots as well as its dynamic sales floor which features a rotating selection of 15 DTC brands at a time which offer unique experiences. The store embraces the digital layer by enabling customers to use its iOS app to explore the brands, make purchases and ask questions (fastcompany.com).

I don't know about you, but I am totally shell-shocked by the toxic red tide that has washed over the markets since the beginning of October. But we have to avoid being blinded by the red glare as the structural disruption forces continue to build below the surface. For example, magazines are re-inventing themselves as Marie Claire is moving its fashion content beyond advertising to launch an online shopping platform. Ironically, the same day the founder of Casper predicts the death of bad retail, the Gap announces plans to aggressively close hundreds of stores. As the Gap downsizes, Canada Goose embraces its accessibility-focused social mission and adds cold rooms to create a unique in-store experience. Even IKEA, which provides one of the best shopping experiences for families, is changing its retail strategy, shifting to smaller-format urban stores and delivery. And soon you might be able to use Amazon Pay at restaurants and gas stations.

Below the Red Tide: November 27, 2018

Canada Goose's new cold rooms create a unique in-store experience

Canada Goose is adding cold rooms to a selection of its 11 corporate-owned stores to enable its customers to test its luxury cold weather outerwear in temperatures as low as -25° Celsius. The cold rooms create a unique sharable experience as they feature sculpted ice blocks lining a glass window (vancouversun.com). More importantly, as the cold rooms advance Canada Goose's accessibility-focused mission to "*free people from the cold — no matter where they live — and empower them to experience more from life*", they will help the company increase the psychological attachment its customers have to the brand. Meanwhile, **Kering**, which formed a joint venture with Yoox in 2012 to power its online sales, is taking its e-commerce back in-house. This isn't surprising given **Richemont** acquired the remaining 50% stake in Yoox Net-a-Porter back in January. More importantly, e-commerce is becoming a critical competitive ground as it is the most important growth engine for the luxury industry, with Bain & Co. expecting e-commerce sales penetration to increase from 10% last year to 25% by 2025. As part of its e-commerce strategy, Kering is working on a suite of apps in partnership with **Apple** to improve the in-store and payment experience (businessoffashion.com). Speaking of Yoox Net-a-Porter, Marie Claire has come up with a brilliant way to leverage the unique advice and curation of its fashion editors to connect customers to retail partners such as Selfridges, **Farfetch**, Yoox Net-a-Porter and Topshop. Marie Claire U.K. is re-thinking how to extract value with its new online shopping platform called Marie Claire Edit. Marie Claire is also planning to launch a campaign with Pinterest and Farfetch to leverage its Pinterest channel, which has 660,000 followers (digiday.com).

Amazon looks to bring Amazon Pay to gas stations and restaurants

Amazon is moving deeper in the banking space, looking to partner with non-retail competitors, such as gas stations and restaurants, to enable their customers to pay with Amazon Pay. As Amazon incentivizes merchants by offering lower payment processing fees and marketing services, this could pose a competitive threat to **Mastercard** and **Visa**. Although digital wallets are still in the nascent stage, comprising less than 1% of all U.S. card transactions last year, Apple Pay is now accepted at 5 million locations across the U.S. (wsj.com). Ultimately, we believe the companies best positioned to transition up to the new crypto-economy over the next decade, creating new ways to extract value, are online marketplace platforms like Amazon and Apple whose digital wallets could evolve into the next digital currencies. The boundaries between banking and retail continue to blur as **Capital One** has acquired Wikibuy, an Austin-based online comparison shopping tool that has grown to 2 million members since it was launched in 2014, to help its customers save time and money while shopping online (cnbc.com). Interestingly, the founder of Wikibuy is Jonathan Coon, who founded 1-800 CONTACTS in his college dorm back in 1992.

Gap plans to aggressively close hundreds of its underperforming stores

After reporting a 7% decline in comparable store sales for Q3 at its Gap namesake brand, **Gap** is looking to close hundreds of underperforming Gap-branded stores. As Gap is looking to close the bottom half of its fleet of 875 Gap-branded stores quickly and aggressively, this could lead to further vacancies at mall-based retail REITs (cnbc.com). On this note, Philp Krim, the co-founder of Casper, predicts the death of bad retail. For example, before Casper came along, people shopping for a mattress had to make the trek to a store where they had to deal with a commissioned salesperson under fluorescent lights in an environment that didn't feel very comfortable. In addition, as legacy companies silo their wholesale, retail and e-commerce retail channels, and they don't have agility in their DNA, he believes they will not be able to deliver what is becoming a very complex customer permutation (wsj.com). For example, the accelerating shift from bricks to clicks is showing up in the Thanksgiving and Black Friday sales data. Foot traffic to U.S. stores fell between 5% and 9% on Thanksgiving and Black Friday, according to RetailNext, which uses cameras to track people in both mall-based stores and stand-alone retailers (wsj.com). At the same time, Adobe Analytics calculated that online sales rose 28% year-over-year to $3.7 billion on Thanksgiving and 24% year-over-year to $6.2 billion on Black Friday. Interestingly, on Black Friday, 33.5% of e-commerce sales came from mobile devices, up from 29.1% a year ago (cnbc.com).

The emergence of robots-as-a-service

Last week I was scrolling through my LinkedIn feed when I noticed a TechCrunch article titled *Kindred's robots help retailers handle fulfillment centers — and take on Amazon.* But it's a small world, as it turns out that Gregg Schoenberg, who shared the article, was also the author of the article. And ironically, it was exactly three years ago that I connected with Gregg, a former Wall Streeter who had back then just launched his radical fintech newsletter, the *Financial Revolutionist*, which he just sold. In the article, Gregg interviews Jim Liefer, the CEO of Kindred AI, is purpose building robots for retail fulfillment centres. Interestingly, instead of selling its robots to retailers, it is embracing a robots-as-a-service model. This is material from a financial perspective as by paying robots on a throughput basis, this shifts the cost of robots from being a capital investment on the balance sheet to an operating expense on the income statement, similar to hiring an employee (techcrunch.com). We note Kindred has raised $44 million since it launched in San Francisco in 2014, with its last $28 million Series B round being led by **Tencent Holdings**. Meanwhile, Geek Plus, a Chinese logistics and warehousing robotics developer launched in Beijing in 2015, just raised a $150 million Series B round. Geek Plus has delivered over 5,000 robots across 100 robotics warehouse projects around the world for customers such as **Alibaba**'s Tmall. Its robots perform functions such as picking, sorting, movement and include unmanned forklifts (techcrunch.com). And AWS has launched RoboMaker, a service to help developers build, test and deploy robotics applications through the cloud. Ultimately, this will help developers simultaneously create and configure multiple virtual worlds, from factories to retail stores, to test software for robots before deploying the code for real (venturebeat.com).

Disney plans to invest $24 billion in theme parks, cruise ships & hotels over next five years

Over the next five years, **Disney** plans to invest $24 billion to leverage its customer and structural capital and enhance the customer experience. Disney plans to add capacity to its most popular theme parks, Disneyland and Tokyo DisneySea, and complete major upgrades at Epcot and Walt Disney Studios Park in Paris. Disney also plans to double its cruise line fleet with the addition of three new ships, at a cost of $1.25 billion each. Disney is also looking to build an experiential hotel, codenamed Project Hubble, which will simulate sleeping on board a luxury "Star Wars" starship as it zooms through the galaxy (nytimes.com). Speaking of Disney, Amazon is looking to deepen its sports video content beyond Thursday Night Football, bidding for all 22 regional sports TV networks that Disney acquired from Twenty-First Century Fox (**News Corp.**). This is a serious threat to traditional media companies that are increasingly relying on sports content, which needs to be watched live, to maintain viewership in the new on-demand world (cnbc.com).

Clorox sees DTC brands as a significant threat

The CMO of **Clorox**, Eric Reynolds, sees DTC brands as a significant threat to its business. To better originate value, Clorox is looking to leverage its customer capital by collecting data on 100 million of its customers through a combination of acquiring DTC brands like Burt's Bees, as well as using social for high engagement categories like vitamins to convert customers into its CRM programs. To better capture value, Clorox is also spending a significant portion of its media budget on Amazon for not just search but also display and sponsored content (adexchange.com).

Walmart testing delivery service in China powered through WeChat

At one of its stores in China, **Walmart** is testing Walmart to Go, a same-day grocery delivery service that enables customers to place orders for a selection of nearly 8,000 products through WeChat (techcrunch.com). We note that back in June, Walmart entered an in-depth strategic partnership with Tencent

Holdings to enhance payment services through "Walmart Scan and Pay", WeChat payment, facial recognition and self-service options. Meanwhile, Coupang, the largest e-commerce firm in Korea, has just raised $2 billion from **SoftBank**, which also invested $1 billion back in June 2015. Coupang, which was founded in Seoul in 2010, claims that half of the adults in Korea have its app on their phone and forecasts its revenue to soar 70% in 2018 to nearly $5 billion (techcrunch.com).

Amazon launches holiday pop-up showrooms in Europe as IKEA re-thinks its store strategy

Amazon is launching "Amazon Loft for Xmas" pop-up showrooms in major European cities to celebrate the holidays. In addition to offering a physical locations to allow consumers to touch and test products from Amazon's marketplace as well as Amazon devices, the showrooms will offer unique and innovative experiences such as book readings, live performances, cooking demonstrations and workshops (pymnts.com). At the same time, IKEA just announced a series of radical changes in its boldest restructuring. It plans to quickly cut 7,500 clerical and administrative jobs but then add 11,500 employees over the next two years as it focuses on increasing delivery options, upgrading its online presence and improving the in-store experience. IKEA is re-thinking how it captures value on a physical level as it moves closer to consumers by opening 30 new stores in city centres as opposed to on the outskirts and one-quarter the size of its traditional store. IKEA is also re-thinking how it originates value on a functional level by investing more in delivery and on the emotional level by featuring more showrooms in its layout, making it a better customer experience (inc.com). We note that IKEA started rolling out this strategic shift in Australia where it is replacing the self-service warehouse experience for bulky furniture items with home delivery from one of three new distribution centres and aggressively rolling out smaller-format city stores.

Could the future of retail see the disappearance of the middleman? This is the shocking scenario that the CEO of a Chinese mall operator paints as he envisions a world where consumers deal directly with manufacturers and malls are repurposed into warehouses. This is already starting to happen. According to JLL, investors are re-developing empty retail big boxes into e-commerce fulfillment centres. And we continue to see the rise in DTC brands as Prose (custom hair care) just raised $18 million, Quip (oral care subscription) raised $40 million and Sleep Country went on the defensive with its $89 million acquisition of Endy. Even Walmart has realized it needs to get closer to its customers — it is starting to shift toward social commerce with the launch of the online interactive Walmart Toy Lab while TD Ameritrade just became the first U.S. brokerage firm to partner with WeChat. And if you're looking to find your perfect watch – look no further than WatchTinder!

The Disappearance: December 4, 2018

Fidelity warns U.K. retail real estate values could plummet 20–70%

We just learned of a big red flag for retail REITs. Fidelity, which manages a £617 million institutional U.K. property fund, is warning U.K. retail real estate values could plummet by 20–70%. This could be driven by a 10–40% reduction in rents to make them affordable for retailers in combination with a 10–30% de-rating of the sector (ft.com). More pain is in store for U.S. retail REITs as **Sears Holdings** has filed a court document identifying over 505 stores it plans to sell, which is more than triple the 142 it originally announced it would close when it filed for bankruptcy on October 15. In addition, Sears will be asking landlords of its profitable stores for rent reductions (fortune.com). This comes as the CEO of Intime Retail, Chen Xiadong, predicts that the future of retail may see consumers dealing directly with manufacturers. As the middlemen retailers are displaced, this will lead to department stores and malls being re-purposed into warehouses (cnbc.com). We note Intime Retail, which operates 62 stores and shopping malls across 33 cities in China, was acquired for $2.6 billion by **Alibaba** in January 2017. Speaking of Alibaba, the biggest department store in Spain, El Corte Ingles, is looking to expand its total addressable market by selling its products worldwide through Alibaba's Tmall and AliExpress platforms. In return, El Corte Ingles is providing Alibaba with valuable structural capital by enabling AliExpress to establish a physical presence in its department stores in Spain (news.abs-cbn.com).

Uber Freight's Lane Explorer tool raises the bar for trucking brokerages

Uber Freight's new machine learning Lane Explorer tool raises the bar for companies operating in the trucking brokerage space by introducing a new level of price transparency. Uber Freight, which launched a platform for SMEs to enable them to manage and track their shipments, is now enabling them to view and book real-time market-rates up to two weeks in advance (truckinginfo.com). We believe the higher level of price transparency will increase the bargaining power of shippers.

Tesco's venture with VW raises obsolescence risk for gas station convenience stores

Tesco is partnering with **Volkswagen** to build the largest free electric car charging network in the U.K. Over the next three years, it will install nearly 2,500 charging points in parking lots at up to 600 Tesco stores across the U.K., or just under 20% of its base of over 3,400 U.K. stores (cnbc.com). Although the rising obsolescence of gas stations is not a new story, the red flag we see is that gas station convenience stores will face plenty of competition from other retailers that will be motivated to leverage their structural capital (i.e., parking lot stalls) to install charging stations to attract customers while automobile manufacturers will be motivated to fund the charging costs.

TD Ameritrade becomes the first U.S. brokerage firm to partner with WeChat

TD Ameritrade is at the forefront of embracing new technologies to bring convenience to its retail brokerage customers. Just a few weeks after it became the first U.S. brokerage firm to allow retail clients to buy and sell stocks/ETFs through Alexa, it has become the first U.S. brokerage firm to partner with **Tencent Holdings**' WeChat. TD Ameritrade is opening a portal on WeChat for U.S. users to enable them to check market data and account balance info as well as chat with agents (cnbc.com). In Japan, **Line** is partnering with WeChat on mobile payments. Japanese bricks-and-mortar merchants with Line Pay terminals will now be able to process WeChat Pay transactions from the over 7 million Chinese tourists that visit Japan each year (techcrunch.com). Speaking of payments, Costa (**Coca-Cola Company)** customers will soon be able to pay for their coffee just by tapping their coffee cup. Costa is introducing the Clever Cup, a £15 reusable coffee cup featuring a detachable contactless chip powered by Barclaycard's (**Barclays**) payment technology (engadget.com). Although this leverages technology to promote sustainability, I'd be worried about spilling my coffee when I tilt my cup to pay.

H&M invests in e-commerce payment firm enabling Millennials to "try before you buy"

H&M just made a $20 million strategic investment in Klarna, a fintech firm which provides e-commerce payment solutions for online merchants and shoppers. By enabling its mostly Millennial customers to "try before you buy", they no longer have to wait for their returns to be credited which is a big problem given apparel e-commerce return rates are 28% versus 9% for traditional stores (theguardian.com). In addition, as fintech expert Gregg Schoenberg pointed out to me "*The key is to think of them as debit card specialists. When younger people, who overwhelmingly use debit cards, make purchases, they don't get the same protections or float that people who use credit cards get*". We note Klarna has now raised a total of $682 million since it launched in Stockholm in 2005.

Personal products CPG companies face threat of new online entrants like Prose & Quip

Prose, a DTC custom hair care brand launched last year in NYC, just raised an $18 million Series B round. As Kirsten Green, founder of Forerunner Ventures and investor in Prose, wisely observes: "*The ultimate luxury is a product that is made just for you*" (fastcompany.com).

Sleep Country goes on the defensive with its $89 million acquisition of Endy

Given the multiple red flags we have seen for mattress retailers in the second half, it is not surprising that **Sleep Country** is going on the defensive and acquiring Endy for $89 million (financialpost.com). Although Endy's sales are forecast to soar over 300% this year to reach $50 million, we note it was only a year ago this DTC mattress-in-a-box brand raised a $1 million venture round on Dragon's Den. Although this acquisition will enhance Sleep Country's online offerings, Endy won't contribute much in terms of customer capital given the low frequency of mattress purchases, and makes us question the success of Sleep Country's own DTC Bloom brand it launched in May 2017. And as Mike Gettis, Endy's founder, pointed out in an interview less than six months ago: "*If you've ever shopped for a mattress in a traditional retail store, you know the experience can be frustrating – at best. There's a commissioned salesperson trying to make a quick sale, it's impossible to price check between retailers or read reviews, and you end up overpaying for a mattress that gives you back pain or sags in a couple of years*" (troymedia.com). Meanwhile, Parachute, a DTC bedding and bath essentials company that raised a $30 million Series C round in June, has doubled its physical footprint to six stores and plans to expand to 20 by 2020. Parachute views bricks-and-mortar as a critical part of its retail strategy as they help it build community and also function as mini-distribution centres. In addition, stores generate a higher conversion rate than online (50% versus 40%) and, most importantly, the presence of a store actually increases Parachute's average online spend in the area by 10 times (digiday.com).

Amazon ventures out of bounds to the final frontier

Amazon is leveraging the infrastructure from dozens of AWS centres to build a network of 12 satellite facilities around the world called AWS Ground Station in a multi-year strategic business agreement with **Lockheed Martin**, which manufactures and operates satellites for the U.S. military. Amazon is also partnering with several satellite companies, including Spire Global, DigitalGlobe (**Maxar Technologies**) and Black Sky, which will use Amazon's ground station- as- a- service to augment the operations of their ground facilities (i.e., achieve faster speeds at lower costs). AWS Ground Station, which will begin operations in mid-2019, will be a vital link for transmitting data to and from satellites in orbit (cnbc.com). Interestingly, as we noted in our October 2 research note, Amazon is partnering with **Iridium Communications** to bring Internet connectivity to the "whole planet" by developing a satellite-based network called CloudConnect for Internet of Things (IoT) applications. And perhaps foreshadowing AWS Ground Station, AWS was looking to hire a software engineer and a product manager "*to help innovate and disrupt the launch, satellite and space world with new AWS products, services and features...for a new AWS service that will have a historic impact*".

AWS brings its servers to traditional data centres

Amazon will also be bringing its AWS-branded boxes to traditional data centres, posing a direct competitive threat to legacy hardware vendors such as **Cisco**, **Dell** and **Hewlett Packard Enterprise**. At the AWS re:Invent conference, Amazon introduced AWS Outposts, its new on-premise service for companies where it will deliver and install its hardware systems, ranging from single servers to multiple racks of data centre equipment, at customers' facilities and provide ongoing services such as maintenance, repair and software updates (cnbc.com). And AWS is offering developers free access to the machine learning courses it uses to train its own software engineers, representing over 45 hours of course material, videos and lab tests across 30 different courses. In addition, it is offering 50% off its "AWS Certified Machine Learning – Specialty" certification (thenextweb.com).

Nike's new store in NYC leverages technology to enhance retail experience

Nike's research reveals that over 80% of its consumers still want the physical experience as part of retail. Its new 65,000-square-foot store on Fifth Avenue in NYC leverages technology to enhance the retail experience. For example, if you're interested in trying on the clothes you see on one of their mannequins, you just need to snap the QR code which pulls up the items and then you can find your size and have it sent to the changing room to try on. The store also features a speed shop which features the trending now clothes. And you can even reserve items online and then pick them up from the smart locker in the store to try on (fastcompany.com). In Japan, GU (**Fast Retailing**) is opening a concept store in Tokyo's Harajuku fashion district that is more of a showroom as it allows customers to try on apparel and then order it online. The GU Style Studio store also features QR codes attached to clothes that customers can scan with their app to view a virtual dressed mannequin on their phone. GU, which is the more affordable and fashion-forward sibling to Uniqulo with nearly 400 stores across Asia, plans to roll out this showroom template to smaller shops in cities that don't have the space to store inventory (businessoffashion.com).

Apple and Amazon deepen their strategic relationship

Apple and Amazon are deepening their strategic relationship. Less than a month after Apple embraced Amazon's marketplace as an e-commerce distribution channel, it is now embracing Amazon's Echo devices as a music distribution channel. Starting in mid-December, Echo devices will be able to stream songs from Apple Music, allowing users to ask Alexa to play specific songs, genres and playlists. The partnership provides Amazon with valuable customer capital in the form of Apple Music's 56 million subscribers (techcrunch.com). Even **Alphabet** seems to be partnering with Amazon on the music front. Although Amazon Prime Video is still not available on Android TV, Amazon Music is coming soon to it (9to5google.com). Meanwhile, to improve the user experience, **Spotify** is testing new features that include allowing you to import your own music directly from your Android phone to Spotify, as well as the option to save a podcast to listen to later (androidandme.com).

Walmart embraces social commerce with its new online interactive Walmart Toy Lab

As part of its strategy to become "*America's best toy shop*", **Walmart** has launched the Walmart Toy Lab, a website that lets kids virtually play with the top toys and then vote to add them to their toy box. Personally, as a mother of two young boys, this seems like more of an interactive commercial exploiting kids to collect data. However, as Chris Walton suggests, this initiative represents the broader shift toward social commerce and the potential for retailers like Walmart to build social media platforms to generate discovery instead of just paying for search advertising. For example, a 7-year old has become a YouTube celebrity and earned over $22 million for just unboxing and playing with toys through his *Ryan ToysReview* YouTube channel which has grown to over 17.3 million followers and generated over 26 billion views since he launched it with his parents in March 2015 (forbes.com). Speaking of exploitation, Amazon, which introduced Amazon Teen back in October 2017 to provide teens with more autonomy by providing them with their own accounts liked to their parent's account, is now aggressively marketing to kids with ads on Snapchat (**Snap**) (fastcompany.com). We note Snapchat started rolling out a visual product search shopping feature in partnership with Amazon in September. Meanwhile, WatchAdvisor, a Swiss platform that connects watch brands with watch lovers and watch stores, has launched WatchTinder. This matchmaking service asks you a number of lifestyle, budget and style questions to provide you with a personalized list of matches which you can then swipe through to find your ideal watch which you can then purchase through authorized e-tailer Troverie (maxim.com).

Big box stores are being re-developed into e-commerce fulfillment centres

According to **Jones Lang LaSalle**, investors are re-developing empty retail big boxes and Class B office buildings in urban locations into last mile e-commerce fulfillment centres (nreionline.com). On the topic of the last mile, **UPS** is forecasting it will handle nearly 800 million packages between Thanksgiving and Christmas this year, up 5% from last holiday season. As this equates to 31 million packages each delivery day, double its average daily volume, UPS has been investing in both its structural and customer capital. On the structural capital side, UPS is looking to increase the number of packages processed through its automated facilities from 50% last year to 70% as a result of the billions it has invested to add 22 new or retrofitted automated sorting facilities. On the customer capital side, UPS is enhancing its relationships by collaborating with customers that represent 80% of its peak volume to improve their shipping forecasts (wsj.com).

Amazon testing cashierless checkout technology for bigger stores

Amazon, which now operates seven Amazon Go stores, is apparently testing its cashierless checkout technology for bigger stores (wsj.com). In Toronto, Uber Eats is hiring a head of grocery product with the goal to "*build the organization and globally scale a brand new product offering which will fundamentally evolve how people purchase their groceries*" (businessinsider.com). And Cleveron, the Estonian-based start-up that developed Walmart's Pick-up Tower, has now developed Lotte, the world's first robotic courier. By autonomously transporting packages to homes/businesses and using its robotics arm to place packages in a pick-up locker, Lotte hopes to reduce the cost of last mile delivery by totally replacing human labour (businessinsider.com).

Chapter Four: The Existential Threat

"There is an existential threat to Fortune 500 companies before the end of this decade" (wsj.com). Investors would be wise to heed this warning by Sean Sullivan, an angel investor who helped coin the term "cloud computing" back in 1996, that companies must realize they can no longer function as non-tech businesses. For example, in the auto space, Uber has filed to IPO next year at a $120 billion valuation while Elon Musk has expressed interest in buying some of the five North American factories that GM is closing. In the health space, Uber and Lyft are expanding into medical transport, Peloton is taking share from SoulCycle, hearables is the next frontier for wearables and Walgreens has partnered with FedEx to offer prescription drug delivery. In retail, Walmart is leveraging AR to transform its aisles into virtual winter wonderlands, the new shopping channel is live video streaming and the hot new trend for luxury is not selling anything. And providing further evidence of WeWork's plan for global domination — it has just partnered with American Express.

The Existential Threat: December 11, 2018

Food retailers could face rising delivery risks as Instacart shoppers protest pay cuts

Our investment thesis that retailers that don't have their own on-demand delivery platform are at risk of losing control over the customer relationship and experience may start to play out. Instacart, which has become the go-to on-demand delivery platform for most food retailers, quietly slashed its delivery and membership rates in November to better compete with Amazon and attract new customers. However, to offset these lower fees, Instacart started to roll out a new payment structure in the U.S. that its shoppers claim has led to a significant cut in their earnings. As a result, Instacart's shoppers are starting to reject jobs that are too low-paying, which is leading to delays in customer orders and rising customer dissatisfaction (businessinsider.com). As we warned back in January 2017, when Instacart reduced its pay structure for the third time in less than a year, this could lead to attrition in its supply base and a negative network effect, and impact the food retailers with which it partnered. Amazon understands this risk which is why it continues to displace Instacart at Whole Foods as its Prime Now two-hour complimentary grocery delivery service is now available in over 60 cities across the U.S. (press.aboutamazon.com). Speaking of Whole Foods, it continues to innovate ways to enhance the in-store experience and is now testing an in-store DIY almond milk bar in partnership with NuMilk. The pilot, which is running in two Whole Foods stores in New Jersey, allows customers to blend and bottle their own almond milk, which they can then buy for $3.99/bottle (thekitchn.com).

Could platforms start to commoditize restaurants?

We are starting to see evidence that platforms are looking to commoditize restaurants, which could lead to a race to the bottom. For example, in India, Uber Eats is testing featuring a "Specials" section, offering restaurants promoted product placement on discounts of bundled meals (techcrunch.com). This is why restaurants need to evolve beyond competing on just the functional level (i.e., price, convenience, variety of choice) to create emotional connections with their customers. To this means, Flipdish, an online ordering and loyalty platform for restaurants, just raised a €4.8 million Series A round. By enabling restaurants to accept online orders directly and manage their online presence and operations, Flipdish is looking to provide a better alternative to platforms such as **Just Eat** and Deliveroo by reducing their costs and increasing their control over the customer experience (techcrunch.com). To take complete control over the customer experience, Pizza Hut (**Yum! Brands**) has gone one step further and is acquiring QuikOrder, an online ordering software and services provider for restaurants. This provides Pizza Hut with valuable structural capital on the digital layer as it gives it control over the software platform it has been using for two decades and processes half of its U.S. sales through. More importantly, it provides Pizza Hut with valuable customer capital and data in terms of the items ordered, time of order and frequency of orders (cnbc.com).

Top four U.S. department stores account for 300 million square feet or equivalent of 300 malls

Green Street Advisors calculates that the department stores still open in the U.S. account for over 350 million square feet of mall space, or the equivalent of 350 average-sized malls. Even scarier is that the top four department stores account for over 85% of this, with **Macy's** 800 stores alone accounting for 160 million square feet, or nearly 50% of the total. **JC Penney** is the second-largest department store, with its 560 stores totaling 55 million square feet, or 15% of the total. **Sears Holdings**, which declared bankruptcy on October 15, is the third-largest, with 330 stores still open, totaling 45 million square feet while **Dillards**' 280 stores take up another 45 million square feet (cnbc.com).

We are starting to see department stores being repurposed into moving company storage warehouses. According to court documents, U-Haul (**AMERCO**) is looking to buy 13 former Sears and Kmart stores from bankrupt Sears Holdings for $62 million which it plans to redevelop into storage centres and places to house their fleet of rental trucks (businessinsider.com). Retail REITs continue to face the risk of rising vacancies as children's clothing company, Gymboree, which filed for bankruptcy in June 2017 and emerged from bankruptcy in September 2017 after closing 350 stores, is now considering closing over half of its remaining 900 stores (chainstorage.com). However, some of the vacancies could be filled by DTC brands like UNTUCKit, which plans to triple its physical footprint over the next five years to 150 stores. Since UNTUCKit launched as a DTC casual men's apparel company in NYC in 2011, it has grown to $150 million in sales and is apparently profitable. UNTUCKit raised a $30 million Series A round in June 2017 and has hired Morgan Stanley to help it raise more capital to fund its aggressive expansion plans, at apparently a valuation of over $600 million (cnbc.com).

Walmart embraces AR with acquisition of Art.com and launch of in-store Christmas Sleigh Ride app

Walmart is expanding its growing portfolio of e-commerce brands with the acquisition of online home décor retailer Art.com. Art.com, which was started near San Francisco in 1998, is one of the largest online sellers of art and wall décor with estimated sales of $300 million. The addition of Art.com's 2 million on-demand designs will enable Walmart to offer its customers increased variety of choice but, most importantly, it will provide Walmart with valuable leverageable AR expertise as its ArtView is used by one-quarter of its customers to view what a piece of art will look like on their walls (cnbc.com).

Walmart is also leveraging the AI layer to enhance the in-store experience and boost customer engagement through its Christmas Sleigh Ride AR app. Walmart has partnered with some of its CPG suppliers (**Clorox**, **Kellogg**, **PepsiCo**) as well as **3M** and Nickelodeon (**Viacom**) to transform its retail aisles into nine virtual winter wonderlands, inviting guests to interact with iconic characters like Tony the Tiger, ride in Santa's sleigh down the aisle, collect presents, throw snowballs and take selfies with holiday-themed filters (mediapost.com).

The new shopping channel: live video streaming

Facebook is testing a home shopping network-like Live video feature for merchants to let them demo and describe items for viewers and then interact directly with customers using Messenger. Although Facebook does not take a commission on transactions, it is hoping that by increasing conversion rates for businesses, they will spend more on ads. Although Facebook is just testing this new feature in Thailand, it could be a future competitive threat for **Qurate Retail Group**'s HSN and QVC. Speaking of live video commerce, **Mogu**, a **Tencent Holdings**-backed Chinese e-commerce mass-market fashion platform, IPO'd on December 6 at a $1.3 billion valuation. As background, Mogu was formed in June 2016 with the amalgamation of China's three oldest e-commerce fashion enterprises: Meilishuo (2009), Mogujie (2011) and Taoshijie (2014). Mogu, which focuses on a "community + content + e-commerce" business model, has embraced China's live-streaming trend as its 48,000 fashion influencers generate content for its 62.6 million+ active users. By enabling its customers to place orders during live video broadcasts, its designers can place the exact orders with manufacturers, eliminating the risk of overstocks or shortages related to the traditional fashion supply chain in which a designer places an order with a factory in anticipation of customer demand in future months. However, Mogu is not yet profitable as it lost $44 million on the $71 million in revenue it generated for the six months ending September 30 (businessoffashion.com).

The hot new trend in luxury: not selling anything

Our thesis that apparel, accessories & luxury goods are uniquely positioned to originate value through investing in experiences to enhance emotional connections with their customers is playing out as the hot new trend in luxury is not selling anything. For example, this summer, Dolce & Gabbana opened a luxurious Instagrammable (Facebook) clubhouse in Soho which hosts monthly cultural events. At the same time, **Tapestry** debuted Life Coach, an experiential pop-up in NYC designed to "lead guests on a journey of self-discovery" through immersive and photogenic rooms such as a NYC subway station where customers can graffiti the walls and a mystical forest where they can get a tarot card reading. And **Hermes International** is opening "Carre Club" pop-ups in NYC, LA, Toronto, Milan and Singapore where customers can have their photo taken, sing karaoke and watch artists and designers at-work (fashionista.com). **lululemon** is looking to capitalize on its cult-like following by introducing a membership program, which it has been testing in Edmonton and plans to expand to other test markets. For a $128 annual fee, members would receive a free pair of pants or shorts, gain access to curated events and workout classes and receive free expedited shipping (cnbc.com). However, lululemon's stock is not immune from the market: on December 7, lululemon's stock price tumbled 13% after guiding to slowing revenue growth in Q4 in the high-single to low-double digits. The company's revenue in Q3 rose 21% to $748 million with comparable sales up 17%, resulting from a 6% increase in comparable-store sales and a 44% gain in e-commerce sales. E-commerce sales represented 25.3% of total revenue, up from 21.2% a year ago.

Are airports the next strategic hub for Amazon?

Amazon Air is expanding its gateway operation at Chicago Rockford International Airport, which is among the top three of its 20 airport hubs across the U.S. Amazon is investing $11 million to add 112,000 square feet to its existing 72,000-square-foot building (airport-technology.com). Amazon isn't just looking to build distribution hubs outside of airports, it now wants to start selling inside them. Amazon has apparently approached officials from LAX and San Jose International Airport to explore the concept of opening Amazon Go inside airports (reuters.com). Personally, I think this is brilliant as Amazon Go's cashierless stores would offer time-pressed travelers a new level of convenience as well as better pricing. On a side note, *Amazon's Best of Prime 2018* update revealed some insightful new data points. Amazon Prime members have ordered over 2 billion products year-to-date for one-day or faster delivery. The nine NFL games livestreamed on Prime Video and Twitch have reached 20 million viewers in over 200 countries.

JD.com partners with Intel to bring IoT technology into retail process

JD.com is partnering with **Intel** to set up a lab to bring IoT technology into the retail process. The technology, which would be based on Intel architecture, would include next-generation vending machines and advertising experiences (techcrunch.com). We note JD.com received a $550 million strategic investment from Google (**Alphabet**) in June and recently announced it would be launching a flagship online store on Google Shopping by year-end. **Alibaba** is opening a warehouse in Liege to help Belgium SMEs sell their products into China as Belgium becomes the first European country to join Alibaba's Electronic World Trade Platform (eWTP) (cnbc.com). We note that since Jack Ma first proposed it in 2016, two other countries have joined: Malaysia in March 2017 and Rwanda in November 2018. Meanwhile, Macy's, which shut down its Chinese website in June, has now closed its online retail store on Alibaba's Tmall marketplace, marking its full exodus from China as it shifts its resources back to the U.S. (zdnet.com).

Adam's face beams as he stands on his tippy toes to reach the mailbox, clutching his precious letter in his mittens. I smile as he excitingly shares with me how his letter is on its way to the North Pole and how the elves will soon be at work, building his Rescue Bots Transformer in Santa's workshop. As he speaks, I can't help but think about how visionary Santa Claus' business model is. First, Santa is DTC (direct-to-consumer) as he manufactures the toys in his workshop and personally delivers them in his sleigh to kids' homes all over the world on Christmas Eve. Second, Santa is C2B (consumer-to-business) as kids place their orders ahead of time with him, either in person when they sit on his lap to pose for the annual photo with Santa, or by writing a letter or e-mailing him, which guides toy production and logistics. And according to Jack Ma, the new e-commerce trend is C2B.

The Letter: December 18, 2018

In Canada, **Dollarama** is crawling up the structural capital pyramid with the pilot launch of its first ever e-commerce store. It is clearly targeting small businesses, not consumers, as you can only purchase items in full-case quantities and there is an

$18 flat shipping fee if you don't want to pick up your order in the store. Dollarama also falls short in terms of variety of choice as it only offers just over 1,000 items and convenience as it doesn't have an app, it will only ship within Quebec and you can't return products ordered online to the store as it has a strict "no exchange, no return" policy (globalnews.ca).

Starbucks' U.S. partnership with Uber Eats positions it to better originate & capture value

Starbucks is strategically partnering with Uber Eats to offer coffee delivery service early next year across the U.S. from 2,000 stores, or nearly one-quarter of its base of over 8,000 corporate-owned stores (fortune.com). We note Starbucks partnered with Uber Eats in Japan last month and has grown its delivery service in China with Alibaba's Ele.me to over 2,000 stores in 30 cities since the launch in August. We expect Starbucks will be able to leverage with Uber the valuable delivery practices it is learning in China, such as creating splash-proof lids and delivery containers to keep drinks hot or cold. In China, Starbucks has also just launched its first-of-a-kind virtual Starbucks store in collaboration with **Alibaba**, unifying its one-stop digital experience across Taobao, Tmall and Alipay (news.starbucks.com). This is critical as Starbucks is starting to face increased competition from new entrants like Luckin Coffee, which just raised a $200 million Series B round, only six months after raising a $200 million Series A round. Luckin Coffee, which offers coffee delivery in under 30 minutes via scooters, has rolled out 1,700 outlets in 21 cities since it launched in January, approaching its aggressive target to reach 2,000 outlets by the end of this year (techcrunch.com).

LVMH acquires Belmond for $2.6 billion to capitalize on shift in luxury market to experiences

As further evidence of the shift in consumer spending from goods to experiences, **LVMH** is buying luxury travel brand **Belmond** for $2.6 billion. Belmond, formerly known as Orient-Express Hotels, will provide LVMH with valuable customer capital in terms of its affluent client base as well as valuable structural capital in the form of the 36 luxury hotels it owns a full or partial stake in, including the famed Cipriani in Venice and Copacabana in Rio de Janeiro, the 21 Club restaurant in NYC, and properties such as its cruise line in France, London-to-Venice train and safari camps in Botswana. LVMH will be able to add these experiential offerings to its existing hospitality portfolio which includes the Courchevel ski resort in the French Alps and six luxury hotels under its Bulgari brand (swift.com).

The new e-commerce trend: C2B

According to Alibaba's founder, Jack Ma, the new e-commerce trend is C2B. During Alibaba's recent Double 12 event, it tested the C2B concept, enabling merchants to promote their offerings through social media from December 3 to 11 and customers to put products they're interested in into their shopping cart. Alibaba's AI systems then provided insights for each product to merchants in terms of online traffic, likes, views, time spent viewing and how many people put it in their shopping cart, with Alibaba announcing the final pricing on December 12. Nearly 100 million people participated in this year's event, putting an average of 15 products in their cart. Essentially, C2B reverses the relationship as consumer demand will guide production, logistics and pricing (ejinsight.com).

Farfetch acquires Stadium Goods for $250 million

Farfetch, the leading London-based online luxury apparel and accessories marketplace, just acquired one of the sellers on its platform, Stadium Goods, for $250 million. Interestingly,

Stadium Goods, an online marketplace for sought-after sneakers and streetwear launched in NYC in 2015, recently joined Farfetch's marketplace in April. The acquisition is strategic as it expands Farfetch's supplier platform from just retailers to individual resellers. In addition, Stadium Goods provides Farfetch with valuable customer capital in the form of Stadium Goods' 1.1 million followers on Instagram (prnnewswire.com).

Mini Amazon Go coming soon to airports, office lobbies and hospitals?

Could **Amazon** be looking to bring a mini-version of Amazon Go to not just airports, but also office lobbies and hospitals? Amazon just opened a tiny 450-square-foot Amazon Go in one of its offices in Seattle which sells mainly pre-made meals (breakfast, lunch, dinner), beverages and snacks. The small-format Go is made of freestanding construction with its own enclosed ceiling which houses its cameras and sensors that it uses to track shoppers and determine when an item has been taken off the shelf (engadget.com). Back in March, Amazon started to squeeze CPG companies by raising transportation fees for suppliers of heavy, bulky products that are expensive to ship and expanded its "add-on" designation to most health and personal care items under $7. Now it is starting to eliminate unprofitable items from its site and pressuring CPG companies like **Coca-Cola** and **Unilever** to change their packaging if they want to continue selling online (wsj.com).

It's not surprising Instacart and Whole Foods are parting ways

Amazon has been aggressively displacing Instacart at its Whole Foods stores with its own Prime Now grocery delivery service since May and is now up to over 60 cities across the U.S. Because of this, it is not surprising to us that Instacart has announced it will no longer do business with Whole Foods as of February 10 (techcrunch.com). We note that back in February 2016, Whole Foods strategically invested in Instacart when it signed a multi-year partnership agreement. Meanwhile, Postmates has unveiled its semi-autonomous rover called Serve. Serve, which looks like a cross between a cooler and stroller, can make about a dozen deliveries a day as it can carry 50 pounds for 25 miles on a single charge. Postmates, which makes 4 million deliveries per month across 550 cities, plans to roll out Serve in LA next year (techcrunch.com).

Sweetgreen looks to create curated personalized menus

In a fascinating *CNBC* interview, the co-founder of Sweetgreen, Jonathan Neman, shared his vision to evolve his company beyond just a restaurant into a **Spotify**-like food platform. By using Sweetgreen's app to build direct relationships with customers and collect data, he is looking to next create curated personalized menus based on each customer's food preferences as well as any allergies (cnbc.com). We note Sweetgreen recently raised $200 million and strategically partnered with WeWork.

North acquires Intel's tech portfolio behind its cancelled Vaunt glasses

North, which recently introduced its $1,000 Focals smart glasses with Alexa functionality that will ship later next year, has just acquired **Intel**'s technology portfolio behind its cancelled Vaunt glasses. North is acquiring the portfolio, which includes 230 patents or applications covering "*everything from new techniques, user interfaces, to ways to interact with the glasses*", as a defensive move and for future versions of Focals (theverge.com). Interestingly, Intel Capital is a strategic investor in Kitchener-based North, having led its $15 million Series A round in June 2013 and $120 million Series B round in September 2016.

Amazon's new patent to pair facial recognition with Ring and create a database of suspicious persons is highly controversial. Although its stated intent is to create safer and more connected neighbourhoods, it is being criticized for looking to create a massive decentralized surveillance network by running real-time facial recognition on people using cameras installed in peoples' doorbells (cnn.com). You will soon be able to use Alexa to quickly check your new e-mails. Amazon is rolling out a new feature across the U.S. that will allow you to link your e-mail account to Alexa. This will enable you to ask Alexa to read you the headlines of your newest emails to which you can then request her to read the full e-mail and reply, archive or delete it (cnbc.com).

Shopify aspires to be one-stop back office shop for DTC merchants

Shopify aspires to be a one-stop back-office shop for DTC merchants, which see the value in building emotional connections with their customers rather than just selling their products on Amazon. To help its merchants with their marketing efforts, Shopify launched a marketing section in October that allows them to create, run and track Facebook and Google ads, as well as text a virtual assistant called Kit to manage their campaigns. However, Amazon still provides a much greater level of convenience from a logistics perspective as Shopify still can't handle the warehouse and shipping for merchants (businessinsider.com).

When I met a UX Designer from Kohler at SXSW last March, it was fascinating to find out how he was integrating Alexa functionality into bathroom mirrors and showers, but I never imagined the technology would find itself in a toilet. So I was shocked to discover that Kohler just introduced an Alexa-powered smart toilet at CES this week that offers a "fully-immersive experience" with surround speakers, ambient mood lighting and even a warmed seat. Interestingly, this year marks the first appearance by Procter & Gamble at CES as it showcases innovative new products like its self-heating Gillette razor and Oral-B smart toothbrush, highlighting how smart technology is creating opportunities for makers of both durable and non-durable consumer products. And Alexa's aspiration to be the Amazonian Queen ruling over the smart home is coming true as over 100 million devices with Alexa have been sold and she now works on 28,000 devices across 4,500 brands and features over 70,000 skills.

The Smart Toilet: January 8, 2019

SBUX has outperformed since we turned positive in August but we're concerned by two new developments

Since we turned positive on **Starbucks** in our August 8, 2018 research note, its stock price has outperformed the NASDAQ by 37%, rising 24% versus the 13% decline in the NASDAQ. However, we are concerned about the negative implications on its growth/risk profile of two new developments. The first is the strategic decision by Starbucks' new CEO, Kevin Johnson, to shelve Howard Schultz's previously announced plans in October 2016 to open 1,000 Reserve coffee bars globally (wsj.com). Although Johnson is trying to bring more financial discipline, we are concerned he is focusing mainly on the functional value proposition (i.e., convenience) and missing the emotional part of the customer capital pyramid as consumers are increasingly looking for unique experiences like those offered by its Reserve stores. The second is that Luckin Coffee is now plotting to overtake Starbucks in China, declaring its ambition to be the largest coffee chain in China by the end of this year, targeting to more than double its number of outlets this year to over 4,500. Although this seems incredibly aggressive, Luckin Coffee has an impressive execution track record, having rolled out 2,000 outlets in its first year of operations. Although it lost $129 million in its first nine months of operations, it seems to have deep pockets supporting its ambitions as it just raised $200 million on top of the $200 million it raised six months ago. (techcrunch.com).

Personal products companies leveraging AI to deliver customized care solutions

Personal product companies are ideally positioned to transform their existing products through the digital and AI layers, enabling them to enhance and even customize care solutions while increasing the emotional connection with customers. For example, **L'Oreal**'s new My Skin Track pH sensor just received the CES 2019 Innovation Award for Wearable Technology Products category. By wearing the sensor on your inner arm for 5–15 minutes, the algorithm on its companion app will compute your pH measurement and rate of perspiration, enabling it to suggest product recommendations for your optimal skin health (fastcompany.com). Neutrogena (**Johnson & Johnson**) is debuting its Neutrogena MaskiD, a customized micro 3D-printed face mask that will be available to the public later this year. The MaskiD uses the TrueDepth camera to take a 3D image of your face so it can customize the mask to align with your face shape and structure. Then it allows you to customize what you put on your face by allowing you to select up to five different ingredients for each of your six facial zones. Then you can order the mask through the app and have it shipped to your home (allure.com). And **Procter & Gamble** is showcasing its SK-II Future X Smart

Store, a pop-up that uses facial recognition, smart sensors and computer vision technology to provide next-gen smart skincare solutions and Ople, a blue light device that scans your face to detect and correct skin imperfections.

In fact, this year marks Procter & Gamble's first appearance at CES which started in 1967. Procter & Gamble is using the trade show to highlight a number of other tech-infused products such as its self-heating Gillette razor, Airia-connected home fragrance that distributes customized levels of scents through your home that you can manage thru an app, its DS3 engineered soap that cleans with less water, and Oral-B Genius X toothbrush that uses AI technology to analyze brushing styles and offer personalized recommendations to achieve better brushing habits (venturebeat.com).

Kohler debuts its Alexa-powered smart toilet

We are starting to see more and more evidence of how household appliance companies are ideally positioned to enhance the functional value proposition of their physical products through the digital and AI layers. At CES, Kohler debuted its Numi 2.0 smart toilet that provides a "fully-immersive experience" with Alexa-powered built-in surround speakers and ambient mood lighting along with a PureWarmth toilet seat (theverge.com). Also at CES, **Whirlpool** is debuting its Connected Hub Wall Oven concept, which uses augmented reality to help you in the kitchen. The front of the oven is a 27-inch transparent LCD interface that enables you to view family calendars, personalize recipe suggestions and will even provide instructions on the screen to what rack and cooking cycle and, most innovative of all, it comes with an internal vision system that allows you to zoom in on your food in the oven. Whirlpool has also transformed Yummly, the recipe and shopping app it acquired in May 2017, into a platform that serves both its Whirlpool and KitchenAid brand appliances, offering ingredient recognition for smart fridges and voice command capabilities (engadget.com).

Amazon Showroom visual design tool raises bar again

Amazon just launched another new feature on the AI layer that further raises the bar for home improvement and home furnishing retailers. Amazon's new Amazon Showroom visual design tool allows you to virtually decorate a living room and then add the items you want to your cart. In addition to being able to place different furniture and décor items in the virtual room, you can even see what they look like with the backdrop of different types of wall colour and flooring. To access the tool just select "Explore Showroom" under the Account & Lists drop-down menu on Amazon.com (techcrunch.com).

Amazon expanding Prime Air fleet from 40 to 50 cargo planes

As further evidence that Amazon will be reducing its reliance on third-party air carriers, it will be adding 10 used **Boeing** 767-300s to Prime Air over the next two years, expanding its fleet from 40 to 50 cargo planes (techcrunch.com). Amazon will be leasing the aircraft from **Air Transport Services Group**, which apparently just secured 20 used Boeing 767s from American Airlines that it will be acquiring over the next three years (seattletimes.com). On the human capital front, Amazon announced it will be creating 600 new technology jobs in Toronto over the next five years, adding to its current base of 800 Amazonians that currently work in the city. It will be hiring technology talent in areas such as software development, machine learning and cloud computing (torontosun.com).

More bad news could come for Apple as Netflix finds a detour around its walled garden

Apple's stock price tumbled nearly 10% on January 3 after its shocking warning that as a result of slowing economy in Greater China it is cutting its Q1 revenue guidance on weaker-than-expected iPhone sales in Greater China (cnbc.com). More bad news could be on the way for Apple...**Netflix** just made an aggressive move to detour new subscribers around Apple's walled garden and go DTC, cutting Apple out of the 15–30% commission it has been charging Netflix for subscriptions made through iTunes. Netflix has quietly removed the iTunes billing option from the Netflix app on Apple's App store, so customers will now need to sign up directly on the Netflix website (businessinsider.com). This could be negative for Apple as Netflix is the top grossing app on its U.S. App Store as it would save Netflix between $350,000 and $700,000 in commissions per day, or $128–$256 million annually (fortune.com). In addition, it could set a dangerous precedent for other companies. However, it looks like Apple is trying to expand into new verticals as it was just granted new patents from the U.S. Patent and Trademark Office, revealing its intent to potentially expand into smart clothing, ride-hailing and multiplayer games (inverse.com).

Retail space announced closures reach 145 million square feet in 2018 – up over 40% from 2017

The mall vacancy rate, which hit a seven-year high of 9.1% in Q3, declined slightly to 9.0% in Q4, but this is still up from 8.3% a year ago. We expect the vacancy rate will resume its upward climb with the new wave of store closures coming from retailers like **Sears Holdings** and the **Gap.** In fact, according to CoStar Group, companies announced plans to close over 145 million square feet of retail space in 2018, up over 40% from 102 million square feet in 2017 (cnbc.com). And the closures will keep coming — we just learned that Charlotte Russe, a privately held mall-based fast-fashion retailer with over 500 stores has hired Guggenheim Securities to explore strategic alternatives, considering a possible sale or bankruptcy (wsj.com).

Big box retailers using sales comps of vacant stores to reduce property tax assessments

As the retail apocalypse accelerates, the underlying value of retail real estate will come down to location, location, location. For example, Enfield Square Mall was just sold at an auction to an undisclosed buyer for $10.85 million, less than half its appraised value of $27.5 million last year. The 788,000-square-foot one-storey regional mall opened in Enfield, Connecticut in 1971 (hartfordbusiness.com). In fact, big-box retailers like **Walmart**, **Home Depot**, **Target** and **Walgreens** are now using aggressive legal tactics to reduce their property tax bills, claiming their tax assessment should be based on recent sales comparables of vacant stores, not the land and building costs or income generated. Essentially, this "dark store" argument reinforces the rising obsolescence risk of big-box stores (nytimes.com). The big threat is that physical retail is becoming no longer about the distribution of goods from cookie-cutter boxes but the building of brand equity. As the functional value proposition (i.e., price, convenience, variety of choice) of shopping from our couches becomes better and better, retailers will need to prioritize context over contents and offer a real emotional experience that goes beyond the flagship model to building a community around a social mission (nytimes.com).

DTC model extends to luxury goods

The DTC model is now extending to luxury goods as you can now buy premium no-label goods straight from the top factories in Europe. For example, Italic, which has raised $13 million since launching in LA last March, is working with

European factories that manufacture for high-end labels such as **Prada**, **Burberry Group** and Givenchy (**LVMH**) to offer its online members designer-branded equivalent goods at a fraction of the cost (theguardian.com).

CPG companies face risk of rising packaging costs as environmental regulations tighten

CPG companies now face the risk of rising packaging costs as a result of rising environmental regulations and consumer activism. For example, China, which imports 45% of the world's plastic trash, will start banning imports of low-grade and single-use plastic this year, forcing rich nations to deal with their own waste. This could lead to tightened environmental regulations as countries follow initiatives like the EU which voted in October to ban single-use plastic in food and drink containers by 2021, and NYC which banned polystyrene foam food and beverage containers starting January 1 (inhabitat.com). At the same time, CPGs are facing a growing backlash from consumers who are looking for CPGs to package their products in recyclable alternatives. As CPGs spend 5–10% of their revenue on packaging costs, having to switch could lead to an increase in their packaging costs, which typically accounts for 5–10% of revenue (wsj.com).

Rise of food halls on fidelity end and delivery platforms on convenience end

A decade after the start of the food truck craze, we are now seeing the rise in food halls. The cookie-cutter QSR mall food court experience is giving rise to the highly Instagrammable and authentic experience offered by food halls filled with stalls from local restaurants (forbes.com). For example, Deliveroo, the restaurant delivery platform that has raised $860 million since launching in London in 2012, recently opened its first bricks-and-mortar food hall in Hong Kong. The Deliveroo Food Market, which is an extension of its "Editions" kitchen-sharing program for restaurants, is home to five restaurants which offer 15 different dining concepts to customers for either delivery or in-store dining. Deliveroo plans to open a second restaurant in Singapore next year (cnbc.com).

While food halls seek to create a high fidelity experience for their patrons, restaurants are also embracing food delivery platforms as they seek to deliver convenience for their customers. For example, **Naspers**, the South African Internet and media giant, led a massive $1 billion Series H round for Swiggy. Other strategic investors include **Tencent Holdings** and **Meituan Dianping**, China's largest service e-commerce platform Since Swiggy launched in Bangalore in 2014, it has grown its supplier base to 50,000+ restaurants in over 50 cities in India (techcrunch.com). **GM**'s Cruise Automation subsidiary is partnering with DoorDash to test driverless restaurant deliveries in San Francisco (cnn.com). We note that **Ford** partnered with Postmates a year ago to test autonomous grocery delivery and expanded the pilot to include Walmart in November.

Amazon looking to build more Whole Foods stores to expand delivery reach

To expand its delivery reach of Prime Now into the suburbs, Amazon is looking to grow its footprint of Whole Foods stores across the U.S. from its current base of 475 stores (wsj.com). Interestingly, Target now offers same-day delivery via Shipt, the delivery platform it acquired a year ago for $550 million, in 200 markets across 46 states on over 55,000 products (e.g., groceries, household essentials, select electronics and toys). Target plans to offer this service for all major categories by the end of next year (techcrunch.com). On the AI front, **Seven & I**

Holdings has collaborated with **NEC** to open a trial 7-Eleven store in Tokyo that utilizes facial recognition technology to enable NEC employees to pay using their face (pcmag.com).

Beverages going DTC with micro-wineries and snackbots

Just like the beer industry was disrupted by the rise in micro-breweries, the wine industry is being disrupted by the rise in micro-wineries, as an increasing number of small wine growers are starting to sell direct-to-consumer instead of wholesale to the big wine houses. Mathieu Julien, the general manager for Europe at Wine Source, sees the emergence of virtual wine tours, where people can visit a winery or take part in a masterclass (cnbc.com). On the direct-to-consumer front, **PepsiCo** is taking the vending machine to a new level of convenience with the debut of the "snackbot", an autonomous delivery robot. PepsiCo is debuting a fleet of snackbots on the University of Pacific campus in California to deliver a selection of healthy snacks and beverages to college students during the school day who just need to place an order on the iOS app. The snackbot, which has headlights and a camera, can run 20 miles on a single charge (theverge.com).

Google Assistant will be on a billion devices by end of January

Google (**Alphabet**) expects its Google Assistant to be running on 1 billion devices by the end of January, up from 400 million a year ago. More importantly, both the daily and monthly active users of its voice assistant have quadrupled the past year. In the past year, Google has added support for Google Assistant for 22 new languages in 66 new countries, bringing it to 30 languages in 80 countries (fastcompany.com). Clearly, Amazon is at a disadvantage with respect to Google and Apple as they can include their voice assistants as the default option on their smartphones, so Amazon is focusing on putting Alexa into the home, car and workplace. For example, this holiday season, Amazon sold millions more Amazon Devices than last year. Alexa's influence continues to grow as the number of customers that used Alexa for shipping more than tripled this holiday season, Alexa delivered more than eight times as many reminders, set over 100 million timers and provided more than three times as many recipes (businessinsider.com).

Over 100 million devices with Alexa have been sold as she reaches over 70,000 skills

Amazon's SVP of Devices and Services, Dave Limp, just disclosed over 100 million devices with Alexa have been sold and 150+ products have Alexa directly built in (theverge.com). Alexa's aspiration to be the Amazonian Queen ruling over the smart home is coming true as she now works on over 28,000 devices across 4,500 unique brands, up from 20,000 devices across 3,500 unique brands in September. In comparison, Google Assistant works on 10,000 devices across 1,000 brands (fastcompany.com). Alexa will soon become a lot smarter. Amazon is rolling out Alexa integration in the U.S. with Wolfram Alpha, a computational knowledge engine that will be able to answer questions related to STEM topics (science, technology, engineering, math), as well as astronomy and history (venturebeat.com). In addition, the NFL has rolled out the *The Rookie's Guide to the NFL* Alexa skill to teach fans about the players, rules and history of American football, including the definition of 1,000 NFL terms (cnbc.com).

Outdoor billboards embracing new ways to capture value

Billboards are embracing new ways to capture value as they move up the structural capital pyramid to the digital and AI layers, leading to a resurgence in outdoor spending. In fact, out-of-home (OOH) is the only traditional media category expected to grow this year, by 3.4% to $33.5 billion, driven by digital outdoor ad spending which is expected to grow 16% this year to $5.7 billion. On the digital layer, screens are becoming more affordable and have the advantage of being location-specific and interactive. On the AI layer, we are seeing the emergence of smart ads that leverage AI. For example, during Fashion Week, New Balance placed digital ads in Soho that used AI to analyze outfits of passerby and determine which ones were stylish and then flashed an image of the person with the heading "exception spotted" (curbed.com).

India's new e-commerce restrictions threaten Walmart & Amazon's expansion plans

Walmart and Amazon are joining forces to lobby against the Indian government's new regulations that seek to level the playing field for domestic merchants by tightening restrictions on foreign e-commerce companies (fortune.com). As of February 1, non-Indian companies will not be able to hold their inventory and ship it to consumers, they will be barred from entering into exclusive online sales agreements and brands will be forbidden to sell more than 25% of their sales via a single e-commerce marketplace (techcrunch.com).

Alibaba launching new B2C used goods platform for brands

Online commerce is becoming more of a two-way street as the ability to return merchandise becomes an expected convenience factor by consumers. In fact, one-third of this season's $123 billion in online sales, or $40 billion, is expected to be returned. This is leading to the growth in supply chains for reverse logistics, which CBRE estimates requires as much as 20% more space for retailers than that required for outbound shipments (wsj.com). To help solve the returns problem, **Al-**

ibaba is launching a used goods platform that expands the closet-sharing economy concept pioneered by start-ups like thredUP, Poshmark and Threadsy, beyond C2C to B2C. Alibaba's new "Idle Fish" platform will enable brands to operate their own online store to sell idle assets such as overstock and samples or secondary goods such as returned or recycled goods while appealing to cost-conscious and socially conscious Millennials. Alibaba plans to pilot with electronic brands before expanding into apparel and other categories (footwearnews.com).

Facebook developing cryptocurrency to transfer money on WhatsApp in India

Other new entrants into the financial services space include social networks such as **Facebook** which is developing a way to use cryptocurrency to transfer money on WhatsApp in India. To avoid the price volatility risk of bitcoin, Facebook is looking to use a stablecoin, which is defined as a digital currency pegged to the U.S. dollar (cnbc.com).

Chapter Five: The Community

In yesterday's research report, I posed the controversial question, "Could Starbucks' Beans Start to Lose Their Magic?", expressing my concern that Starbucks' beanstalk could start to wilt with Schultz no longer around to cultivate his high-fidelity community-based social mission to "inspire and nurture the human spirit—one person, one cup and one neighborhood at a time", which brings the real magic to its beans. The key emerging risk is that Starbucks faces a highly aggressive disruptive entrant, Luckin Coffee, which could start to flash red on investors' radar screens as it is apparently looking to IPO on the Hong Kong Stock Exchange. Interestingly, in 1998, 11 years after Howard Schultz planted the magic beans for his Starbucks movement, another community-based social mission took root, with Chip Wilson starting his lululemon movement to "create components for people to live a longer, healthier, and more fun life". Although Chip Wilson was forced out of his company in early 2015, which he recounts in his new tell-all book, "Little Black Stretchy Pants", the cult-like following he built is bearing real fruit as lululemon is able to leverage it to build DTC distribution channels and the company just raised its Q4 guidance. And 11 years later, in 2009, Adam Neumann and Miguel McKelvey put together the pitch deck for "The we brand companies", planting the seeds for their WeWork movement, inspired by their community-based social mission to empower people to "Make a Life. Not Just a Living." A decade later, guided by their original vision, they have re-branded WeWork to The We Company, signaling their intent for global domination as they advance beyond office leasing.

The Community: January 16, 2019

Luckin Coffee could start to flash red on the radar screen for investors in Starbucks

Luckin Coffee is apparently looking to IPO on the Hong Kong Stock Exchange. Investment banks have begun to prepare listing materials, according to an anonymous source. Luckin Coffee, which now operates 2,073 stores across China, has a pre-IPO valuation of $2.2 billion based on its $200 million Series B funding round in December. The company claims to have sold over 85 million cups of coffee in 2018 to 12 million customers (technode.com).

lululemon raises Q4 guidance on strong holiday sales momentum

lululemon's stock price rose 6% after it raised its fourth-quarter guidance on January 14, disclosing its sales momentum remained strong over the holidays. lululemon raised its comparable sales forecast from the high single-to-low double digits to the mid- to high-teens and increased its average EPS guidance 5%, from $1.65 to $1.73 (financialpost.com).

GNC Holdings, JC Penney & Pier 1 Imports among 10 retailers on bankruptcy watch

The National Law Review has put ten retailers under watch for a possible Chapter 11 filing this year. The list includes 2 retailers that have already gone through the bankruptcy process (Gymboree and Payless Shoes), 3 publicly traded retailers (**GNC Holdings**, **JC Penney**, **Pier 1 Imports**) and 5 privately held retailers (Guitar Center, J Crew, Neiman Marcus, 99 Cents Only, PetSmart) (natlawreview.com). As the retail apocalypse continues, we expect to see the re-development of malls in prime locations. For example, the Westside Pavilion mall in West LA, owned by **Hudson Pacific Properties** and **Macerich**, is being re-developed into a creative office campus. Google has signed a 14-year lease to take possession of the entire 584,000-square-foot office complex, called One Westside, starting in 2022. As a foreshadowing of the fate to befall many more malls, Westside Pavilion, which was built in 1985, lost its key anchor tenants **Nordstrom** in September 2017 and **Macy's** in May 2018 (hollywoodreporter.com).

Kroger partners with Microsoft as start-ups look to help retailers compete with Amazon Go

Kroger is beta testing Kroger EDGE (Enhanced Display for Grocery Environment), which it developed in partnership with **Microsoft** Azure, in two pilot stores. Its new digital shelf technology shows pricing, nutritional information, video ads and coupons. In addition to enabling stores to dynamically change prices and activate promotions, it also connects with customers' shopping lists on their Kroger app (cnet.com). Although this "connected store" experience is promising, we note that Kroger announced a year ago it would have EDGE in nearly 200 stores by now. Explorer.ai, a start-up founded in July 2017 with the vision to create a mapping platform for the autonomous vehicle world, is pivoting to mapping retail stores. Explorer.ai is joining Standard Cognition, which raised a $40 million Series A round in November to fund its ambitions to become the go-to cashierless checkout platform to help retailers compete against Amazon Go (venturebeat.com). And Caper just raised a $2.2 million seed round to help grocery retailers compete against Amazon Go with its smart shopping cart. Caper, which is trialing its smart shopping carts in two grocery stores in NYC, is looking to bring them to 150 grocery stores this year. The smart shopping cart includes a touchscreen with a store map that can highlight daily deals and the soon-to-be launched next version will include image-recognition cameras and weight sensors to automatically ID items when you put them in the cart (digitaltrends.com).

Amazon shelves 365 by Whole Foods stores as Postmates preps for an IPO

Now that Amazon has lowered prices at Whole Foods stores, the price gap has narrowed with its 365 by Whole Foods store, so it has made the strategic decision to keep operating them but not open any more. Since Whole Foods launched the first 365 by Whole Foods store in May 2016, it has grown its footprint to a dozen locations, targeting Millennials with a differentiated functional value proposition of lower prices than Whole Foods but less variety of choice, with a smaller store footprint (25,000–30,000 square feet versus 38,000–50,000 square feet) and fewer SKUs (7,000 versus 20,000+) (supermarket.com). However, as we discussed in last week's research note, Amazon is looking to build more Whole Foods stores to expand its Prime Now delivery reach. Interestingly, Postmates, which makes 5 million food deliveries per month from 550 U.S. cities, is starting to prep for an IPO. It just raised a $100 million Series F round, shortly after its $300 million Series E round in September. Postmates is expected to report $400 million in revenue in 2018 on $1.2 billion in gross food sales, implying a 30% commission (techcrunch.com).

Amazon pilots "Product Sampling" as it rolls out Key for Garage and Key for Business

Amazon is venturing deeper into the advertising space with

the quiet pilot of its new "Product Sampling" program which lets new and established brands send free samples to Amazon customers based on their purchasing history (cnbc.com). If you don't feel comfortable having Amazon deliver packages into your home or your car, you now have a third option — your garage. Amazon will roll out its Key for Garage program in Q2 to Prime members in 37 cities across the U.S. It will be available to those Prime members who purchase a Chamberlain or LiftMaster myQ garage door for $180 or affix their existing door opener with an $80 hub (geekwire.com). An even bigger game changer could be Key for Business, a fob that gives Amazon access to offices and apartments to make deliveries, which Amazon is apparently testing with commercial property managers (zdnet.com).

IKEA ventures deeper into the smart home

IKEA is extending its portfolio of smart home offerings beyond light bulbs and wireless charging lamps with the quiet debut of two models of €99 smart blinds to its Germany online store. The smart blinds, which work with Amazon Alexa, Google Assistant and **Apple** HomeKit, will be available in the U.S. in early April (mashable.com). Google (**Alphabet**) is looking to expand its ecosystem of smart devices by making it easier for device manufacturers to integrate with Google Assistant. Google is launching a new set of developer tools called Google Assistant Connect, which is similar to the Alexa Connect Kit that Amazon launched back in September. It will be broadly available to developers later this year (techccrunch.com).

Could voice be the next big interface for gaming?

Razer, the world's leading lifestyle brand for gamers, will be integrating Alexa into its gaming platform starting in the second quarter (techcrunch.com). Interestingly, Amazon is apparently looking to create the "**Netflix** of Gaming" as it has been talking to publishers about the idea of streaming games on its platform that it plans to launch next year. In addition to complementing Amazon's existing media portfolio of videos, music and photo storage, adding a gaming platform could help it attract more Prime members and provide it with a new way to leverage Alexa (techcrunch.com).

Three Minecraft Lego sets. Two Minecraft towels. One Minecraft-themed bedding set. As my 8-year-old opened his massive pile of birthday presents yesterday, I realized that clearly he is not the only Minecraft-obsessed kid in his class. While Brady's younger brother, Adam, still loves watching Netflix, Brady now just wants to play Minecraft on his iPad — literally all the time. This shift in media consumption is starting to play out in the markets as Netflix just revealed that it views Fortnite as a bigger threat than HBO. In fact, Fortnite is becoming the new coveted "third place" for its core 18–24-year-old demographic to virtually meet up, displacing the mall and even Starbucks. This explains why game streaming is emerging as the next battleground as tech giants Microsoft and Alexa prepare to capitalize on this obsession and launch the "Netflix of Games".

The Obsession: January 22, 2019

World's biggest resource firms starting to invest in AI

One of the world's largest mining companies is ascending the structural capital pyramid to the AI layer. **Vale SA** is opening its first AI centre in Brazil as it looks to "*leverage the adoption of innovative and disruptive technologies in all areas of the business*", specifically to optimize the maintenance of assets like off-road trucks, as well as improve the management of ore processing (cnbc.com). In the energy sector, **Royal Dutch Shell** is investing heavily in the R&D of AI. Upstream, it is using reinforcement learning to control its drilling equipment, which is a form of semi-supervised machine learning. Downstream, it is rolling out AI at its public EV charging stations to monitor and predict demand so it can better manage shifting demand for power throughout the day (forbes.com). In the agricultural space, **John Deere** is leading the agtech revolution, embracing the AI level of the structural capital pyramid. At CES, it showcased its autonomous tractor as well as its giant combine harvester which uses AI, machine learning and camera technology to not just harvest grain, but to also harvest data (engadget.com).

Scottish mall being auctioned for £1 as smartphone shopping set to overtake malls

Fidelity's warning back in December that U.K. retail real estate values could plummet 20–70% is starting to play out. A Scottish shopping mall is being auctioned off next month with a reserve price of only £1. The pension fund Columbia Threadneedle is selling the mall after 15 years of ownership as 14 of the 21 shops lie vacant, resulting in the annual upkeep being more than the £152,000 generated from the rent (theguardian.com). And we expect this will not be an isolated incidence as smartphone shopping is set to hit a tipping point this year, with British people expected to spend more money shopping on their smartphones than in shopping malls. According to U.K.-based price comparison service, uSwitch, British smartphone users are expected to spend £25 billion this year, up 66% from £15 billion last year. Shopping via smartphone offers a superior functional value proposition in terms of both convenience (two-thirds like to be able to shop at any time from any location) and pricing (one-third like being able to save money through online comparison shopping). The most popular e-commerce sites are **Amazon** (89%), **eBay** (63%) and Argos (**J Sainsbury**) (41%) (techradar.com).

Netflix sees Fortnite as bigger threat than HBO, Microsoft looks to create "Netflix of Games"

Netflix views Fortnite as a bigger competitive threat than HBO. It made this shocking statement in its Q418 shareholder letter as it disclosed it earns around 10% of TV screen time in the U.S. Since Fortnite was released by Epic Games (40% owned by **Tencent Holdings**) in July 2017, it has attracted over 200 million players and had 78.3 million monthly active players as of September. It's interesting as Fortnite, an online video game set in a post-apocalyptic, zombie-infested world, has become the new coveted "third place" for its core 18–24-year-old demographic to virtually meet up, displacing the mall and Starbucks (techcrunch.com). **Microsoft** sees this opportunity as it is looking to transform XBox into a "Netflix for Games". It is testing its Project xCloud cloud-based streaming gaming service privately on an invite-only basis with plans to launch public trials this year (businessinsider.com).

But Alexa could be Amazon's secret weapon for its "Netflix of Games"

But Microsoft isn't alone in this concept as if you recall, I wrote last week about how Amazon is looking to create the "Netflix of Gaming" and suggested that voice could be the next big interface for gaming as Razer is integrating Alexa into its gaming platform starting in the second quarter. Related to this, Nolan Bushnell, the founder of Atari and Chuck E. Cheese, sees Alexa creating a white space between video games like Atari's Pong and movies as using your voice is more natural than holding a remote. At VoiceFirst.FM's Alexa Conference, he announced plans for his

X2 Games company to release six Alexa-centric board games this year and observed he believes we are about to enter a new era of interactive board and card games you can play using Alexa (cnet.com).

Netflix raises rates as Walmart jumps ship & Disney reports >$1 billion loss from streaming

Netflix is raising monthly subscription rates between 13% and 18%. As a sign of its confidence in the value it delivers for its subscribers and resulting strong pricing power, this marks Netflix's fourth and largest rate hike since it launched its streaming service twelve years ago. The rate hikes will take effect immediately for new customers and be rolled in over the next three months for existing subscribers (cnbc.com). Meanwhile, **Walmart** is abandoning its plans to enter the increasingly competitive video-streaming space. Although Walmart had been exploring the idea of creating an Amazon Prime-like service for its price-conscious core middle-America customer base, it wisely decided it was too risky a venture given it was outside its core competency and the significant capital investment required to create original content. Instead, Walmart will focus on enhancing its existing Vudu on-demand movie streaming service (cnbc.com). But **Disney** still plans to launch its Disney+ video-streaming service later this year, even after reporting a loss of over $1 billion from streaming last year. Disney reported a $580 million loss in equity investments from its 30% stake in Hulu and $469 million in losses from its BAMTech streaming technology, which powers ESPN+ that it launched in April (cnbc.com).

Microsoft changes strategy for Cortana – no longer a voice assistant, just a skill

Cortana no longer wants to be friends with Alexa, she wants

to be her servant. Microsoft's CEO, Satya Nardella, has changed his strategy for Cortana — viewing her no longer as a standalone voice assistant but as a valuable skill that Microsoft 365 subscribers can access using Alexa, Google Assistant or Siri (zdnet.com). Reflecting back, it seems like he has been making this shift as in November we discussed how Alexa was invading the turf of her new friend, Cortana, as Microsoft had started to sell Amazon's Echo devices in its retail store. And Alexa is becoming more human. Thanks to new neural text-to-speech technology, she will be able to deliver a more natural-sounding voice. As a first step, Amazon will be rolling out a "newscaster voice" for Alexa in the U.S. when she broadcasts news or recites Wikipedia entries (geek.com).

Amazon Prime U.S. membership crosses 100 million as it ranks as top tech spender

Amazon Prime membership just crossed the 100 million mark in the U.S. According to *Consumer Intelligence Research Partners* (CIRP), Amazon's U.S. Prime membership base reached 101 million in Q418, up 11% from 92 million in Q417 and up 4% from Q3. There was no change from last quarter in terms of spending, as Prime members continue to spend an average of $1,400 per year while non-Prime members spend an average of $600 (cirp.com). Not surprisingly, Amazon was the biggest corporate spender on technology in 2018, spending $13.8 billion on IT, ahead of **Alphabet** and Walmart, who spent just under $12 billion each. According to IDC, the top 10 companies, which each spent at least $6 billion on IT, accounted for 7% of the total $1.1 trillion by the 4,800 firms it tracks. Among the top 10 were four banks (**JPMorgan**, **Bank of America**, **Wells Fargo**, **Citigroup**) and three tech firms (Microsoft, **Facebook**, **AT&T**) (wsj.com). Interestingly, Amazon is hosting a public version of its invite-only MARS conference for tech elites and billionaires to bring together business leaders and experts in MARS (machine learning, automation, robotics, space). The re:MARS event will be held from June 4–7 in Las Vegas (cnbc.com).

Could the sharp drop in consumer expectations foreshadow a consumer spending slowdown?

The University of Michigan Consumer Sentiment Index plummeted from 98.3 in December to 90.7 in January, reaching the lowest level since October 2016. According to Richard Curtin, Chief Economist for the Surveys of Consumers, the sharp 7.7% decline was "*due to a host of issues including the partial government shutdown, the impact of tariffs, instabilities in financial markets, the global slowdown, and the lack of clarity about monetary policies*". Even more concerning is the even larger 10% drop in consumer expectations from 87.0 in December to 78.3 in January, which could start to impact consumer spending (cnbc.com).

Spotify launches Car View mode as it preps to launch voice-controlled in-car music player

Spotify just launched a new Car View mode on Android smartphones to make it easier for you to manually control the music while you're driving which supersizes the song info, track controls and shuffle button (theverge.com). Spotify, which was supposed to launch an in-car music player last April, is apparently looking to launch one later this year. The $100 single-purpose device would come with voice control capabilities and synch with the car stereo through Bluetooth (theverge.com). We believe bringing its music direct to consumers would be a positive move for Spotify as one of its biggest risk factors is customer disintermediation as it increasingly depends on platforms like Amazon Echo and Google Home.

Stop & Shop will soon deliver not just groceries to your door,

but the grocery store itself

Stop & Shop (**Koninklijke Ahold Delhaize**), which operates a chain of over 400 supermarkets in the Northeast U.S., will soon deliver not just groceries, but the grocery store itself, to the front doors of its customers in Boston. Stop & Shop, which was founded in 1892, is ascending the structural capital pyramid to the AI level, partnering with Robomart to deploy its fleet of self-driving mini-grocery stores to bring a new level of convenience and accessibility to customers. The mini-grocery store, which stocks produce, meal kits and convenience items, can be summoned using a smartphone (cnbc.com). Interestingly, Robomart was founded in 2017 and has only raised a seed round in February 2018.

Google buys some of Fossil's smartwatch IP for $40 million

Meanwhile, in the smartwatch space, Google is collaborating with **Fossil Group** to launch a new product line within its Wear OS family. Under the $40 million deal, Google will acquire some of Fossil's R&D team members as well as some of Fossil's smartwatch IP under development. Interestingly, the IP is based partly on the technology from Fossil's $260 million acquisition of Misfit Wearables in late 2015 (wareable.com).

Mattress space becomes more crowded with entry of DTC bedding co Parachute Home

As a further red flag for **Sleep Country Canada**, Parachute Home, the online DTC bedding and bath essentials company, is expanding into the mattress category. Unlike new entrants in this increasingly crowded space, Parachute Home will be able to leverage the customer base it has built up over the past five years, especially its core customers between the age of 30 and 45 who are beginning to prioritize self-care and sleep and looking for a premium organic eco-friendly mattress (fastcompany.com).

We note Parachute Home raised a $30 million Series C round in June to fund the expansion of its physical footprint from 5 to 20 stores by 2020.

Gillette is guilty of "halo polishing" but Coinstar's new move is truly exploitative

As the mom of two young boys, I have to admit I got tears in my eyes watching Gillette's inspiring commercial, *We Believe: The Best Men Can Be*. However, it didn't resonate with me on the same level as **Nike**'s recent campaign which was strategically brilliant as Kaepernick's message, "*Believe in something. Even it means sacrificing everything*", is both authentic and socially conscious, advancing Nike's social mission "*to bring inspiration and innovation to every athlete*". **Procter & Gamble**'s Gillette commercial, however, seems opportunistic, reminding me of what I wrote back in 2016 in my *Ubernomics* book: "*Just as the rising popularity of corporate social responsibility over the last decade led companies to engage in greenwashing, the rising popularity of having a social mission is leading some companies to engage in what I call 'halo polishing'*". But at least P&G is well-intentioned, which is more than I can say for Coinstar, who just made an incredibly exploitative and fiduciarily irresponsible move to add a feature enabling its customers to convert their spare cash into Bitcoin at their cash-counting kiosks. Coinstar has partnered with Coinme, a start-up with a small network of cryptocurrency dispensing ATMs, to start rolling out this new feature to thousands of its cash-counting kiosks at retail locations. However, the limit is $2,500, so you'll only be able to buy just over two-thirds of Bitcoin, which is currently trading at nearly $3,600 (techcrunch.com). If you remember, last May Amazon partnered with Coinstar to roll out its Amazon Cash deposit capability at its kiosks. The reason Amazon did this was to target lower-income unbanked customers who should not be investing in such a highly speculative financial instrument as Bitcoin, which has plummeted over 80% since peaking at $20,000 in December 2017.

What if we could keep ice cream cold by storing it in metal containers? What if toothpaste came in tablets instead of a tube? What if you only needed to replace the head of your toothbrush? What if sound could be part of the future design of our homes? What if we could blur the lines between coworking and retail by opening a public "town square"-like space? What if we added luxury designer residences above our flagship store?

What If?: January 29, 2019

Circular economy creates innovation opportunities for CPGs
Loop, a new circular economy shopping platform developed by TerraCycle in partnership with **UPS**, has the potential to introduce a subscription model on the e-commerce layer for CPG companies. Loop, which launches in Paris and NYC this spring, features over 300 products in re-usable packaging from a wide coalition of CPG companies. The exciting part is that it enables CPG companies to design innovative re-usable containers and packaging, improving the functional and aesthetic features on the physical layer. For example, Haagen Daaz (**General Mills**) has created metal containers to keep contents frozen, Oral B (**Procter & Gamble**) has designed toothbrushes with replaceable heads, **Clorox** has created a stainless steel package to keep wet wipes wetter and **Unilever** has invented toothpaste tablets that you can chew instead of squirt out of the tube (fastcompany.com). This creates an additional opportunity for personal products

companies, which are also ideally positioned to leverage the digital and AI layers to transform their product portfolio.

Increasing brand loyalty through better packaging design would help CPG companies compete against Brandless, which is known as the "Procter & Gamble for Millennials". This is important as Brandless is launching an optional subscription service to increase the emotional connection with its customers and improve retention rates. The subscription is similar to Amazon's Prime Pantry as it enables customers to set up regular deliveries of household essentials, but unlike Amazon its customers don't need to be members to subscribe. Brandless offers free shipping for orders over $39 and a flat $5 delivery fee under this threshold but there is no minimum for its members, which pay $36 a year (pymnts.com). Brandless also announced that it is adding baby and pet products to its portfolio. Although this introduces a new price point of $9, 90% of its products will still fall in the $3 category (techcrunch.com). We note that Brandless raised a massive $240 million Series C round led by **SoftBank** at the end of July.

Circular economy could lead to increasing threat of substitutes for packaging companies

While Loop could save CPGs from the growing backlash from sustainability-focused consumers, the shift to the elimination of single-use disposable packaging could lead to a rising threat of substitutes for packaging companies. As we discussed in our January 8 research note, we are seeing tightened environmental regulations as countries like China start to ban imports of low-grade and single-use plastic this year, and the EU which will ban single-use plastic in food and drink containers by 2021.

Starbucks' China growth story comes under scrutiny as its traffic declines 2%

Starbucks' revenue rose 9% to $6.6 billion in Q119, driven by 7% unit growth and a 4% growth in comparable-store sales, comprising gains of 3% in average ticket and 1% in traffic. Starbucks achieved comparable-store sales growth of 4% in the U.S., driven entirely by higher average ticket, but only 1% in China as the 3% increase in the ticket was nearly offset by the 2% decline in traffic. Although there was no specific mention of Luckin Coffee on the conference call, its China growth story is starting to come under increasing scrutiny as Kevin Johnson did concede that "*we expect competition to remain highly promotional and disruptive*" (starbucks.com). Starbucks also announced it has launched Uber Eats delivery service for $2.49 in San Francisco with plans to expand it in the coming weeks to select stores in NYC, Boston, D.C., Chicago and LA (cnbc.com). Starbucks is also partnering with Uber Eats in London and will be piloting its delivery service there for £2.49 (telegraph.co.uk). However, as we previously discussed, since Starbucks offers a high-fidelity value proposition, we are concerned its new partnership with Uber Eats could erode its brand equity as it will lose control over the customer relationship and experience.

Amazon seeks to gain share of residential parcel delivery market from FedEx & UPS

Amazon is no longer just looking to reduce its reliance on the USPS, **UPS**, **FedEx** and DHL (**Deutsche Post**), but to gain share of the residential parcel delivery market from them with a new promise to eliminate accessorial fees such as residential and fuel surcharges. These extra fees can add 30% to the shipping cost in many cases, with FedEx and UPS charging residential surcharges just under $4 and adding on another 7% for a fuel surcharge (wsj.com). To help lower the cost of the last mile, Amazon has developed a delivery robot in-house called Scout.

The six-wheeled blue delivery robot is the size of a beach cooler and cruises along at walking pace. Amazon will be piloting its robotic delivery service in Snohomish County, Washington with six Scouts to start, each of which will be escorted by an Amazon employee (techcrunch.com). Amazon has also been slowly ramping up its ocean shipping business under the radar. In 2016, Amazon China was granted a license from the U.S. Federal Maritime Commission to operate as an ocean freight forwarder for shipments between China and the U.S. Although Amazon China only shipped a small number of containers in 2017, last year it shipped 5,300 shipping containers, holding 4.7 million cartons of consumer goods, from ports in China to Long Beach and Seattle. In Q4, it opened up its program to U.S. sellers (usatoday.com).

UPS and FedEx fight back by pushing the edges of the convenience frontier

However, UPS and FedEx are not sitting still. In addition to partnering with TerraCycle on its new Loop circular economy shopping platform, UPS is expanding its program with Latch to gain digital access to multi-residential buildings without a concierge from NYC and San Francisco to 10 additional U.S. cities (techcrunch.com). This follows Amazon's unveiling a few weeks ago of its Key for Business, a fob that gives Amazon access to offices and apartments to make deliveries, which it is apparently testing with commercial property managers. We note Brookfield Ventures led a $70 million Series B round for Latch back in July; as part of the strategic investment, **Brookfield Property Partners** will be installing Latch systems in its multi-residential properties that are under development. FedEx is also pushing the edges of the convenience frontier with its new Extra Hours delivery service that extends the cut-off for online ordering for consumers to 2 am for next-day local delivery in select cities and 2-day shipping anywhere in the U.S. More importantly, FedEx is empowering traditional retailers to compete with Amazon Prime by picking up the ordered products directly from the retailers' stores instead of from their regional distribution centres, thus reducing the shipping process by 2–3 days (businessinsider.com).

Walmart's departure from Google Express raises a number of questions

Walmart has abandoned **Alphabet**'s Google Express, Google's online shopping platform which it strategically partnered with back in August 2017 to offer voice shopping via Google Assistant. Apparently Walmart was not seeing any meaningful volume from Google Express, so it has strategically decided to prioritize its own website and delivery infrastructure (forbes.com). With the loss of one of its anchor partners, we question what this implies for the future of Google Express, which has positioned itself as the go-to online mall for retailers looking to compete with Amazon by offering voice-based ordering and home delivery. We note Google Express has partnered with major retailers such as **Target**, **Costco**, **Home Depot**, **Kohl's**, **Bed Bath & Beyond**, PetSmart, **Staples** and **Walgreens.** Although Walmart can compete on the e-commerce layer, we do not believe it has the resources, in terms of both capital and talent, to build or buy its own Alexa. Especially since we just learned that Amazon has 10,000 employees working on Alexa, focusing on AI and machine learning as well as developing her knowledge base, personality, interaction and conversational skills (digitaltrends.com).

Could sound be part of the future design of our home?

IKEA is combining its home furnishing expertise with **Sonos**' sound expertise to make us think about sound as part of the design for the home. Although they have not disclosed the details of their upcoming launch in August of the new IKEA Symfonisk line, they have hinted that they are innovating on how to build sound into the furniture itself (fastcompany.com). We expect more innovations to come from IKEA as back in August it announced it was collaborating with **adidas** to bring together designers from both companies to explore connections between living spaces and sport to understand how homes can better enable active lifestyles.

TomTom sells telematics division to Bridgestone to refocus on mapping

TomTom is selling its telematics fleet-management division to tire manufacturer **Bridgestone** Europe for €910 million. This is a strategic move for TomTom, which faces the near-term threat of increasing competition from Google and HERE (majority-owned by **Audi**, **BMW**, **Daimler**) in the mapping space and the disruption from the longer-term structural shift toward autonomous driving. TomTom will be refocusing its efforts toward its core mapping, navigation software, real-time traffic info and services businesses (venturebeat.com). **Garmin**'s new golf GPS is more than just a GPS to help you improve your game — it also includes a new games feature that lets you compete in virtual golf tournaments. The GPS, which retails for $500, includes new launch monitoring skills, enabling you to track the speed of your ball and club head, the estimated distance and your swing tempo (engadget.com).

Armani Group adds luxury residences to flagship store on Manhattan's UES

As further evidence of the shift in luxury from consumer goods to experiences, the Armani Group is adding 19 luxury residences designed by Giorgio Armani to its flagship Giorgio

Armani store on Manhattan's UES. **SL Green Realty Corp.**, which owns the 79,000-square-foot building at 760 Madison, plans to start re-developing the property in 2020 and finish it by 2023 (chainstoreage.com).

Conde Naste embraces paywalls as it shifts toward the subscription model

Conde Naste, the publisher of popular magazines such as Vogue, GQ and Bon Appetit, announced that it will put all of its titles behind paywalls by year-end. Conde Naste currently has three titles behind metered paywalls — The New Yorker, Wired, Vanity Fair — which allow readers access to up to four free articles per month. The paywall seems to be working as The New Yorker generated $115 million in paid subscription revenue last year, up 69% from $68 million in 2015. It put Wired behind the paywall in February and Vanity Fair in April. The biggest concern of putting up a paywall is the loss of readers, but Conde Naste actually intends to charge advertisers a premium as its paid subscribers are worth more as they represent a more engaged audience (wsj.com).

Amazon's new private-label accelerator program already has its first graduates

Amazon is driving down the time to development for new private label brands from 12–24 months to 90 days through its "Our Brands" accelerator program which it launched in October. This program was designed to attract manufacturers to make products exclusive for Amazon over a wide range of categories and is already producing its first graduates: Tuft & Needle (new mattress brand called Nod), **GNC Holdings** (two new brands of supplements) and Merisant (new brand of sweetener called Sugarly Sweet by Equal) (wsj.com). While Amazon looks to expand its exclusive brand portfolio, an Austin-based start-up is looking to build a new type of consumer products company on top of Amazon's FBA (Fulfilled by Amazon) platform. 101 Commerce raised $12.7 million in June to create a global e-commerce platform by acquiring or investing in 101 Amazon FBA businesses over the next two years. 101 Commerce is looking to capitalize on the operating leverage provided by Amazon's FBA platform resulting from the outsourcing of traffic, conversion, fulfilment and shipping. 101 Commerce is looking to grow the businesses and maximize their sales by creating additional operating leverage through technology, supply chain economies of scale and big data-driven marketing (entrepreneur.com).

Netflix joins MPAA as it receives a record 15 Oscar nominations

Netflix, which just received a record 15 Oscar nominations, has joined the Motion Picture Association of America (MPAA). Netflix is the first Internet streaming service to break into the Hollywood elite, which comprises major studios such as **Disney**, Paramount (**Viacom**), **Sony**, **21st Century Fox**, Universal (**Comcast**) and Warner Bros. (**AT&T**) (techcrunch.com). Meanwhile, Hulu is opportunistically dropping the price of its popular streaming service by 25%, from $7.99 to $5.99 per month, to attract new customers that are looking for more affordable alternatives to Netflix, which just hiked its rates by 13–18%. However, Hulu is maintaining the price of its ad-free streaming service at $11.99 per month and is raising the price of its Live TV service, which streams live programming for over 60 channels and includes an on-demand library of over 85,000 TV episodes, by 13%, from $39.99 to $44.99 per month (techcrunch.com). We note Hulu is a joint venture with Disney, Century 21st Fox and Comcast each owning 30%, and AT&T the remaining 10%. **Shopify** is the latest retailer to venture into entertainment with a new division called Shopify Studios to develop entrepreneur-focused, feature-length documentaries and docu-series. It is launching with 20 short documentaries featuring a variety of the small businesses on its platform and an accompanying podcast called Vanguard by Shopify Studios (fastcompany.com).

Albertsons becomes the latest retailer to partner with Microsoft

As a defensive move against Amazon and following in the footsteps of **Kroger** and Walgreens, Albertsons has entered into a three-year agreement with **Microsoft**. Under the agreement, Albertsons will use Azure as its preferred public cloud and roll out Microsoft 365 to its employees. Albertsons will also use Microsoft's AI technology and could team up with it on its cashierless system (cnbc.com). On the e-commerce layer, according to a new Capgemini study, 40% of U.S. consumers already order groceries online at least once a week. But the services are not meeting their functional value proposition expectations in terms of pricing (59% are not happy with the high prices) and convenience (47% are unhappy when same-day delivery is not an option and 45% complained about late deliveries). In fact, almost half would stop buying from a retailer if they are not satisfied and over half would be willing to switch to a competitor that offers faster deliveries (forbes.com).

Another mall-based retailer bites the dust

We expect the mall vacancy rate to continue its upward climb as Things Remembered, a mall-based retailer that specializes in personalized gifts and engraving, is preparing to file for bankruptcy and close most of its ~400 stores. Things Remembered is burdened by $120 million of debt resulting from its LBO in 2012 (chainstoreage.com). At the same time, we are seeing the demise of start-ups like Munchery. The on-demand food delivery start-up, which has raised $125 million since launching in San Francisco in 2011, is shutting down effectively immediately (techcrunch.com). We note back in May, Munchery closed its operations in LA, NYC and Seattle, and cut 30% of its workforce.

Chapter Six: The Empowerment

I was thrilled to learn that Google just launched a new feature called Live Transcribe as it will empower deaf people, like my brother, by transcribing audio in real time. I'm also excited to order Casper's new Glow Light for my kids to help them fall asleep better and wake up. It's exciting to see Aetna partner with Apple on a new health-tracking and motivation app as it could be really valuable to help people engage in healthy behaviours. It's also very encouraging to see health insurers like Health Care Service Corp. try to help low-income consumers living in food deserts by offering them subsidized health meal delivery services. While Uber Freight is looking to empower its drivers through its new Yelp-like feature for shipping and receiving facilities, Amazon is empowering its sellers with its Amazon Live Creator app which enables them to livestream for free on its platform to promote their products. And even Foot Locker seems to be gaining a social conscience with its new community-driven mission "to inspire and empower youth culture", which coincides with its $100 million strategic investment in the sneaker resale marketplace GOAT Group.

The Empowerment: February 13, 2019

Starbucks faces another disruptive new entrant in China: We-Work

Luckin Coffee could be the first of a new breed of venture-financed hybrid coffee shops to challenge **Starbucks** through the ability to achieve exponential growth by leveraging the customer, structural and supplier capital of food delivery start-ups. And we just spotted a second one - Fore Coffee, which launched in Indonesia last year and has already reached 100,000 deliveries per month and expanded to 15 outlets by leveraging the structural and customer capital of both Go-Jek and Grab (it is available on their apps). Fore Coffee's app itself is scoring at the top the Food & Beverage category for both iOS and Android, ahead of Starbucks, **McDonald's** and Pizza Hut (**Yum! Brands**), and the company just raised an $8.5 million Series A round to accelerate its expansion efforts (techcrunch.com). Although Fore Coffee itself is immaterial to Starbucks as Indonesia represents just over 1% of Starbucks' global store count, we believe this emerging breed of coffee shops could pose rising competition on the convenience front.

CEO of Simon Property Group warns the retail apocalypse is not over

The CEO of the largest mall owner in the U.S. just warned the retail apocalypse is not over. David Simon, CEO of **Simon Property Group**, warned on the company's Q418 conference call that he expects more closures and bankruptcies this year, stating: "*There are some retailers out there that we're nervous about*" (cnbc.com). For example, **Mattel**'s American Girl, which is facing double-digit declines, is closing two of its stores in March as part of a move to cut costs. American Girl is closing its experiential 22,000-square-foot stores in Minnesota's Mall of America and Boston's Natick Mall, which both opened in November 2008 in the heart of the economic downturn (startribune.com). In the U.K., the British Retail Consortium reports that footfall fell by 0.7% in January, marking the 14th consecutive month of decline, while the vacancy rate rose to 9.9% versus 8.9% a year ago (marketwatch.com). Given the rising store closures, we expect to see more re-purposing of retail into industrial space. For example, CBRE reports that since 2016, there have been 24 retail-to-industrial projects in the U.S., resulting in the conversion of 7.9 million square feet of retail space into 10.9 million square feet of industrial space. Not surprisingly, most of the conversions have been freestanding big-box stores in low income areas close to population centres with industrial vacancy rates under 5% (cbre.us).

Instacart faces class action lawsuit while Deliv terminates partnership with Walmart

Instacart is getting hit with more bad publicity as it turns out it has started using customer tips to subsidize the earnings to its shoppers. Instacart shoppers are fighting back and urging customers to just leave a nominal $0.22 tip and tip them with real cash instead (businessinsider.com). It is becoming worse as on February 4, NBC reported that Instacart is facing a class-action lawsuit, with allegations that it "*intentionally and maliciously misappropriates gratuities in order to pay plaintiff's wages, even though Instacart maintained that 100 percent of customer tips went directly to shoppers*" (nbcnews.com). As we have been warning, this could lead to an attrition in its supply base and a negative network effect, and impact the food retailers with which it partnered. More bad news on the grocery delivery front: Deliv has terminated its same-day grocery delivery partnership with

Walmart. Walmart apparently couldn't process the orders fast enough, resulting in Deliv drivers often having to wait over 40 minutes at the store to collect orders. We note this follows the termination last May of Walmart's partnerships with Uber and Lyft, which it entered into at the same time as Deliv back in June 2016. Walmart has also ended its in-home delivery service pilot it launched in October 2017 with August Home and Deliv (businessinsider.com). In Australia, the supermarket giant Coles (**Coles Group**) is partnering with Uber Eats to increase its convenience value proposition. Coles is trialing home delivery of ready-to-eat meals in a Sydney suburb for a delivery fee of $5 per order (dailytelegraph.com.au).

Postmates files for IPO, DoorDash is raising $500 million & SoftBank invests $940 million in Nuro

As expected, Postmates has confidentially filed for an IPO; however, it has not disclosed the time frame or size and price range. We note that Postmates, which makes 5 million food deliveries per month from 550 U.S. cities, raised a $100 million Series F round in January, following closely behind its $300 million Series E round in September (wsj.com). DoorDash, which raised a $250 million Series E round in August, is now in the process of raising a $500 million round at a $6 billion pre-IPO valuation (techcrunch.com). **SoftBank**'s Vision Fund just invested $940 million in Nuro, a robo-delivery start-up founded in Mountain View in 2016 that partnered with **Kroger** back in June to test the world's first driverless grocery delivery service (inc.com). This investment is massive considering Nuro had previously only raised a single $92 million Series A round last January when it revealed that it had built an initial fleet of six purpose-built fully autonomous delivery vehicles "*designed to transform local commerce*" by bringing things you want from local businesses directly to your home.

iRobot now has a Roomba to mow your lawn for you

The **iRobot** Terra Robot Mower, which took nearly a decade to make, and incorporates a technology called Imprint Smart Mapping, can be controlled from its Home app like its vacuuming and mopping Roombas. It will launch first in Germany later this year and in the U.S. next year, although it will be doing a beta program test in the U.S. this year (fortune.com).

Alexa reaches over 80,000 skills and acquires home mesh router Eero

Alexa, who now has over 80,000 skills, was once again claimed Queen of the Super Bowl for *Not Everything Makes the Cut* which mocks Bezos' strategy to hide his growing army of Alexa Amazonian Warriors inside Trojan horses disguised in the form of a wide range of new smart hardware devices. It starts with the new Alexa microwave, which made the cut, and then showcases the hilarious rejects: a toothbrush, a dog collar and a hot tub (cnet.com). We note the ad has been viewed over 39 million times since it was posted on YouTube on January 30. It will be interesting to see if this will surpass the record Amazon set last year for its *Alexa Loses Her Voice* Super Bowl ad, which was the most viewed ad on YouTube, with over 50 million views, and introduced a human aspect to Alexa, elevating the company to a new emotional level. Amazon has a new Trojan horse — Eero — the home mesh router start-up it just acquired that enables you to spread Wi-Fi around your home instead of having to rely on a single Wi-Fi router. This acquisition is highly strategic as in addition to providing Amazon with another entry point into your home, Wi-Fi is the essential foundation of the smart home and Amazon could also potentially build the technology into the Echo, which could double as a Wi-Fi spot (cnbc.com). Interestingly, according to CIRP, the U.S. installed base for smart speakers reached 66 million in December, up 78% from 37 million in December 2017 and 25% from 53 million in September 2018. Amazon Echo continues to be the dominant player with a 70% share, followed by Google Home at 24% and Apple HomePod at 6% (techcrunch.com).

Alexa now wants to become friends with your baby

Amazon just launched the Baby Skill Activity API to help developers to build Alexa skills for baby apps and baby care devices for activities such as tracking a baby's weight, sleep, diaper changes and feedings. Through the Amazon Alexa Fund, Amazon is also making a strategic investment in Hatch Baby, which makes the popular Grow baby smart changing pad and scale and the Rest sleep light (techcrunch.com). American publishing company ChooseCo is collaborating with Amazon's Audible to bring Choose Your Own Adventure stories to Alexa as a new skill. It is starting with two stories, narrated by voice actors, titled *The Abominable Snowman* and *Journey Under the Sea*, which have 28 and 37 endings, respectively (techcrunch.com).

Amazon guides lower for Q1 as it steps up its capital investments

Amazon issued lower-than-expected guidance for Q119 as a result of a step-up in capital investments as well as the impact in India of the government rule change on e-commerce. Amazon's net sales in Q418 rose 20% to $72.4 billion and it beat on the bottom line, reporting a record quarterly EPS of $6.04 versus $3.75 a year ago. The big driver continues to be its high-margin AWS division, where net sales rose 45% to a record $7.4 billion and operating margin rose 280 bp to 29.3%. The company's overall operating margin increased 170 bp to 5.2% as its operating margin in North America, which accounts for 61%

of its net sales, rose 60 bp to 5.1%, and its International operating margin improved by 200 bp to -3.1%. Interestingly, Amazon's "Other" revenue, which is mainly advertising revenue, rose 97% to $3.4 billion, totalling over $10 billion for the year. As evidence of Amazon's growing influence in advertising, **Facebook** cited Amazon for the first time as a competitor in its 10-K for 2018: "*we compete with Apple in messaging, Google and YouTube in advertising and video,* ***Tencent*** *in messaging and social media, and Amazon in advertising*" (facebook.com).

Retailers are now venturing into the advertising world

Interestingly, retailers like Walmart, **Target**, **Kroger** and **Ahold Delhaize** are looking to create new revenue streams by following Amazon into the advertising business, launching in-house media networks as they look to capitalize on their supplier capital (i.e., long-standing relationships with big brands) and customer capital. For example, according to Forrester Research, Walmart receives 300 million monthly visitors to its U.S. stores and 140 million U.S. visitors to its website, exceeding the online U.S. traffic to Google (240 million), Facebook (200 million) and Amazon (200 million). Like Amazon, Walmart knows what consumers actually buy whereas Google only knows what they want and Facebook only knows what they like (bloomberg.com).

Watch out HSN & QVC: Amazon is invading the home shopping channel space

As a direct competitive threat to **Qurate Retail Group**'s HSN and QVC, Amazon has launched its own home shopping channel called Amazon Live. It has also launched the Amazon Live Creator app, enabling brands to livestream for free directly to Amazon.com and the Amazon app with the option to pay to boost their livestream. As Amazon states on the Apple app store: "*Livestreaming allows you to tell your brand story, showcase your* *products, and interact with shoppers in real time, all while driving sales*". The app, which is currently available to U.S. Professional Sellers enrolled in Amazon's Brand Registry, includes built-in analytics (techcrunch.com). We note that back in December, Facebook started testing a home shopping network-like Live Video feature for merchants in Thailand. This comes as QVC launches a new Q Anytime app and introduces a new brand identity and logo in the U.S. ahead of its international rollout as part of its mobile and social first strategy to video shopping (fashionunited.uk).

NBC's Golf Channel launches GolfPass subscription services

NBC Sports' Golf Channel (**Comcast**) is going direct-to-consumer, launching a GolfPass subscription service. For a cost of $9.99 per month or $99 per year, members will receive a dozen TaylorMade golf balls, a complimentary round of golf once per month at any of 7,000 global golf clubs, discounts on golf resorts, apparels and accessories, and exclusive access to over 4,000 on-demand instructional videos on the GolfPass app. To enhance its content, the Golf Channel is partnering with four-time champion golfer Rory McIlroy, who will provide instructional and autobiographical videos and host an exclusive monthly podcast with Carson Daly (cnbc.com).

Amazon goes on a spending spree at Sundance Film Festival

To boost its Amazon Prime content, Amazon went on a spending spree at the 2019 Sundance Film Festival. Amazon spent a total of $46 million for four films: two comedies, one drama and one semi-autobiography (forbes.com). To enhance its content, **Disney**+ will include non-Disney programming when it launches and it will buy certain outside products opportunistically (techcrunch.com). Now even ride-hailing companies are venturing into the video-streaming space. Grab, the ride-hailing giant in Southeast Asia that has raised $7.3 billion since launching in 2012, is partnering with HOOQ to let its customers stream movies and TV shows on its app. Grab's customers will receive access during a three-month free trial to over 10,000 hours of content from HOOQ, a joint venture established in 2015 between Singel, **Sony** Pictures Television and Warner Bros. Entertainment (**AT&T**) to offer over-the-top video service in Asia (techcrunch.com).

Spotify aspires to become the "Netflix of Audio" with podcast acquisitions

Spotify is expanding its total addressable market from music to all of audio as it aspires to become the "**Netflix** of Audio". On February 6, Spotify acquired Gimlet Media and Anchor and in his blog article, *Audio First*, Daniel Elk, Founder & CEO of Spotify, shared his plans to spend up to $500 million this year on more podcast acquisitions. As he discusses in his article, there seems to be a value creation opportunity in audio as currently the market for music and radio is only one-tenth of that for video ($100 billion versus $1 trillion), but as he astutely points out, why should our eyes be worth over 10 times our ears? Spotify is uniquely positioned to capture share of the rapidly growing podcast market through leveraging its customer capital (i.e., 207 million active users and 96 million paid subscribers), structural capital (i.e., in October it launched the beta of its Spotify for Podcasters platform) and acquiring high-quality original content (newsroom.spotify.com). Anchor, which has raised $14 million since launching in NYC in 2015, provides Spotify with an audio creation platform and over 15 billion hours of content. Gimlet Media, which has raised $28 million since launching in NYC in 2014, provides Spotify with a network of high-quality narrative podcasts. As we've previously mentioned,

Barry McCarthy, CFO of Spotify, was the CFO at Netflix from 1999 to 2010.

Food Locker invests $100 million in sneaker resale platform GOAT Group

It seems like **Foot Locker** is trying to ascend to the peak of the customer capital pyramid and create a psychological attachment with its customers through its new community-driven mission "*to inspire and empower youth culture*", which is much more soulful than its previous stated mission "*to be the leading global retail of athletically inspired shoes and apparel*". As part of this strategic shift, it is making a $100 million investment in GOAT Group, an authentic sneaker resale marketplace. Since GOAT Group launched in 2015 in California, it has grown its platform to 750,000 sneaker listings, with 150,000 vendors and 12M active users. Foot Locker expects this will lead to the two companies combining their efforts across digital and physical retail platforms as GOAT Group's technology will help Foot Locker enhance its digital capabilities and sneaker buying experience while Foot Locker will provide GOAT Group with valuable structural capital in terms of physical access points for buyers and sellers (forbes.com). On the sports retail front, Walmart has entered into a non-exclusive long-term partnership with Fanatics (**eBay**), the online retailer which holds exclusive licensing rights to produce and distribute merchandise for all major professional sports leagues. Under the deal, Walmart will start selling thousands of sports-related merchandise on Walmart.com, including NFL jerseys and NBA t-shirts (cnbc.com).

Casper debuts Glow Light, Warby Parker adds "virtual try-on"; Rebag raises $25 million

New Guard retailers like Casper, Warby Parker and Rebag continue to innovate and make strides down the retail field while

Old Guard retailers like Canadian Tire fumble the ball. Apparently three **Canadian Tire** stores in Toronto have pulled their decade-old self-checkout machines as they are inefficient and keep breaking down (cbc.ca). Meanwhile, Casper is advancing its mission to improve sleep with the debut of the Glow Light. The Glow helps you fall asleep at bedtime by filing your room with a warm LED light and then dim to darkness the next 45 minutes and you can schedule it with an app to wake you up in the morning through the reverse process. The $89 Glow is also small and portable so you can use it in the middle of the night without waking anyone up (techcrunch.com). Warby Parker is leveraging the AI layer to enhance convenience and the customer experience with its new "virtual try-on" feature. The new feature on its iPhone app allows you to see the virtual glass frames on your face and also snap a screenshot to share with others (techcrunch.com). Rebag, an online reseller of luxury handbags launched in NYC in 2014, just raised a $25 million Series C round. Unlike most closet-sharing companies, Rebag is not a marketplace as it buys second-hand handbags directly from consumers, who just need to upload photos of their handbag on its app to receive a free quote and then ship it to Rebag's headquarters to receive immediate payment. In addition to using the funds to expand its physical footprint from 5 stores in NYC and LA to 35 in the medium term, we expect Rebag will use it to buy more inventory as it currently has just over 3,700 luxury handbags for sale from over 50 designers on its site, ranging from a low of $315 for a Christian Louboutin pink leather wallet to $54,000 for a **Hermes** Birkin Bag Limited Edition (techcrunch.com).

Walmart launches new private label online furniture brand

Walmart is following Amazon into the online home furnishings space with the launch of a new private-label furniture brand that promises "*elevated style without the elevated price*". MoDRN features nearly 650 items of furniture over three stylish collections — Retro Glam, Refined Industrial, Scandinavian Minimal — and is affordably priced at between $199 and $899 (digiday.com). Facebook is also venturing into the home furnishings space with its acquisition of GrokStyle, an app that uses AI to identify furniture and home décor from any picture or angle. Interestingly, last year GrokStyle partnered with IKEA on its AR furniture app (in.mashable.com). However, the acquisition was likely not material as GrokStyle had only raised $2.5 million since launching in San Francisco in 2016.

1. *A wristband that not just opens the door to our hotel room but links to our credit card to make it easier for us to spend money – SMART.*
2. *Adding a massive digital screen to the stage set to enhance the nightly entertainment shows for guests – SMART.*
3. *Replacing the paper version of the daily activities schedule with an app so we need to carry our expensive smartphones all around the resort – NOT SMART.*

As I experienced during my recent family holiday at Club Med Ixtapa, and explore in next week's in-depth research report, there is an exciting opportunity for companies to leverage the digital and AI layers to better originate and capture value and enhance the customer experience. For example, LG wants to make sure you never run out of detergent again — its new line of smart washers, dryers and dishwashers not only works with Alexa, but also synchs with Amazon Dash. To help you sleep better, Eight Sleep has launched a new smart mattress that will automatically adjust the temperature on your side of the bed. MSC Cruises is debuting the first virtual cruise assistant to answer passengers' questions and help them book services. But just like they should fire the genius at Club Med who did away with the paper daily activities schedule, sometimes companies should leave well enough alone. And one of these is Lego, who is sadly trying to kill the magic of kids' imagination by bringing augmented reality to its new line of Lego sets.

Smart?: February 19, 2019

Canada Goose revenue soars 50% as DTC sales climb 78%
Our thesis that vertically integrated, high-margin apparel, accessories & luxury goods companies with social missions are uniquely positioned to originate value by leveraging their cult-like following to build DTC distribution channels continues to play out. For example, **Canada Goose**'s revenue rose 50% to $399 million in Q3 and its EPS 66% to $0.98. But, more importantly, its DTC sales soared 78% to $235 million, accounting for 58.9% of total sales, up from 49.5% a year ago. Although the higher gross margin for Canada's Goose DTC versus wholesale channel (76.1% versus 47.7%) led to positive mix shift, its overall gross margin only rose 80 bp to 64.4% as a result of changes in product mix and increased manufacturing labour costs. Canada Goose also plans to open its second Quebec manufacturing facility in Montreal, bringing its number of manufacturing facilities in Canada to eight (investor.canadagoose.com).

More bad news for retail REITs as Payless announces plans to close all 2,100 U.S. stores

Just weeks after the CEO of the **Simon Property Group** warned the retail apocalypse is not over, Payless announced what will be the largest-ever liquidation in terms of number of stores with its plan to close all 2,100 U.S. locations. Payless, which closed 700 stores after filing for bankruptcy in April 2017, is preparing to file for bankruptcy again (wsj.com). And economic, not just structural headwinds, could soon come into play for retailers and retail REITs. U.S. retail sales tumbled 1.2% in December, the largest decline since September 2009. Core retail sales, which exclude autos, gasoline, building materials and food services, performed even worse, declining 1.7%. The largest declines were in miscellaneous store retailers (-4.1%), online retailers (-3.9%) and department stores (-3.3%) (cnbc.com).

LG synchs its new home appliances with Amazon Dash while Samsung opens retail stores

LG is leveraging AI to better originate and capture value with the upgrade of its product line of 2018 and 2019 smart washers, dryers and dishwashers. Not only will they work with Alexa, but now also synch with Amazon Dash, enabling them to track and automatically re-order detergent or dryer sheets from Amazon when you run low (cnet.com). Meanwhile, **Samsung**, the top home appliance maker in the U.S., is opening its first stand-alone retail stores. Two years after opening its Samsung 837 flagship store in NYC to let visitors test Samsung products and share them on social media, it is opening Samsung Experience Stores in Long Island, LA and Houston — and unlike its 837 store, these will actually sell Samsung products (techspot.com). It will be interesting to see what these stores are like. As I previously shared, when I visited its 837 flagship store in NYC back in the fall, I found it gorgeous and loved how it showcased many innovations such as Samsung's VR and its Bixby-powered home appliances, but the experience itself fell flat as the staff didn't seem that knowledgeable or passionate.

Apple entering video streaming, acquires PullString

Apple is planning to launch a streaming video service in April or early May. It is expected to offer free original content for its device owners and a subscription platform for its existing digital services (cnbc.com). Moving up from the digital to the AI layer, Apple just acquired PullString to help improve Siri's strength and powers. PullString, formerly known as ToyTalk, has raised $45 million since being launched by former Pixar executives in San Francisco in 2011. PullString, which helps companies design and publish voice apps, partnered with **Mattel** in 2015 to create Hello Barbie (techcrunch.com).

Amazon Go coming to London, Whole Foods raising prices, Kroger launches Kroger Pay

Amazon is bringing its cashierless Amazon Go to London as apparently it has secured a central retail location for it (reuters.com). We could soon see rising grocery costs as Whole Foods is raising prices on hundreds of products as it bows to pressure from CPGs to pass on rising inflation costs for packaging, ingredients and transportation (wsj.com). On the payments front, **Kroger** has launched its own QR-based mobile payment system called Kroger Pay. In addition to providing customers with a greater level of convenience and reducing checkout times, Kroger is looking to increase the emotional connection with its customers through linking it to its loyalty program (businessinsider.com). Meanwhile, to increase convenience for Chinese tourists, **Walgreens** is more than doubling the number of U.S. locations accepting Alipay (**Alibaba**) from 3,000 to 7,000 by April. According to Nielsen, over two-thirds of Chinese tourists use their smartphones to pay while traveling abroad (pymnts.com).

MSC Cruises is debuting the first virtual cruise assistant

As further evidence to our thesis that cruise lines are ideally positioned to use the digital and AI layers to leverage their physical assets and enhance the customer experience, MSC Cruises is debuting the first virtual cruise assistant on the maiden voyage of its new 4,400-passenger MSC Bellissima cruise ship next month. Zoe, which MSC developed in partnership with **Samsung**, is fluent in seven languages, can answer over 800 of the most commonly asked questions and even help passengers book a specific service, as well as interact with the in-cabin TVs (telegraph.co.uk).

Innovation continues in the mattress space

Eight Sleep, a sleep fitness start-up that has raised $30 million since launching in NYC in 2014, is launching a new smart mattress. The Pod, which Eight Sleep's co-founder & CEO, Matteo Franceschetti, describes as "Nest for your bed". In addition to integrating with smart home devices such as **Alphabet**'s Nest, Philip Hue smart lights and Alexa. The Pod automatically adjusts its temperature during the night to improve your sleep and features a thermal alarm which wakes you up by cooling down your side of the bed. The Pod starts at $2,000 and will begin shipping in April (theverge.com).

Do our kids really need augmented reality Lego sets?

Lego is bringing augmented reality to its Lego sets. Its new Hidden Side line of eight augmented reality-focused sets blur the line between the physical and virtual worlds by enabling kids to play with Lego as they hunt for ghosts with the app on their smartphone. Although this is innovative, as the mother of two young boys who spend countless hours playing with Lego blocks, I have to agree with Mark Wilson, who states in his Fast Company article, *Lego is betting on the wrong future*: "*I'd argue that the real magic of Lego occurs in that gap between the physical product and your mind–a gap where the imagination lives...*" (fastcompany.com).

Amazon breaks up with NYC on Valentine's Day

On February 14, Amazon announced it will not be locating its second headquarters in Long Island City. Although Amazon has the support of 70% of New Yorkers, it is facing increasing vocal opposition from state and local politicians. Amazon still intends to grow its base of employees in the New York area, which already total over 5,000, but focus on establishing its second headquarters in North Virginia and Nashville (cnbc.com). On the consumer front, Amazon is bringing a new level of convenience to festival goers, installing Amazon Lockers at the music festival and launching a dedicated Coachella storefront on its site (techcrunch.com). To facilitate cross-border shopping, Amazon is launching PayCode in partnership with **The Western Union Company**. Using PayCode, people will be able to pay for Amazon items in their local currency at Western Union outposts. Amazon is starting PayCode in 10 countries (Chile, Columbia, Hong Kong, Indonesia, Kenya, Malaysia, Peru, Philippines, Taiwan, Thailand), expanding its total addressable market beyond its existing 14 developed countries with their own Amazon websites (techcrunch.com). And on the supplier capital front, Amazon is seeking to empower its Brand Registered third-party sellers with the release of its new free Amazon Brand Analytics dashboard. The dashboard provides access to data points that were previously only available through a $30,000+ subscription for its Amazon Retail Analytics in Vendor Central (forbes.com).

Chapter Seven: The Scooters

Last week the value of sustainability shone through with Amazon rolling out Amazon Day to its 100 million+ U.S. Prime members, Elon Musk announcing the launch of Tesla's long-awaited standard Model 3 electric vehicle for $35,000, achieving the ambitious vision he set out back in 2006 in "The Secret Tesla Motors Master Plan", and Lyft, which is driven by its sustainability-focused mission "to take cars off the road", filing to go public at an expected valuation of between $20 billion and $25 billion. This reminded me of what I wrote back in 2016 in my Ubernomics book:

"Business as usual is changing. While once companies saw sustainability issues as risks to be managed, many now also see sustainability as a source of innovation that drives growth and profitability. These words appeared in The Value Driver Model: A Tool for Communicating the Business Value of Sustainability, a paper released in December 2013 by the UN Global Compact and PRI initiative. It highlights the recent advancement in its thinking about sustainability in terms of growth opportunities versus risk management. Notably, it is a radical departure from the

ESG-centric focus of its previous papers..."

$USTAINABILITY: March 5, 2019

Amazon is looking to disrupt and gain share in transportation & logistics

On February 28, **Amazon** rolled out its Amazon Day delivery option to all its +100 million Prime members in the U.S. (techcrunch.com). I was so excited when I learned of the pilot of this project that I featured it in our November 14, 2018 research note, *The Amazon Man*, and explored the concept further in our February 26, 2019 research report, *The Alpha Playbook to the Sensual Revolution.*

During XPO Logistics' Q418 conference call, its CEO, Brad Jacobs, disclosed: "*We had a major impact in the fourth quarter when our largest customer decided to curtail its postal injection... We can't ignore the fact that our largest customer is curtailing about two thirds of its business with us.... We had substantial capacity dedicated to this customer in brokerage, last mile and logistics.*" He also revealed that its largest customer represented 5% of total revenue in 2018 — which is believed to be Amazon.

The other big development is that **Stamps.com** has ended its long-standing exclusive partnership with the USPS, stating it wants to expand its relationship with Amazon from Australia and the U.K. to the U.S. (businessinsider.com). As Ken McBride, CEO of Stamps.com, stated during the company's Q418 conference call: "*as we look to the future of shipping, we no longer see an exclusive partnership with the USPS as the right strategy for Stamps.com*" as USPS does not offer two-day guaranteed delivery and he is concerned USPS will become even less competitive over time as it is constrained operationally by regulations and financially by its pension/healthcare liabilities. I encourage you to read the transcript, in which he mentions "Amazon" 49 times, and shares valuable insights into Amazon: 1) Amazon's current fleet of 27 Amazon Air cargo planes carry 25% of Amazon's own North American packages and its flight routes could potentially compete with 67% of the routes of volumes flown by UPS and FedEx combined; 2) he believes Amazon's marginal cost of carrying additional packages will be low so he expects Amazon to expand its Shipping with Amazon service and be able to make good margins while offering low prices; and 3) Amazon's public acknowledgement in its recently filed 10-K of its intent to compete in shipping and logistics was one of the major reasons behind Stamps.com's decision to end its relationship with the USPS.

Amazon launching a new grocery chain in U.S. as Marks & Spencer invests in Ocado

As a direct competitive threat to grocery retailers, Amazon is in talks to launch a new grocery chain that would likely appeal to a wider base of customers than upscale Whole Foods by offering a wider variety of choice and likely lower prices. Amazon is in talks to open dozens of grocery stores in major U.S. cities such as LA, San Francisco, Seattle, Chicago, D.C. and Philadelphia, with the first one scheduled to open in LA as early as the end of this year. The grocery stores will be 35,000 square feet, nearly half the typical supermarket size of 60,000 square feet, and Amazon is seeking flexibility with leases in terms of the type of store and the type of products it will be allowed to sell (wsj.com). In the U.K., **Marks & Spencer's** is investing £750 million for a 50% stake in **Ocado Group**'s retail business. However, Marks & Spencer won't be able to offer online grocery delivery to its customers until September 2020, when Ocado's partnership with Waitrose ends, but it needs to fund the deal now by doing a £600 million rights issue and cutting its dividend by 40%. In addition, it is only investing in Ocado.com and will not receive any equity in Ocado Solutions, which will continue to develop new robotics warehouse technology for retailers like **Groupe Casino**, **Kroger** and Sobeys (**Empire Company**). In addition to offering Marks & Spencer an online grocery ordering and delivery platform, Ocado will provide valuable supplier capital, increasing the variety of choice of products. In return, Ocado will receive valuable customer capital in the form of access to Marks & Spencer's database of 12 million food shoppers (bbc.com).

Delta and Samsung embrace the Sensual Revolution

Delta (**Masco**) is introducing a new line of smart kitchen faucets that measure water usage over time that you can also use your voice to turn the water on/off and specify how much water you want. Delta's VoiceIQ technology works with both Alexa and Google Assistant (digitaltrends.com). **Samsung** unveiled a number of AI devices at the Kitchen & Bath Industry Show in Las Vegas (news.samsung.com).

- *Samsung Bot Chef*: Chef's assistant is a collaborative robot arm, or "cobot", that responds to simple voice commands to perform a wide range of kitchen tasks (chopping, whisking, pouring, cleaning).
- *Chef Garden*: AI farming platform integrates with the Samsung Family Hub, using the power and water connections already provided to the fridge, to grow fresh and pesticide-free fruits and vegetables.
- *Air & Bot Clean*: Autonomous robot uses sensors to identify areas with low air quality to move to and purify.

The retail apocalypse deepens as HBC, L Brands & The Gap announce store closures

Hudson's Bay Company is closing its Home Outfitters housewares chain of 37 stores across Canada. It is also conducting a fleet review of its 133 Saks OFF 5th locations across the U.S. and Canada, with expectations to close 20 stores in the U.S. (financialpost.com). **L Brands** is closing 53 Victoria's Secret stores, representing 4% of its global fleet of 1,143 stores. This comes as Victoria's Secret's same-store sales declined 3% in Q418 as a result of competition from traditional retailers and new DTC brands (cnbc.com). And the competition is intensifying as **Target** is launching three new private-label lingerie and sleepwear brands, targeting over $1 billion in sales this year (cnbc.com).

The Gap is tossing a lifesaver to Old Navy as it announces a massive downsizing of its drowning fleet of Gap namesake stores. The Gap is spinning off Old Navy, which generated $8 billion, or nearly half of its sales last year, into its own publicly traded company as it announces the closure of 230 of its Gap-branded stores, on top of the 68 it has already closed this year. The NewCo will hold the remaining brands – Gap, Banana Republic, Athleta, Intermix, HillCity — which generated $9 billion in sales last year (wsj.com). The Gap is serious about enhancing its brand image as just days after announcing the Old Navy spin-off, it is acquiring Gymboree's Janie and Jack high-end kids clothing brand for $35 million (businessinsider.com).

McDonald's franchisees complain about Uber Eats, DoorDash raises $400 million round

McDonald's franchisees are complaining the 20% delivery fee they need to pay to Uber Eats is pressuring their already tight profit margins. Since McDonald's first pilot-tested a partnership with Uber Eats in January 2017, it has expanded this to offering delivery at over 19,000 locations worldwide, including 8,000 restaurants in the U.S. But franchisees are concerned that delivery, which accounts for 10% of sales in some markets, will continue to cannibalize their on-premise restaurant sales and reduce their cash flow (adage.com). DoorDash just raised a $400 million Series F round at a $7.1 billion pre-IPO valuation. We note this follows closely behind its $250 million Series E in August (techcrunch.com).

FedEx tests a delivery robot, Rakuten partners with JD.com

As the last mile accounts for over 50% of delivery costs, we are seeing the debut of more and more delivery robots. For example, FedEx has partnered with Deka Development & Research Corp., whose founder created the Segway. FedEx is testing the delivery robot, which resembles a cooler on wheels with a top speed of 10 mph, between its FedEx stores in its hometown of Memphis with plans to roll it out for its SameDay service which operates in 1,900 cities around the world (venturebeat.com). **Rakuten** is partnering with **JD.com** to accelerate the development and commercialization of its last-mile delivery efforts. Under the partnership, JD.com will bring its drone delivery system and autonomous vehicles to Japan (techcrunch.com).

Walmart uses its own train containers as it doubles super-centers as fulfillment centers

To gain more control over its supply chain, **Walmart** started piloting a program in Southern California last summer to use its own intermodal train containers instead of going through third-party rail companies or middlemen (businessinsider.com). We are starting to see the utilization of stores as distribution centres: on Walmart's Q419 conference call, President & CEO, Doug McMillon, stated: "*It looks to me like there's a long runway* *here where our supercenters can double as fulfillment centers*". Meanwhile, Travis Kalanick, the founder and ex-CEO of Uber, has acquired $40 million in commercial real estate in Manhattan and Queens for City Storage Systems, which he invested $150 million in and became CEO of last March. He is also looking to expand the operations of City Storage Systems to Europe and Asia (therealdeal.com).

P&G launches Tide Cleaners as Amazon retires Amazon Dash button

Procter & Gamble is launching Tide Cleaners, opening "full-service, on-demand laundry solutions" in 2,000 locations across North America. Tide is looking to offer a new level of convenience to consumers by expanding from product into services as laundry is the fifth most disliked household chore. In addition to stand-alone retail stores, Tide is looking to add drop-box locations in apartment buildings, retail stores and even delivery vans on college campuses (adweek.com). Interestingly, Amazon is retiring its physical stick-on Amazon Dash button which it debuted only three years ago. The physical button has become obsolete thanks to innovations on Amazon Dash on both the e-commerce layer (i.e., the introduction of Subscribe & Save) and the AI layer (the hundreds of smart devices that now sync with Amazon Dash and the ability to re-order household and personal products using Alexa) (techcrunch.com).

Farfetch's stock price soars on strategic partnerships with Harrods and also JD.com

Farfetch's stock price has risen over 30% the past week on news of two significant strategic partnerships. On February 26, Harrods, the iconic British department store, announced it is strategically partnering with Farfetch to enhance its e-commerce platform. Harrods is revamping its e-commerce site using Farfetch's white-label Farfetch Black & White Solutions, which will provide Harrods with e-commerce management and operations, international logistics and tech support (digital-commerce360.com). Two days later, JD.com announced it is merging its high-end Toplife platform, which it introduced in mid-2017, with Farfetch China. This strategic move comes as Chinese consumers, which account for one-third of global luxury goods purchases, increasingly shift their spending from stores in European capital cities to mainland China and from physical stores to online. In addition to JD.com providing Farfetch with valuable supplier capital in the form of luxury brands such as **Kering**'s Saint Laurent and Balenciaga, it is contributing valuable structural capital in the form of its app and customer capital in terms of its 300 million Chinese customers (reuters.com). We note that JD.com is the largest shareholder in Farfetch, having been the sole investor in its $397 million corporate round in June 2017, its last funding round before Farfetch IPO'd on September 21, 2018.

Nordstrom, Foot Locker, Target, Pinterest & Office Depot make strategic moves on e-commerce layer

Nordstrom is increasing its commitment to moving up the structural capital pyramid to the e-commerce layer with the appointment of retail visionary Kirsten Green to its Board of Directors. Since founding Forerunner Ventures in 2010, she has invested in highly successful DTC brands such as Jet and Bonobos (acquired by Walmart for $3.3 billion and $310 million in 2016 and 2017) Dollar Shave Club (acquired by **Unilever** for $1 billion in 2016), Warby Parker, Outdoor Voices and Glossier (press.nordstrom.com). To avoid the fate of mall-based retailers such as Gymboree and Payless, **Foot Locker** is making strategic investments to quickly advance up the structural and capital customer pyramids. Just weeks after investing $100 million in sneaker resale platform GOAT Group, Foot Locker is leading the $19.5 million Series C round for Rockets of Awesome, a DTC kids clothing brand launched in NYC in 2016, with an investment of $12.5 million. Interestingly, one of the other investors is Forerunner Ventures, which previously invested in its $12.5 million Series A round in January 2017. **Target** is actively reaching out to brands on an invitation-only basis to create a curated online shopping platform called Target+ (cnbc.com). Pinterest, which confidentially filed for an IPO last month at an expected valuation of $12 billion, is introducing new tools for merchants to drive its e-commerce business. Through its new Catalogs tool, merchants can create a virtual storefront by uploading and converting their entire product catalog into shoppable pins. In addition, they can now post Shopping Ads straight from their feeds (engadget.com). To compete against Amazon Business, **Office Depot** has entered into a strategic partnership with **Alibaba** and launched a co-branded e-commerce site on Alibaba.com (techcrunch.com). Under the agreement, Office Depot will gain valuable supplier capital as its U.S. business customers will now have access to Alibaba's global network of over 150,000 suppliers. In return, Office Depot will give Alibaba valuable customer capital in the form of access to its 10 million U.S. business customers and supplier capital in the form of its 1,800 sales agents (techcrunch.com).

Levi, Walmart and Facebook make strategic moves on AI layer

Levi Strauss, which filed to go public last month on the NYSE under the ticker "LEVI", is hiring its first chief AI officer (mytotalretail.com). Walmart is acquiring Aspectiva, an Israel-based AI start-up that provides shoppers with product recommendations, both in the store and online, by analyzing user-generated content such as product reviews and combining it with shoppers' browsing behaviour. Walmart plans to add Aspectiva to its Store No. 8 in-house incubation arm it founded in 2017 (techcrunch.com). We note Aspectiva had raised $8 million since launching in Tel Aviv in 2013. **Facebook** aspires to build its own digital assistant. In addition to partnering with **Intel** last month to develop a specialized and powerful AI chip, Facebook is working on developing its own custom ASIC chip to support its AI programs, which include monitoring video in real-time and moderating content (ft.com).

My mind is still a whirlwind as I reflect back on the four days I just spent down in Austin at the SXSW Interactive conference learning about the latest societal, technological and economic trends, but there is one image I keep seeing: the scooters. These new stork-like two-wheeled species, which come in a variety of four-letter names (Bird, Spin, Lime, Jump [Uber] and Lyft), were everywhere I looked — sleeping in the middle of the sidewalk, flocking together in front of buildings, and charging dangerously toward me at all angles. It truly felt like the Wild West and I couldn't help think about what caused the birth and explosion in population of this new invasive and disruptive form of transportation species? One word: convergence.

As Mary Webb discussed in her session "2019 Emerging Tech Trends Report", the number of tech trends she observed last year rose 40% to 315 tech trends across 26 industries as a result of the convergence of different technologies and inflections across the board. As Alex Spinelli, the former Global Head of Alexa OS at Amazon, discussed during his session "The End of Websites is Nigh", we have shifted from a linear to a branching world. And I loved the analogy proposed at the session "The Future of Augmented Reality in Sports": when you connect devices together, it is like a symphony as the sum of the parts is more than the whole.

To understand the exponential rise in scooters, we need to look at the convergence of the three forms of capital. For example, from the customer capital perspective, scooters achieve dual social missions of accessibility and sustainability as they help solve the first and last-mile challenge as we shift from vehicle ownership to transportation as a service. From a structural capital perspective, the scooters are not just physical objects but connected devices on the digital layer. And in terms of economic capital, the scooters are able to capitalize on the sharing economy mindset established by Uber and Lyft.

The Scooters: March 13, 2019

Software is starting to eat the mining world

"We've already seen software start to eat the world in previously hardware-only — or otherwise entrenched industries — such as transportation, finance, education, and more. Now it's for mining." Investors in the mining industry would be wise to heed these words written by Connie Chan, a General Partner at Andreessen Horowitz. In her article she discusses her firm's new investment in KoBold Metals, which is building a digital prospecting engine that represents a *"software overlay over the physical world"*, essentially a *"Google Maps for the earth's crust"*. Interestingly, it uses *"computer vision, machine learning, and sophisticated data analysis"* that *"combines previously unavailable, dark data with conventional geochemical, geophysical, and geological data to identify prospects in models that can only get better over time, as with other data network effects" (a16z.com).*

Connected urban farms could start to disrupt the food distribution chain

We are starting to see a shift toward a localized supply chain for fresh produce. Gordon Food Service is partnering with Square Foots, an urban farming accelerator launched by Kimbal Musk (Elon's younger brother) in Brooklyn in 2016. Under the agreement, Square Roots will set up campuses containing ten shipping container farming systems on or near Gordon Food's distribution and retail locations. Each container, which can grow 50,000 pounds of produce a year, is part of the connected farm, which will be able to harvest the data to increase the yield of crops and operating efficiencies (fastcompany.com). Meanwhile, Bumble Bee Foods is using blockchain technology supplied by **SAP** to track yellow fin tuna and bring transparency to consumers. Consumers will be able to scan the QR codes on 12-ounce bags of ahi tuna steaks to discover where the tuna originated, size of catch and why it is certified as fair trade (fortune.com).

Amazon working with Mexico's central bank on QR-based mobile payment system

Amazon is working with Mexico's central bank to beta test a mobile payments system called CoDi that lets customers pay for online purchases using QR codes. The Mexican government is hoping CoDi will help lift its citizens out of poverty by increasing online payment convenience. Only 3.9% of retail sales are made online in Mexico as less than one-third of adults in the country have credit cards (cnbc.com). Interestingly, a year ago, Amazon launched its first-ever debit card — in Mexico — the Amazon Rechargeable debit card, which it created in partnership with **MasterCard** and **Grupo Financiero Banorte**. And in November, Amazon brought Alexa to Mexico.

Diesel USA files for bankruptcy as Levi files to IPO

Diesel USA has filed for Chapter 11, blaming changing consumer buying habits, increasing losses and expensive leases. The jeans maker and retailer is a subsidiary of privately held Italian retail clothing company Diesel SA (fashionunited.uk). Ironically, this comes as Levi Strauss looks to go public on the NYSE with the plan to raise $587 million, selling 36.7 million shares between $14 and $16 per share (fortune.com).

Z Gallerie files for bankruptcy as West Elm partners with Rent the Runway

Z Gallerie, an upscale home furnishings and décor retailer, is following in the footsteps of Gymboree and Payless — filing for bankruptcy for the second time. As part of its restructuring process, it will be closing 17 stores, representing 13% of its base of 76 stores. Z Gallerie previously filed for bankruptcy in 2009 (chainstorage.com). To avoid this fate, West Elm (**Williams-Sonoma**) is experimenting with new economic models as it partners with Rent the Runway, which is expanding its rental platform beyond apparel & accessories to home décor soft goods. Rent the Runway's +10 million members will be able to select from over a dozen bundles of 3–4 items like quilts, shams and coverlets curated by West Elm (cnbc.com).

The dominoes continue to fall for mall-based apparel retailers

Charlotte Russe, a privately held mall-based fast-fashion retailer that filed for bankruptcy on February 4, will liquidate and close all its 416 stores by the end of April (fortune.com). Following a 3.8% decline in same-store-sales in Q418, **Chico's FAS** has announced it will close 60–80 stores this year. We note this is part of its previously announced plans to close 250 stores over the next three years, representing 17% of its current base of 1,431 stores in the U.S. and Canada (chainstorage.com). Interestingly, Chico's started selling its apparel and accessories on Amazon last May. According to App Annie, consumers actually spent 18 billion hours on shopping apps in 2018, up 45% from 2016 (businessinsider.com). Given this, it's not surprising that Google (**Alphabet**) is following the lead of Instagram (**Facebook**) and Pinterest, testing shoppable ads within its image search results. Google is testing the feature on a small percentage of traffic with select retailers (digitaltrends.com).

Tesla backs off store closure plans after pushback from shopping centre landlords

After facing strong pushback from Class A retail REITs such as **Simon Property Group**, **Macerich** and **Taubman Centers**, Elon Musk has decided to only close half as many **Tesla** stores as previously announced. However, he hasn't changed his strategy to shift all sales online as the Tesla stores will now just function as showrooms. To help offset the costs, he will be raising prices by 3% on all models, with the exception of the Model 3 (wsj.com). On the transportation front, Grab, the Southeast Asian ride-hailing giant that has expanded into payments and food delivery since launching in 2012, has raised $1.5 billion from **SoftBank**'s Vision Fund. This brings Grab's ongoing Series H round to $4.5 billion, which includes strategic investors **Toyota**, **Hyundai**, **Microsoft** and **Booking Holdings** (techcrunch.com).

Amazon closing all 87 pop-up stores as it expands bricks and mortar foundation

As Amazon expands its bricks-and-mortar footprint with Amazon Books, Amazon 4 star and Amazon Go, it has decided to close all its 87 pop-up stores in the U.S. Amazon has been using these pop-up kiosks, which measure a few hundred square feet, to showcase its devices like the Echo, tablets and Kindle in locations such as malls, Kohl's stores and Whole Foods stores (wsj.com). Speaking of **Kohl's**, it is serious about getting in shape as it shrinks its store footprint. Less than a month after partnering with Weight Watchers (**WW**) on a series of wellness initiatives, Kohl's is now partnering with **Planet Fitness**. Under the agreement, Kohl's will lease vacant space next to ten of its stores this year with the potential to expand to more (fortune.com).

You can now control your Roku TV with Alexa

Roku just launched an Alexa skill that enables you to use voice commands to control your Roku TV through your Echo device. However, for now, you are limited to simple commands like turning your Roku TV on or off, adjusting the volume, pausing the content, or searching for something (theverge.com). Apple will be holding a press event on March 25 where it is expected to debut new services, such as its new streaming video service and a bundled Apple New subscription offering and new products such as a low-cost iPad and a new version of AirPods (cnbc.com).

Walmart develops new AI scanning app as Costco raises minimum wage to $15 per hour

Sam's Club (**Walmart**) has developed new scanning technology that recognizes products using computer vision and machine learning. Sam's Club will be testing this technology at its new Dallas test store this spring. If the test is successful, the new AI scanning app will replace the Scan & Go app it launched two years ago that requires you to scan the barcode (techcrunch.com). And **Costco** is raising its minimum wage to $15 per hour, following the lead of Amazon which raised its minimum wage for its 250,000+ employees in the U.S. to $15 per hour on November 1. Interestingly, this is Costco's second minimum wage hike in less than a year — back in June, it raised its minimum wage from $13 to $14 per hour (fortune.com).

Amazon spends record $14.7 million lobbying, Senator War-

ren is seeking to break up tech

Last year, Amazon spent a record $14.2 million lobbying 42 entities on 24 general issues, up just over 10% from its spending last year. Amazon was the second–largest spender of the tech companies, behind Google who spent $21 million, and accounted for 17% of the total $77 million spent by the nine tech companies. Amazon lobbied 42 entities on 24 general issues (bloomberg.com). The tech companies may need to up their spending as we're seeing a rise in anti-trust regulatory risk. On March 8, Senator Elizabeth Warren published a highly controversial article on Medium, *Here's how we can break up big tech,* detailing her aggressive plan to break up tech giants like Amazon, Google, Facebook and Apple. She proposes imposing new rules on tech platform companies with over $25 billion, arguing they cannot own both the "platform utility" and own a participant on their platform. Her radical plans include unwinding high-profile mergers, which she deems as anti-competitive, such as Amazon+Whole Foods, Google+DoubleClick and Facebook+Instagram+WhatsApp (cnn.com). When questioned later, she also said she would also break apart the App Store from Apple (cnbc.com).

Airbnb acquires last-minute hotel booking app HotelTonight

Airbnb is acquiring HotelTonight for just over $400 million. HotelTonight, a last-minute hotel booking app, has raised $127 million since launching in San Francisco in 2010 (skift.com). Although HotelTonite will provide Airbnb with valuable customer and supplier capital, enabling it to expand its total addressable market beyond home-sharing, it could be a bit of a red flag as Airbnb seems to be buying growth before going public and moving away from its community-driven social mission "*to belong anywhere*". Meanwhile, co-living is starting to create opportunities in the residential real estate market. For example, Proper Development is investing $100 million to build seven co-living apartment buildings over the next 2–3 years in LA. This will create 600 beds, which will be operated by Common, a New York-based co-living operator. The accommodation is targeted toward Millennials that make between $40,000 and $80,000 per year (latimes.com).

When I sketched out an outline of all the emerging structural disruption developments I was seeing to create my first "Ubernomics Fault Lines Update" back in January 2017, I never imagined that just over two years later I would be writing my 100th research note as Lyft and Uber prepare to IPO at valuations of over $20 billion and $120 billion, respectively. As some of you will remember, I opened that research note with the warning, "the price of taxi medallions is eroding as private driver companies like Uber render the core activities and assets of the taxi industry with obsolescence". As you know, Uber and Lyft have not only disrupted taxis and rental cars, but are now also investing in scooters and autonomous vehicles as they seek to disrupt the entire auto ecosystem, shifting society from vehicle ownership to Transportation-as-a-Service (TAAS). And Uber is now seeking to bring a new level of disruption to the food delivery and restaurant space with Uber Eats ghost kitchens. As I cautioned in my first in-depth research report, "Where do the Ubernomics fault lines lie in your portfolio?": "If the Content Quake last decade measured a four to five on the Richter scale, the Ubernomics Quake will be a nine on the scale".

The Ubernomics Quake: March 19, 2019

Hudson Yard real estate developer acquires logistics and warehouse provider

Retail real estate development firms are starting to vertically integrate into the logistics and fulfillment centre space. Quiet Logistics, a third-party logistics provider offering fulfillment services for digital-first brands, has been acquired by Related Fund Management, the private equity arm of the real estate developer behind the $25 billion Hudson Yards neighbourhood in NYC which just opened to the public. It's interesting as Quiet Logistics works with 60 DTC brands, including Away, Bonobos (**Walmart**), Tuft & Needle and Outdoor Voices, which are opening stores in Hudson Yards. The real insight is that as retail shifts away from chain stores, the new DTC tenants need logistical support from their retail landlords. To meet this increasing demand and to be able to offer faster delivery, Quiet Logistics is expanding its fulfillment facilities footprint beyond Boston and St. Louis to Dallas, Chicago and LA (fastcompany.com). Meanwhile, Nuro, the robo-delivery start-up that recently raised $940 million from **SoftBank**'s Vision Fund, is expanding its self-driving grocery delivery service with **Kroger** from Scottsdale to Houston (techcrunch.com).

DoorDash gains share from GrubHub but Uber Eats is introducing a new level of disruption

DoorDash, fueled by $1.3 billion in venture capital raised the past year, has nearly doubled its market share in the past year and is now the top player in the U.S. online food delivery market. DoorDash seems to be taking share from **GrubHub** — according to Edison Trends, DoorDash's share has risen from 15% to 28% while GrubHub's has fallen from 38% to 27%. Uber Eats and

Postmates have seen their share stay relatively flat, at 25% and 12%, respectively (wsj.com). However, Uber Eats could bring a new level of disruption to both the food delivery and restaurant business. Uber is piloting a program in Paris where it rents out fully equipped commercial-grade kitchen space to restaurants selling food through Uber Eats. This could "uberize" the restaurant industry as the problem is most restaurants are facing operational issues trying to fulfill online orders as they treat delivery as an add-on rather than a business. Ironically, Uber's ousted founder, Travis Kalanick, has also been testing the ghost kitchen concept in LA with plans to bring his CloudKitchen to Chicago, San Francisco and China (restaurantdive.com).

Dick's Sporting Goods increasing e-commerce capex to compete with Amazon

According to CNBC's Jim Cramer, **Dick's Sporting Goods** "*dropped a bomb*" during its earnings call, basically admitting that it needs to increase its capex on the e-commerce layer to compete with **Amazon**. Specifically, it plans to spend more on digital marketing with **Facebook** and Google (**Alphabet**) to increase online traffic as well as open two new dedicated e-commerce fulfillment centres to reduce freight and shipping costs. Like many retailers, Dick's Sporting Goods is starting to lose customers who are turning to Amazon to buy non-exclusive products (cnbc.com). Meanwhile, dollar stores could face increasing competition from Wish, the discount shopping e-commerce app targeted toward low-income consumers. Wish is the third-largest e-commerce platform in the U.S. and globally, it has grown to 90 million monthly active users and was the most downloaded shopping app last year. Wish, which has raised $1.3 billion since it launched in San Francisco in 2010, has more than 300 million items on its platform supplied by over 1 million merchants that offer cut-rate pricing by shipping directly from Chinese manufacturers (forbes.com).

Amazon launches first beauty product from accelerator program

Amazon just launched the first beauty product from its "Our Brands" accelerator program. Fast Beauty Co., which was founded by Latvian models who also happen to be sisters, includes face masks and makeup removing wipes (cnbc.com).

Burger King introduces coffee subscription program

Burger King (**Restaurant Brands International**) has just launched the BK Café subscription program. The program, which is only available through its app, seems like incredible value as members can receive one small cup of brewed coffee a day, which retails for $1, at a minimal cost of only $5 per month (today.com). Meanwhile, restaurants are starting to question who actually owns the customer relationship as OpenTable (**Bookings Holdings**) is now blocking restaurants from giving competitors access to diner data (wsj.com).

Spotify files anti-trust complaint against Apple, Apple Music comes to Amazon Fire TVs

Spotify has filed an anti-trust complaint against **Apple** with the European Union (EU). Spotify is arguing Apple Music has an unfair advantage as it doesn't have to pay the 30% fee on purchases made through Apple's in-app payment system. After Spotify opted out of the payment system in 2016, it had to pull its premium subscription service from Apple's app store. In addition, Apple restricts the distribution channels as it does not allow Spotify to be played on Siri, HomePod and Apple Watch (wired.com). While Spotify clashes with Apple, Apple is cozying up to Amazon. Apple is launching Apple Music on Amazon Fire TVs in the U.S. to allow its subscribers to access its catalog of over 50 million songs with their voice (cnbc.com). The two tech giants seem to be deepening their relationship as back in mid-December Apple partnered with Amazon to enable Echo devices to stream songs from Apple Music. And Alexa just won the newly created "Game Changer Tech Award" at the iHeartRadio Music Awards. As she humorously states in her acceptance speech: "*It feels electric...I couldn't have done this without my fans, especially all you ceiling and bathroom fans out there. And a big shout out to Wi-Fi for always supporting me. Without it, I'd be speechless.*"

Amazon is now providing intros between private investors and AWS clients

Amazon is launching the AWS Pro-Rate Program to introduce private investors and family offices to start-ups seeking capital that use AWS and VCs whose portfolios feature AWS customers. The first three start-ups include: 1) Boom, a supersonic jet manufacturer that is raising $100 million; 2) Roman, a men's health products maker that is raising $50 million; and 3) FreightWaves, a data and analytics provider for the freight market that is raising $20 million (cnbc.com). The program is being run by Brad Holden, whose LinkedIn Profile states his role as "Angel & Seed Business Development Manager" for AWS "*working with top tier angel/seed investors and their portfolios to help them grow, thrive, and leverage the Amazon Web Services cloud platform*" and Jason Hunt, whose title is "Business Development, Early Stage Start-ups" for AWS.

Chapter Eight: The Kool-Aid

It was fun covering business trusts over a decade ago as it was a hot sector and there was a constant stream of IPOs. A freshly printed prospectus is like candy to me — I love digging into it trying to figure out a company's revenue drivers, cost structure, competitive position and economic moat. Unlike most of the analysts back then, I was skeptical and cautioned investors against many of the companies, which I classified as "wolves in cash-cows' clothing". Given there is a scarcity of publicly traded companies operating at the peak level of all three sides of the value pyramid, I'm excited about the new herd of unicorns that are queueing up, waiting for their turn to prance into the public arena. For example, Pinterest and Zoom filed their S-1s on Friday, and Peloton just hired investment bankers for its IPO. But as you can tell from the special research report I published yesterday, "Why I'm Not Drinking the LYFT Kool-Aid & New Insights from SXSW", I'm still not one to follow the herd.

The Unicorns are Coming: March 26, 2019

Levi's stock soars 32% on its first day of trading
It wasn't a unicorn, but an old gray mare called **Levi Strauss** that took the lead and saw its shares soar 32% after making its debut in the public arena on the first day of spring. Interestingly, Levi Strauss, who invented the blue jean in 1873, actually went public

for the first time back in 1971 but was then taken private by the Haas family in 1985 so they could focus on the long term. This explains the family's decision to use a dual-class share structure, which provides them with 99% voting control even though they only own two-thirds of the shares. Unlike many unicorns, Levi's is actually profitable, generating a 5.1% net margin on $5.6 billion of revenue last year, and trading at 30 times last year's earnings (wsj.com). Levi's is ideally positioned to capitalize on its iconic brand to enhance its emotional connection with consumers, which it should be able to leverage to build DTC distribution channels. However, the company still operates primarily on the base of the structural capital pyramid, with wholesale still comprising 65% of its revenue and only 4% coming from e-commerce.

Pinterest and Zoom file their S-1s

On March 22, two unicorns filed their S-1s: Pinterest and Zoom. Zoom, the cloud video conferencing start-up that has raised $161 million since launching in San Jose in 2011, seems to be a rare breed of unicorn: one that is profitable. Zoom, which operates at the peak level of the value pyramid with its accessibility-based mission "*to make video communications frictionless*", more than doubled its revenue to $331 million and reported net income of $8M million (techcrunch.com). Pinterest operates at the peak level of the value pyramid as a creative idea social network with the community-based mission "*to bring everyone the inspiration to create a life they love*". Pinterest has created a valuable structural asset base, comprising 175 billion saved pins on over 4 billion boards with its 265 million+ monthly active users doing over 2 billion searches a month. Pinterest is starting to monetize this through advertising, mostly in the U.S., with its revenue rising 60% last year to $765 million. Like many unicorns, it still operates in the red as its net operating loss was $75 million last year, but the good news is it seems to be gaining operating leverage as its net operating loss margin narrowed from -30% to -10% (sec.gov). However, as a direct competitive threat to Pinterest, Instagram (**Facebook**) is rolling out a new checkout feature in the U.S. that will enable you to buy products inside the app with just a few clicks. Instagram expects there is a lot of pent-up demand for this feature given the number of people that look at product tags has risen from 90 million in September to 130 million. This essentially transforms Instagram into an online retail marketplace, as it will receive a small "selling fee" each time a user transacts with one of the retailers/brands on its platform. The new checkout feature is being trialed with a limited group of retailers and brands, including **Burberry Group**, **Michael Kors**, **Nike** and Warby Parker (recode.net).

Peloton selects its bankers to lead its IPO

Peloton, which has raised $995 million since launching in NYC in 2012, has selected **JPMorgan Chase** and **Goldman Sachs Group** to lead its IPO, which is expected to achieve a valuation of $8 billion. Peloton has attracted a cult-like following and more than doubled its customer base last year through its accessibility-focused social mission "*to use technology and design to connect the world through fitness, empowering people to be the best version of themselves anywhere, anytime*". Although Peloton started as a DTC brand, retail sales accounted for 30% of its $800 million in sales last year and it plans to more than double its physical footprint from 60 to 160 showrooms (finance.yahoo.com).

The rise of the pink unicorns: Glossier and Rent the Runway

Glossier just raised a $100 million Series D round, valuing the DTC beauty brand, which started less than a decade ago as a beauty blog, at $1.2 billion. Back in 2010, Emily Weiss, who was working in NYC as a fashion assistant at Vogue, launched her own beauty blog called "*Into the Gloss*" which quickly grew to a readership of 10 million views per month. In 2014, she decided to leverage her customer capital and launch Glossier (forbes.com). In November, Glossier opened its first flagship store in Soho in NYC which offers the experience of "*conversation, story-telling and community building*", embracing what Weiss terms "*emotional commerce*". Another pink unicorn has emerged on the scene as Rent the Runway just raised a $125 million venture round from Franklin Templeton Investments and Bain Capital Ventures, valuing the apparel and accessories rental company that was launched in NYC in 2009 at $1 billion (techcrunch.com). We note Rent the Runway recently entered into strategic partnerships with WeWork and West Elm (**Williams-Sonoma**). According to thredUP's newly released *2019 Resale Report*, the number of women in the U.S. shopping second-hand rose 27% last year, from 44 million to 56 million. thredUP forecasts resale will continue to capture share of the apparel market, nearly doubling over the next five years from 6.3% ($24 billion of $378 billion in sales) to 11.8% ($51 billion of $431 billion in sales). We are seeing a societal shift toward cost-conscious and social-conscious consumerism as the percentage of female adults willing to buy second-hand has risen from 45% in 2016 to 52% in 2017 to 64% in 2018 (thredup.com).

Google looks to disrupt gaming industry with its new streaming game platform — Stadia

On March 19, **Alphabet**'s Google unveiled its new streaming game platform: Stadia. Google is looking to disrupt the $140 billion gaming industry through its new "game platform for everyone" as it turns Google's data centres into consoles that provide instant access to high-end games that you can play on any device with an Internet connection with no need to purchase expensive consoles or computers. In addition to being screen agnostic, you will be able to switch between devices and click on any YouTube game video to play. Google is further leveraging its structural capital with its new Stadia Controller, which has a special button to enable you to save and share your game on YouTube as well as a Google Assistant to enable you to get help using your voice. Although Google did not disclose any pricing or release dates, it said it will be launching Stadia this year in the U.S., Canada, U.K. and most of Europe (cnbc.com). Even **Walmart** may be looking to join the race to create the "Netflix of gaming". Walmart has apparently been in discussions with developers and publishers about launching its own gaming service (pcgamer.com). However, we note Walmart recently abandoned its plan to enter the video streaming space as it decided it was too risky a venture given it was outside its core competency and the significant capital investment required to create original content. And WeChat (**Tencent Holdings**) is opening up its mini games platform to developers worldwide. The mini games platform, which is featured in a tab inside the WeChat app, enables users to play basic games like Tetris. It is currently used by nearly half, or 400 million of WeChat's over 1 billion monthly active users (theverge.com).

Apple unveils three on-demand media subscription services

On March 25, at the Apple Special Event, Tim Cook unveiled **Apple**'s three new on-demand subscription services, emphasizing how they will transform media by empowering creators and providing privacy for members:

- **Apple News Plus**: Apple is launching a premium news subscription service, providing members with access to over

300 magazines, including newspapers like the WSJ and LA Times. It is available today in the U.S. for $9.99 per month and Canada for $12.99 per month and will launch later this year in Australia and the U.K.

- **Apple Arcade**: Apple is launching a curated game-streaming subscription service, providing access to over 100 exclusive games accessible on a new tab on the App store.
- **Apple tv Channels**: Apple is launching a Netflix-like platform to enable you to subscribe to individual streaming services and channels. Apple is also partnering with a number of high-profile celebrities such as Steven Spielberg and Oprah Winfrey to offer original video content through Apple tv+.

In addition, Apple is transforming the credit card experience, partnering with **MasterCard** and **Goldman Sachs** to launch Apple Card, which will be available in the U.S. this summer (cnbc.com). Apple is also positioned to capitalize on the rise in social commerce. Fans at the Quicken Loans stadium in Cleveland can now order drinks directly to their seats thanks to a new pilot conversational commerce pilot between **Aramark**, the Cleveland Cavaliers and Apple. Using Apple Business Chat, fans can scan the QR code on the back of their seat and then interact with an order bot in Messenger to access the drink menu and order drinks to be delivered directly to their seat (techcrunch.com).

Just what we need: a Keurig machine to make at-home cocktails

Keurig Dr. Pepper has partnered with **Anheuser-Busch InBev** to create a Keurig machine to make at-home cocktails: Drinkworks. The machine retails for $399 and a four-pack of liquid-filled pods sell for $15.99. The Drinkworks appliance adds water and carbonation to the pods, which are filled with a shot of alcohol and flavoring (wsj.com). From a strategic perspective, Drinkworks enables Anheuser-Busch InBev to move up the structural capital side to the e-commerce layer (i.e., you can purchase pods through the Drinkworks app and they are easier to ship than bottles of booze) and the AI layer (Drinkworks is a connected device so it could provide the two companies with valuable customer data). From a customer perspective, it enables the two companies to establish direct relationships with customers, deepening the emotional connection, creating the foundation for a subscription model. The e-commerce experience is being powered by Thirstie, which just raised a $7 million Series A round. Thirstie, which launched in NYC in 2013 to offer on-demand local alcohol delivery, is shifting its business model from consumer to enterprise, now working with alcohol brands to create e-commerce and delivery experiences (techcrunch.com).

Emirates and Netflix each see themselves as more of media companies

Emirates sees itself as more of a media company than an air carrier. While most airlines are promoting BYOD, Emirates is doubling down on in-flight entertainment. In addition to investing heavily in media and licensing, Emirates worked with U.K. audiophile brand Bowers & Wilkins to create customized noise cancelling headphones and its app enables passengers to create a wish list to select among the 6,000 hours of content for the media and movies they want to see on their upcoming flights. In addition to creating an enhanced emotional connection with customers, Emirates is able to capitalize on its valuable customer capital (i.e., it has nearly a half-million first and business class passengers per month) through advertising, as evidenced by the fact that brands are creating specific ads for the airline and its ad revenue is up 26% (skift.com). As tech companies come under increasing scrutiny from government and regulators on privacy and anti-trust concerns, Reed Hastings is making the timely argument that **Netflix** is more of a media company than a technology company. His rationale is that as Netflix spends only $1.2 billion on technology versus $10 billion on video content, Netflix is more of a "*content company powered by tech*" (cnbc.com). Netflix sees interactive shows as the next innovative frontier in TV shows and movies. Following the success of its recently released first choose-your-own-adventure film for adults, *Black Mirror: Bandersnatch*, it is now exploring interactive shows in genres like romance, adventure and horror (fastcompany.com). This is a smart strategy as interactive shows create a customized experience, increasing the level of engagement and emotional connection viewers have to the show.

As shopping shifts online, the bricks continue to fall...

According to CouponFollow's *2019 Millennial Shopping Report*, Millennials are shifting their shopping habits online as brick-and-mortar shopping declined from 53% to 40%. They are shopping increasingly on mobile, which now represents 60% of online shopping, nearly double the 34% last year. Millennials also love **Amazon** as 97% shop on the platform and two-thirds make one-half or more of their purchases on Amazon (theladders.com). In fact, according to a study by Feedvisor, 66% of consumers start their search for products on Amazon, but, more importantly, 74% go directly to Amazon when they are ready to buy a product. Feedvisor also found that 45% of Prime members buy from Amazon at least once a week with 5% buying once a day (cnbc.com). As shoppers shift online, the bricks continue to fall. Shopko Stores, a Wisconsin-based general merchandise retailer, is closing what remains of its 363 stores after failing to find a buyer following its bankruptcy filing in January (cbsnews.com).

Amazon is leveraging the power of its platform as it grows its private label business

Amazon is increasing its control over its platform at the expense of its advertising business. Amazon is aggressively blocking ads for vendors who sell products that Amazon can't make a profit on (cnbc.com). As further evidence of Amazon's power of owning its platform, it has been testing pop-up features on its app promoting its private-label products. For example, when you search for "AAA batteries", the sponsored listing comes up for Energizer (**Energizer Holdings**) batteries but when you click on it, a pop-up window appears for Amazon's lower-cost AmazonBasics AAA batteries (wsj.com). Speaking of private label, Amazon is entering the high-growth, high-margin skin care space. It is launching its first dedicated private-label skin care line called Belei, which features products such as moisturizers, eye creams and spot treatments, ranging in price from $9 to $40. According to NPD Group, the skin care category, which comprises 30% of the $18.8 billion U.S. prestige beauty market, grew 13% last year, more than double the 6% growth rate for the market (cnbc.com).

Co-living, but for families

Common, a New York-based co-living operator, is partnering with real estate developer Tishman Speyer to meet the unmet and rising demand for family-friendly urban condos. In the past five years, the focus has been on singles. According to CoStar Group, nearly 60% of all new units built in the top 54 metros since 2014 have been studios or 1-bedrooms, up from 45% from 2000 to

2013. Although their new brand, called Kin, isn't really a co-living concept as it won't feature shared kitchens or bathrooms, the units will be more compact with larger common areas such as playrooms and offer on-demand child care (wsj.com). Tishman Speyer is adapting to the rising expectations for its tenants as a year ago it launched its Zo app, which provides office workers with on-demand access to amenities such as haircuts, educational talks, child care and yoga classes.

Keatz raises €12 million to expand cloud kitchens in Europe

Keatz, a cloud kitchen provider launched in Berlin in 2015, has raised a €12 million Series B round. Keatz operates 10 cloud kitchens across Europe, ranging in size from 1,000 to 2,000 square feet, and leverages delivery platforms like Deliveroo, Uber Eats, **Just Eat** and **Delivery Hero** to serve a 1–2-km delivery radius (techcrunch.com). Grab Financial, the fintech arm of the Southeast Asian ride-hailing and food delivery giant Grab which has raised $4.5 billion to-date for its ongoing Series H round, is rolling out lending for small businesses and micro-entrepreneurs and micro-insurance for its drivers in Singapore under its "Grow with Grab" road map (pymnts.com).

San Francisco might look to ban Amazon Go stores

Ironically, San Francisco, the tech capital of the world, might soon ban Amazon Go stores. San Francisco is considering following in the footsteps of Philadelphia and New Jersey which have recently introduced into law new legislation banning cashless stores on the grounds they discriminate against low-income consumers that don't have bank accounts or credit cards (cnbc.com). According to market research firm ETR, Amazon and **Microsoft** are the preferred vendors in over half of the IT spending intentions by over 800 CIOs. These include basic IT needs like cloud infrastructure and software, AI, robotics and data analytics (wsj.com).

My heart pounded as I sat in the WeWork conference room on Thursday, staring at the Skype screen, waiting to be interviewed live on Yahoo! Finance's morning show by its host, Alexis Christofouros, on why I wasn't drinking the LYFT Kool-Aid. I wish I could go back on the show as since I published my report just a week ago, there have been five major strategic developments, adding to the toxicity of the LYFT Kool-Aid. But I'm excited about the upcoming stampede of unicorns as my mindset is what Heidi Grant Halvorson and E. Tory Higgins call "promotion focus", as they describe in their book "Focus: Use Different Ways of Seeing the World for Success and Influence": "Promotion focus is about maximizing gains and avoiding missed opportunities. Prevention focus, on the other hand, is about minimizing losses" Just like we saw with the dotcoms nearly two decades ago, promotion-focused investors are now in danger of getting caught up in the "cult-like following" of these unicorns and drinking what I call the "pink Kool-Aid".

Prevention-focused investors are also at risk of drinking the Kool-Aid. But the Kool-Aid in this case is blue, not pink, and the danger is the toxicity of "blue Kool-Aid" increases as the rate of structural disruption increases. For example, back in January 2008, I warned investors to stop drinking Yellow Pages' "blue Kool-Aid" as I was worried the accelerating shift to online and emergence of the then new online disruptors like Facebook and Craigslist would increase its business risk profile. And I continue to caution investors against drinking the "blue Kool-Aid" of Canadian retailers like Dollarama and Sleep Country Canada as they still operate mainly at the base of the value pyramid.

The Two Flavours of Kool-Aid: April 2, 2019

lululemon further leveraging its cult-like following as DTC reaches nearly 30% of sales

In my research report last week, I shared how **lululemon** stood out as being at the forefront of experiential retail as the only non-tech company with a "house" at SXSW. As evidence of how lululemon is uniquely positioned to leverage its cult-like following to build DTC distribution channels, its e-commerce sales rose 39% in Q4, accounting for nearly 30% of sales — up from 25.3% in Q3. Its overall revenue in Q4 rose 26% to $1.17 billion, with comparable-store sales up 7%. On lululemon's Q418 conference call, CEO Calvin McDonald stated, "*when looking at our digital ecosystem, we are still in the early stages of our development with so much potential ahead*", and he also shared how lululemon expanded the testing of its membership program from Edmonton to Denver and will "*continue to test as we look into expanding the program and ultimately leading into a national program in the coming quarters to year*".

Dollarama & Sleep Country Canada continue to operate at base of value pyramid

In sharp contrast, as we shared in our March 28 flash research note, **Dollarama** is still focusing on the base of the value pyramid, as evidenced by this statement by Neil Rossy, President & CEO, in its Q419 results: "*In fiscal 2020, our priority is to continue to re-invest in our strong value proposition and enhance our product assortment, always with the consumer in mind. We also continue to focus on the execution of our growth strategy by adding 60 to 70 net new stores for the year, and on initiatives to increase store traffic and sales.*" The other Canadian retailer we continue to caution against as being a value trap is **Sleep Country Canada**, whose structural disruption risk continues to rise as Casper just raised a $100 million Series D round and announced it is seeking to hire underwriters in April for an IPO (cnbc.com).

Home furnishings retailers re-think how they capture value on physical layer

Wayfair is moving down the structural capital side of the value pyramid, opening its first permanent retail store at the Natick mall in Natick, Massachusetts this fall, with plans to also open four pop-up stores this summer. Interestingly, this mall was the site of one of its two holiday pop-up stores (techcrunch.com). Like with its pop-up stores, we expect its new store will staffed by its customer service and home design employees who will be available to recommend products and show customers how to use its online design services marketplace. IKEA is re-thinking how it captures value on a physical value by moving closer to consumers. IKEA is opening the IKEA Planning Studio in NYC on April 15 — its first city centre location in the U.S., with plans to open 30 of these smaller-format urban stores over the next three years (curbed.com). Meanwhile, Muji is moving beyond the traditional retail box. Muji (**Ryohin Keikaku Co**.), which opened its first hotel above one of its largest stores in China last January, is opening its first hotel in Japan in April, above its global flagship store in the Ginza neighbourhood of Tokyo. The 79-room hotel enables Muji to create an experiential immersive destination for its fans as it will offer them the opportunity to experience over 700 products sold at the Muji store, including furniture, bedding sets and toiletries (fastcompany.com).

Molson Coors finally embraces DTC with launch of e-commerce sites

Molson Coors Brewing is starting to crawl up the customer and structural capital sides of the value pyramid, launching e-commerce sites for Coors Light and Blue Moon with plans to embed shopping capability into ads on **Facebook**, Instagram and Snapchat (**Snap**). The alcoholic beverage industry has been slow to adopt e-commerce as players are restricted from being involved in more than one tier of the three-tiers of alcohol distribution (i.e., manufacturer to wholesaler to retailer to consumer). Consequently, according to Molson Coors, only 1% of beer purchases take place online and 80% of consumers aren't aware you even can purchase beer online. To get around the restriction, Molson Coors is partnering with third-party delivery platforms like Drizly and Minibar Delivery. By going DTC, Molson Coors hopes to gain visibility into consumer behavior (i.e., preferences, purchase patterns, time of day) (digiday.com). This is a good first step, but we think Molson Coors should look at **Anheuser-Busch InBev** which is further deepening the emotional connection with its customers and creating the foundation for a subscription model by partnering with Keurig Dr. Pepper to launch Drinkworks, a Keurig machine to make at-home cocktails.

McDonald's pays $300 million for AI start-up as 7-Eleven opens lab store selling organic fare

McDonald's is serious about ascending the customer and structural sides of the value pyramid as it just made its biggest acquisition in two decades, paying over $300 million for Dynamic Yield. Dynamic Yield, which has raised $83 million since launched in NYC in 2011, is an AI-powered customer personalization platform. McDonald's will use Dynamic Yield's AI technology to personalize digital promotions and create real-time digital displays at its drive-through (wsj.com). Meanwhile, 7-Eleven (**Seven & I Holdings**) has opened a lab store that offers beer on tap and organic fare and features an in-store taqueria and coffee bar. This highlights how even convenience stores are starting to adapt to shifting consumer preferences toward local, healthy and organic food (grocerydive.com).

Amazon working on ad-supported video news app for Fire TV

Just a week after **Apple** unveiled Apple tv Channels, it is rumoured that **Amazon** is working on an ad-supported video news app for Fire TV to offer live and on-demand programming from TV networks (fastcompany.com). On the gaming front, Amazon is offering Twitch Prime subscribers a free year's subscription to Nintendo Switch Online, the online service for Switch games launched by **Nintendo** in September (theverge.com). **Spotify** is investing in original podcasting content with the acquisition of Parcast, a small but highly successful podcast studio founded in 2016 that has published 18 podcast titles focused on true crime, with 20 more in the pipeline (techcrunch.com). Although Spotify did not state how much it paid for Parcast, which doesn't seem to have raised any funding, we note that back in early February, when Spotify acquired Gimlet Media and Anchor, it announced its intention to spend a further $500 million this year on podcast acquisitions this year as it aspires to become the "**Netflix** of Audio".

Bad news for Shopify as Mailchimp ends partnership and Square enters e-commerce

Mailchimp has ended its partnership with **Shopify** over a disagreement about who has the right to customer data. As a result, Mailchimp is removing its Mailchimp plug-in from the Shopify App Store which let users create targeted e-mail campaigns (techcrunch.com). More bad news for Shopify as **Square** is entering the e-commerce space, invading Shopify's territory, with the launch of Square Online Space, which enables merchants to sell through their own digital storefronts, offering shipping and in-store pick-up features, as well as marketing and social selling through Instagram. Square Online Store integrates the technology of Weebly, the website-builder it acquired for $365 million last April, into its existing payments ecosystem (fastcompany.com).

World's first smart shopping mall coming to Abu Dhabi as flagship stores close in NYC

"*With digital transformation currently disrupting retail boundaries and on-demand shopping delivered wherever and whenever you want, the days of the traditional shopping mall are over*". Investors in retail REITs would be wise to heed these cautionary words spoken by Milat Sayra Berirmen, digital experience manager for Reem Mall, the world's first smart shopping mall in Abu Dhabi. The 2 million-square-foot leasable area, which is targeted to be completed by late 2020 at a cost of $1.2 billion, will feature 450 stores, 100 dining options and a range of experiences like Snow Park Abu Dhabi. Most importantly, it will feature innovative data analytics, combined with a 23,000-square-foot integrated e-commerce logistics hub with the capacity to deliver 30,000 parcels a day (arabianbusiness.com). The days of the traditional flagship store to promote a brand may be over too as in the past few months, we have seen flagship store closures by **Gap**, Lord & Taylor (**Hudson's Bay Company**) and **Ralph Lauren**. Notably, last week, **PVH** announced it will be closing its Tommy Hilfiger global flagship store on Fifth Avenue and its Calvin Klein flagship store on Madison Avenue in NYC (businessinsider.com). In addition, Barneys is looking to downsize its iconic flagship store on Madison Avenue, giving up five of the nine floors it occupies to reduce the annual $30 million rent cost (forbes.com).

Amazon launches Alexa for Business as Skype replaces Cor-

tana with Alexa

Amazon is launching Alexa for Business, empowering companies to create their own voice skills exclusively for their employees to use while in the office. Companies can create skills for processes such as onboarding employees and answering common questions by using one of dozens of blueprints rather than having to spend months writing code (engadget.com). This comes as Skype replaces Cortana with Alexa, removing the Cortana bot, the chatbot version of Cortana, from Skype as of the end of April (cnet.com). This is not surprising given **Microsoft**'s CEO, Satya Nardella, recent change in his strategy for Cortana — viewing her no longer as a stand-alone voice assistant.

UPS launches first commercial drone delivery service at hospital campus

UPS has partnered with Matternet to launch the first regular commercial drone delivery service at the Wakefield hospital and campus in Raleigh, North Carolina. The first route for the drone, which can carry up to five pounds, is between the surgery centre and the lab, which takes the drone only 3 minutes versus 30 minutes for a courier to travel one-third of a mile (fastcompany.com). We note Matternet, the drone delivery company, has raised $26 million since launching in Menlo Park in 2011, including strategic investors like Daimler (participated in $10 million seed round in August 2016), **Boeing**'s VC arm (led $16 million Series A round in June 2018) and Swiss Post (participated in Series A round). On the grocery delivery front, **Meituan Dianping**, China's largest service e-commerce platform that is a combination of **Groupon**, **Yelp** and Uber Eats, is entering the increasingly crowded grocery delivery space. Meituan is testing a new grocery delivery feature in Beijing that offers under 30-minute delivery on 1,500 items (techcrunch.com).

Alexa, who has not yet turned five, just earned her MD — she is now HIPPA-compliant. As W. Chan Kim and Renee Mauborgne wrote in 2005 in their book Blue Ocean Strategy, "Blue oceans... are defined by untapped marketspace, demand creation, and the opportunity for highly profitable growth." Amazon is creating new blue oceans in the $3.5 trillion healthcare space by meeting needs and desires we didn't even know we had by empowering us to use our voice to manage our health improvement goals, check the status of home delivery prescriptions, get blood sugar readings and schedule doctor appointments. Likewise, through "Project Kuiper", Amazon is looking to launch over 3,000 satellites to bring global Internet access from space to the 4 billion non-customers. And Amazon is starting to attract new tiers of non-customers in the advertising space, as large advertising buyers such as WPP and Omnicom Group are starting to shift their ad search spending from Google to Amazon.

From a DCF perspective, accessing these new blue oceans will enable Amazon to expand its total addressable market. The critical point for investors is that Amazon is able to create new blue oceans as a result of the convergence of intangibles it has been investing in higher up the value pyramid, like customer relationships, R&D and platform ecosystems. Likewise, WeWork is creating new blue oceans as it seeks to become the operating system for offices with acquisition of office services management platform, Managed by Q. And lululemon is leveraging its cult-like customer following by expanding its total addressable market beyond apparel, accessories and footwear into self-care products.

Dr. Alexa: April 9, 2019

Amazon cuts produce prices 20% at Whole Foods as it partners with Oxxo in Mexico

Amazon just announced its third round of price cuts at Whole Foods. It is reducing prices by an average of 20% on hundreds of items, with an emphasis on produce. In addition, it is doubling the number of exclusive deals and deepening the discounts for Prime members and offering customers $10 off a $20 purchase when they sign up for a 30-day free trial of Amazon Prime (cnbc.com). In Mexico, Amazon is now accepting cash payments at Oxxo (**FEMSA**), the largest Mexican convenience chain with nearly 18,000 locations. This will enable Oxxo, which had already offered a pick-up partnership with Amazon at nearly 3,000 locations, to further leverage its structural capital to capitalize on the rise in e-commerce in a country where over 60% of the population is unbanked. With the new service, called Amazon Cash, Mexican shoppers can deposit between $5 and $260 in cash per transaction to their Amazon accounts (pymnts.com). We note Amazon first launched Amazon Cash two years ago in the U.S. in partnership with convenience stores.

lululemon expands into self-care products

lululemon is expanding beyond apparel, footwear and accessories, with the upcoming launch this spring of its own self-care products. This is a brilliant strategic move as its new self-care line-up of exclusive deodorants, lip balms and face moisturizers meets the demand from its athletes, ambassadors and customers to "*transition from sweat into daily life*" and advances its community-based mission "*to create components for people to live a longer, healthier, and more fun life*" (shop.lululemon.com).

Amazon plans to provide global Internet access from space

Space is the final frontier for Amazon, which just announced "Project Kuiper", its plan to launch a constellation of 3,236 low Earth orbit satellites to "*provide low-latency, high-speed broadband connectivity to unserved and underserved communities around the world*" (cnbc.com). This follows Amazon's announcement in late November that it would be leveraging the infrastructure from dozens of AWS centres to build a network of 12 satellite facilities around the world called AWS Ground Station in a multi-year strategic business agreement with **Lockheed Martin**, which manufactures and operates satellites for the U.S. military. Amazon is also partnering with several satellite companies, including Spire Global, DigitalGlobe (**Maxar Technologies**) and Black Sky, which will use Amazon's ground station-as-a-service to augment the operations of their ground facilities (i.e., achieve faster speeds at lower costs). AWS Ground Station, which will being operations in mid-2019, will be a vital link for transmitting data to and from satellites in orbit (cnbc.com). Interestingly, as we noted in our October 2 research note, Amazon is partnering with **Iridium Communications** to bring Internet connectivity to the "whole planet" by developing a satellite-based network called CloudConnect for Internet of Things (IoT) applications. And perhaps foreshadowing AWS Ground Station, AWS was looking to hire a software engineer and a product manager "*to help innovate and disrupt the launch, satellite and space world with new AWS products, services and features...for a new AWS service that will have a historic impact*".

WPP & Omnicom Group shift their ad spending from Google to Amazon

Large ad buyers are starting to shift their ad search spending from Google to Amazon, which is not surprising given over half of people now start their product search on Amazon. For example, **WPP PLC**, the world's largest ad buyer, has more than doubled its spending on Amazon search ads from $125 million in 2017 to $300 million last year; however, this still only represents 10% of the $3 billion it spends globally on Google search ads. Amazon seems to be gaining more penetration in the U.S. as **Omnicom Group** has shifted 20–30% of its U.S. search ad spending for clients from Google to Amazon (wsj.com).

Amazon creating rival to Apple's AirPods as DTC hearing aid company Eargo raises $52 million

Amazon is reportedly creating an Alexa-powered rival to **Apple**'s AirPods. Amazon is working on developing a more affordable set of wireless earbuds with built-in controls and a mic so you can talk to Alexa, along with a case that doubles as a charger. However, you would have to tether the earbuds to your smartphone to access Alexa (techcrunch.com).

U.S. online retail sales reach tipping point as shopping mall vacancy hits 8-year high

U.S. online retail sales have reached the tipping point — in February, for the first time in history, online retail sales surpassed general merchandise sales. The Commerce Department reported the market share of online retail sales climbed to 11.813% versus 11.807% for general merchandise sales, which includes department store sales (cnbc.com). Given this, it is not surprising that the U.S. shopping mall vacancy rate hit an 8-year high of 9.3% in Q1, up from 8.4% a year ago, according to real estate research firm Reis. The vacancy rate is likely to climb higher as Coresight Research calculates that U.S. retailers have announced plans to close 5,480 stores to date this year, reaching nearly the total of 5,730 store closures for all of 2018 (ft.com). And this week, we learned of more store closures. For example, Robert Cavalli is liquidating its North American operations and closing all its U.S. stores — comprising seven full-line stores and four outlet mall stores — as its North American business, Art Fashion Corp., files for Chapter 7 bankruptcy (businessoffashion.com). **Signet Jewelers**, which operates the trio of Kay, Zales and Jared jewelry stores, is closing over 150 mall-based stores in fiscal 2020 as part of its turnaround plan (businessinsider.com). **Ascena Retail Group** is unloading its women's value fashion brands. It is selling a majority interest in Maurices, its women's apparel chain of 943 stores, for $300 million to a London-based PE firm. In addition, it is exploring options for Dress Barn (digitalcommerce.com).

Leasing activity drops 26% for big-box industrial spaces over 1 million square feet

According to Jones Lang LaSalle, leasing activity for big box industrial spaces over 1 million square feet declined by 26.1% last year versus only a 3.6% decline for spaces between 100,000 and 500,000 square feet as companies seek smaller warehouses closer to cities. For example, **Walmart** recently opened a 200,000-square-foot warehouse in the Bronx to handle e-commerce fulfillment for Jet.com and Amazon's new 855,000-square-foot warehouse on Staten Island is able to handle 50% more inventory than its traditional warehouses which are 20% bigger (wsj.com). This supports the thesis we introduced in our February 26 research report, *The Alpha Playbook to the Sensual Revolution,* that the race for the last mile is starting to be offset by supply-side developments such as increased efficiency with the growth in smart warehouses and increased space utilization as warehouses expand vertically.

Walmart offers grocery shopping via Google Assistant – but still missing its own Alexa

Although Walmart recently left **Alphabet**'s Google Express, it turns out it does have a voice-commerce strategy — partnering with voice assistant platforms, like Google Assistant. Walmart has partnered with Google to offer voice-activated online grocery shopping via Google Assistant but Walmart will be responsible for handling the processing and delivery of orders (cnbc.com). Although this is a positive move, we continue to remain bearish on Walmart in the long term as it still doesn't have its own Alexa. Walmart is looking to capitalize on the demise of Babies 'R' Us with its upgraded baby registry. The baby registry includes new mobile features and a chatbot called Hoot the Owl which will provide personalized recommendations based on your answers to the baby's due date, gender and nursery theme (cnbc.com).

Pinterest looks to be a downward-facing unicorn as Poshmark joins the IPO queue

Pinterest is setting an IPO price range for its shares between $15 and $17 per share, which implies a $2 billion discount to the $12.3 billion valuation it achieved when it raised a $150 million venture round back in June 2017 (techcrunch.com). More concerning is that Pinterest was actually valued at $11 billion four years ago, back in May 2015, when it raised a $186 million Series G round. The problem is this valuation was based on the expectation the company would generate $2.8 billion in revenue by 2018, but in reality it ended up generating only $756 million. While Pinterest has been able to grow its revenue per monthly active user in the U.S. to $9.04, close to its forecast of $9.34, it hasn't been able to yet monetize its international user base, resulting in its average revenue per monthly active user being only $3.14, one-third of its forecast (techcrunch.com). Poshmark, the closet-sharing platform, has hired Goldman Sachs and Morgan Stanley as it prepares to go public as early as this fall. Poshmark, which appeals to the Millennial group of cost-conscious and socially conscious females, generated nearly $150 million in revenue last year with narrow losses. Poshmark, which has raised $153 million since launching in Redwood City in 2011, was last valued at $1.25 billion on the secondary market (wsj.com).

Slack plans to enter the public arena unescorted

Slack has elected to do a direct listing on the NYSE, following in the footsteps of **Spotify**, which entered the public arena unescorted last April (wsj.com). I actually shared my thoughts on direct listings back in January, when I was invited to contribute to the TechCrunch article, *Direct Listings: Six leading IPO experts talk about the revolution in how tech start-ups go public*:

Realistically, the direct listing route is most suitable for companies meeting the following three criteria: 1) consumer-facing with strong brand equity; 2) easy-to-understand business model; and 3) no need to raise capital. Even if a company meets this criteria, the "escorted" IPO route could provide a positive return on investment as the IPO roadshow is designed to provide a valuation uptick through building awareness and preference versus competitive offerings by enabling a company to: a) reach and engage a larger investment pool; b) optimally position its story; and c) showcase its skilled management team.

Although the concept of democratizing capital markets by providing equal access to all investors is appealing, if a large institution isn't able to get an IPO allocation, they may be less willing to build up a meaningful position in the aftermarket. The direct listings option also introduces a higher level of pricing risk and volatility as the opening price and vulnerable early trading days of the stock are left to the whims of the market. Unlike with an IPO, with benefits of stabilizing bids and 90 to 180 days lock-up agreements prohibiting existing investors from selling their shares, a flood of sellers could hit the market.

Shopify could face another competitor as Microsoft looks to enter e-commerce space

Shopify, which just lost Mailchimp as a strategic partner and could face increased competition as **Square** moves into e-commerce with the launch of Square Online Space, could face another competitor — **Microsoft**. Microsoft is rumoured to be looking at a building an e-commerce online store to meet growing demand from some of its larger customers (zdnet.com).

Nickelodeon acquires early learning platform Sparkler

Nickelodeon (**Viacom**) is acquiring Sparkler, an early learning platform, to advance its goal to become the premier interactive learning destination for preschoolers and their families. Nickelodeon is integrating Sparkler's platform, which "*measures child development and delivers personalized content and coaching to parents to improve child outcomes*", into its app-based video subscription service Noggin to leverage its content which includes over 1,500 videos and 30 series, including PAW Patrol, Peppa Pig and Dora the Explorer (fastcompany.com).

Chapter Nine: A Different Species?

I still remember taking my first Uber ride — I was visiting NYC with my husband and then one-year-old. I was so inspired by that experience that I wrote the LinkedIn article, "Social Capital: The Secret Behind Airbnb and Uber", which went viral and led to the creation of my Ubernomics book two years later. It has been a long wait as my baby is now in kindergarten and Uber's valuation has since increased 10-fold from $10 billion to an expected $100 billion. So I was totally excited to dig into Uber's newly-filed S-1.

Although I really want to want to buy UBER, I'm cautious about drinking the Kool-Aid - especially since LYFT is now trading 22% below its $72 IPO price and 35% below its $87 opening price. After an initial review of Uber's S-1, you might want to take a look at Uber. In addition to being one of the rare publicly traded companies to operate at the peak of all three sides of the value pyramid, it offers a global platform play on the future of transportation and delivery. Although Uber is still not profitable, it actually seems to have operating leverage as all its line expense items declined last year on a per-ride basis. I still need to do more digging into Uber's S-1 but I'll leave you with this question:

Could Uber be a different species of unicorn than Lyft?

A Different Species?: April 16, 2019

Disney unveils Disney+ streaming service as Netflix publishes its first magazine

Disney unveiled details of its long-awaited Disney+ streaming service, which will launch in the U.S. on November 12. Disney+ offers an appealing value proposition, especially to families on a functional value basis in terms of pricing ($6.99 per month is nearly half the price of Netflix), variety of choice (access to Disney's massive library of existing content from Disney, Pixar, Star Wars, Marvel, National Geographic) and convenience (streaming with ability to download content). More importantly, on the emotional level, Disney will be able to leverage its iconic brand and the huge incredibly powerful connection that both parents and their kids have to the Disney brand. The good news is that Disney+ will be available in Canada in Q120 with plans to roll it out to Western Europe in the first half of 2020 and across Europe, Asia-Pacific and Latin America throughout 2021 (techcrunch.com). Personally, I'm excited that my boys will soon be able to access Disney's rich media library at such a low cost and it will be a great complement to Netflix. To enhance its emotional connection with academy members in advance of this year's Emmys, **Netflix** is embracing the physical layer, publishing its first magazine called Wide. Netflix plans to distribute Wide, its 100-page journal that features interviews, essays and features about and by people that work on Netflix series, at academy events in June (bnnbloomberg.ca). This is a strategic move as Netflix won 23 Emmy awards last year, tying for the first time in history with HBO (**AT&T**), and is moving deeper into Hollywood as it recently joined the Motion Picture Association of America.

U.S. retailers have announced nearly 6,000 store closures YTD – more than all of last year

According to a new report from data analytics firm Thasos, U.S. mall foot traffic peaked in August 2018. In fact, according to Coresight Research, U.S. retailers have now announced more store closures year-to-date than in all of last year, at 5,994 versus 5,864. Although there have been 2,641 new store openings announced this year, this will leave a net 3,353 store closures year-to-date, exceeding the net 2,625 store closures for all of last year (cnbc.com). For example, **Christopher Banks**, a women's apparel retailer with 457 stores across the U.S., has hired a lease structuring specialist as it prepares to close 40 stores by year-end (chainstoreage.com). **Fred's** is rationalizing its physical footprint by closing 159, or nearly one-third, of its 557 discount stores. Fred's is focusing on closing underperforming stores with shorter lease durations and has hired PJ Solomon to evaluate further "strategic alternatives" (chainstorageage.com). In the U.K., Debenhams, which just went into administration, has sold its business to lenders (wsj.com). Interestingly, it was only back in October, less than two weeks after the bankruptcy of Sears Holdings in the U.S., that Debenhams announced it would be closing 50, or nearly one-third, of its 166 department stores in the U.K.

Amazon & Microsoft are finalists for $10 billion Department of Defense cloud services contract

The Pentagon has narrowed down the list of contenders for the $10 billion Department of Defense cloud services contract to **Amazon** and **Microsoft**, eliminating **Oracle** and **IBM** (geekwire.com). To improve its warehouse operations, Amazon has acquired Canvas Technology, a robotics company that has raised $15 million since it launched in Denver in 2015 with the mission "*to provide end-to-end autonomous delivery of goods*". Amazon is likely most interested in deploying Canvas Technology's robotics like its Canvas Autonomous Cart which works like an autonomous driving car in warehouses (techcrunch.com). Amazon will begin accepting cash at its Amazon Go stores (techcrunch.com). This comes as San Francisco, Chicago and New York consider following in the footsteps of Philadelphia and New Jersey which have recently introduced into law new legislation banning cashless stores on the grounds they discriminate against low-income consumers that don't have bank accounts or credit cards.

Walmart goes on the defensive against Amazon

Walmart is buying Polymorph Labs, an advertising tech company that has raised $14 million since launching in 2013. Walmart is hoping Polymorph Labs will help enhance its Walmart Media Group in-house advertising business and enable it to better compete with Amazon via online digital ads using targeted shopper data (techcrunch.com). Walmart de Mexico is also going on the defensive, penalizing food companies that supply groceries to Amazon. Walmart is Mexico's largest grocery retailer, with over 2,400 stores (Walmart, Sam's Club, Superama, Bodega Aurerra) accounting for nearly 60% of Mexico's supermarket sales. However, as only 1.4% of Walmart's sales are online, it is worried about the threat from Amazon, which entered Mexico in 2015 and started to sell non-perishable groceries online in August (reuters.com).

Faced with rising wage pressure, Walmart is moving up the structural capital side of the value pyramid to the AI layer as it automates low-skilled jobs. Walmart is adding machines that can scan shelves for out-of-stock produce to at least 300 of its stores and bringing autonomous floor scrubbers, which can save 2–3 hours per day, to 1,500 of its stores. In addition, it is doubling the number of conveyer belts that can scan and sort products coming off trucks to 1,200, enabling it to cut the number of required workers for each truck in half from 8 to 4. To fulfill online orders, it is hiring 40,000 store workers to pick groceries from shelves, as well as bringing self-service Pick-up Towers to an additional 900 stores (wsj.com). After spending $2.2 billion on remodeling 500 stores last year, Walmart plans to remodel another 500 this year, adding features such as wider aisles, self-checkouts and brighter lighting (pymnts.com).

Rent the Runway expands to girls' clothing as Neiman Marcus empowers its stylists

Rent the Runway, the women's apparel & accessories rental platform, is expanding into girls' clothing, creating the next generation of fashionistas. The initial offering will focus on high-end clothing for girls aged 3–10 from designer brands such as **LVMH**'s Little Marc Jacobs and Fendi, Chloe (**Compagnie Financiere Richemont**) and Stella McCartney (**Kering**) (vogue.com). We note that **Stitch Fix**, the subscription apparel company, expanded into kids clothing last June. Meanwhile, Neiman Marcus is empowering its stylists to create shoppable Instagram posts through Salesfloor's new SocialShop feature (footwearnews.com). We note that Salesfloor, a people-powered e-commerce platform, has raised $3 million since launching in Montreal in 2013. But before you post your next selfie on Instagram, you should know that **Facebook** was just granted a patent for "*computer-vision content detection for sponsored stories*". It is totally Big Brother as it would let Facebook's "*image object recognition algorithm*" scan through your photos to detect brands and then send that data to advertisers to sell you more product or promote it to your friends as a sponsored story (fastcompany.com).

Amazon in talks to launch a free, ad-supported music streaming service to rival Spotify

According to Billboard, Amazon is in discussions to launch a free, ad-supported music streaming service. As Amazon would be able to promote this on its Echo devices, this would be a direct competitive threat to **Spotify** by increasing its risk of customer disintermediation through platforms such as Amazon Echo (billboard.com). We note Spotify had 207 million monthly active users in Q418, with 54% being non-Premium Subscribers. Meanwhile, Casper is embracing the sense of sound, launching the "Casper Sleep Channel" on Spotify and YouTube, which it describes as "*a magical slumberland of sounds, meditations, and bedtime stories to help you wind down and drift off*". This is a brilliant strategy as it will enhance the emotional connection to Casper and could serve as an innovative customer acquisition strategy, further differentiating Casper from traditional mattress retailers like **Sleep Country Canada.**

IKEA is growing its own lettuce in shipping containers outside its stores

IKEA is embracing environmental sustainability, growing lettuce in shipping containers outside two of its stores in Sweden to serve local sustainable salad greens to customers. IKEA's vertical urban farm, which yields up to 3,600 heads of lettuce, features a four-level hydroponic growing system that uses no soil, up to 90% less water and renewable energy LED light (fastcompany.com). This underlines the shift we are starting to see toward a localized supply chain for fresh produce. For example, in March, Gordon Food Service partnered with an urban farming accelerator to set up campuses containing 10 shipping container farming systems, each yielding 50,000 pounds of produce a year, on or near Gordon Food's distribution and retail locations.

One of the red flags that totally scared me off drinking Lyft's Kool-Aid was the discrepancy I discovered with its reported U.S. market share. It turns out the skepticism I shared with you in my March 25 research report was warranted as Lyft is now facing two class-action lawsuits from investors claiming it exaggerated its U.S. market share at 39% in its prospectus. It will be interesting to see what happens, especially since Uber disclosed in its April 11 S-1 filing that it currently has over 65% of the ride-sharing category in the U.S. and Canada. But most red flags take much longer to play out. For example, back on January 15, I warned about the threat of the new disruptive entrant Luckin Coffee to Starbucks' China growth story – but Starbucks' stock has continued to climb since then, up 18.6% versus the 15.6% gain in NASDAQ. And the red flag just flashed brighter as in the past week, Luckin has raised a $150 million Series B+ round, on top of the $200 million it raised in December – and even more significantly, filed to IPO on NASDAQ. So it will be interesting to see whether its Starbucks' China growth story comes under scrutiny from analysts when it reports its Q219 results today after market close. And a new red flag just developed for the U.S. dollar stores as the USDA has launched a two-year pilot program in New York state to enable SNAP recipients to buy groceries online from Amazon and Walmart.

The Red Flag: April 25, 2019

Starbucks' China growth story threatened as Luckin Coffee files to IPO and raises $150 million

On April 22, Luckin Coffee filed to go public on the NASDAQ, increasing our concern about the threat this new aggressive disruptive entrant poses to **Starbucks**' China growth story. Even more concerning, this announcement comes less than a week after it raised a $150 million Series B+ round, which follows closely behind its $200 million Series B round in December. Since Luckin Coffee launched in January 2018, it has attracted over 16.8 million customers with a 54% customer repurchase rate and grown its physical footprint to 2,370 stores in 28 cities across China with the ambitious plan to reach 4,500 stores by year-end. Like many young unicorns, Luckin Coffee seems more focused on growth than profitability as it had a negative operating margin of 110% in Q119 on revenue of $71 million (ft.com). Speaking of China, Amazon is shutting down Amazon.cn, its third-party marketplace which connects mainland Chinese buyers and sellers. However, Amazon is only partially retreating from China as it "*will continue to invest and grow in China across Amazon Global Store, Global Selling, AWS, Kindle devices and content*". Amazon entered China in 2004 with the $75 million purchase of Joyo.com, the then-largest online bookseller in China (wsj.com).

Fortress surrounding dollar stores could start to crumble with new SNAP pilot program

The fortress surrounding U.S. dollar stores could start to crumble as the USDA just launched a two-year pilot program that will enable 3 million SNAP (Supplement Nutrition Assistance Program) recipients in the state of New York to buy groceries online from **Amazon**, **Walmart** and ShopRite. Under the pilot program, Amazon will offer SNAP recipients free delivery on AmazonFresh orders over $50 with no Prime membership required while Walmart will enable them to order groceries online and pick them up at nearly 275 stores. The USDA plans to expand the pilot in the future to the states of Alabama, Iowa, Maryland,

Nebraska, New Jersey, Oregon and Washington (cbnc.com). This could be negative for retailers like dollar stores that serve these lower-income consumers given these 42 million people, representing 13% of the population, receive a total of $65 billion in annual SNAP benefits.

Kohl's is rolling out Amazon Returns nationwide to all its department stores

Kohl's and Amazon are deepening their relationship - on both the investment and operational fronts. On the investment side, Amazon N.V. Investment Holdings has received warrants to buy up to 1.75 million shares of Kohl's, or 1.1% of the company, at an exercise price of $69.68 over a 5-year vesting period that starts in January 2020. On the operational side, Kohl's will expand its Amazon Returns service, which it launched in October 2017 at 82 of its department stores in LA and Chicago, nationwide to all of its 1,150 department stores (chainstorage.com). This seems to be a win-win partnership as Kohl's provides Amazon with valuable structural capital by carving off space in its stores to serve as drop-off hubs for customers to return Amazon merchandise, which Kohl's staff will then package and forward to Amazon's return centres. In return, Amazon provides Kohl's with valuable customer capital by driving traffic to its stores. Although this is a good defensive move for Kohl's, we question whether this marks the beginning of the repurposing of department stores into e-commerce distribution warehouses.

Amazon deepens its strategic partnership with Groupe Casino in France

In France, Amazon is deepening its strategic relationship with **Groupe Casino**, which it partnered with last March to launch Prime Now grocery delivery service in Paris for Monoprix. Under the new agreement, Groupe Casino will provide Amazon with valuable structural capital in terms of placing Amazon Lockers in 1,000 of its grocery store locations across France by year-end and valuable supplier capital in terms of adding more of its Casino-branded products on Amazon's website. In return, Amazon will provide Groupe Casino with valuable structural capital by expanding its Prime Now grocery delivery service into new cities outside Paris in the next 12 months. France is a strategic market for Amazon as it is its third-largest market, after Great Britain and France, and it is the leading e-commerce player with a 17.3% share but its grocery share is only 2% (cnbc.com).

Walmart partners with KidBox to offer its first subscription apparel service

Walmart is launching its first subscription apparel service in partnership with KidBox, a kids' clothing subscription start-up. Walmart is hoping to offer a unique value proposition in terms of variety of choice (customers will be able to purchase six themed boxes a year offering 4–5 items, one box for each season plus back-to-school and Christmas, and the boxes will be curated based on a styling quiz) and pricing (the cost will be $48, 50% off the retail price). However, the offering lacks convenience as customers either have to keep all the items or return everything for a complete refund (cnbc.com). We believe this will increase the awareness of emerging apparel retail platforms like **Stitch Fix** and Rent the Runway, which recently expanded into kids' clothing, and act as a positive catalyst to expand demand.

Facebook is developing its own voice assistant as Amazon introduces Alexa skills certification

During an interview with CNBC, venture capitalist Mark Tluszcz shared his view that "*voice is the opportunity of a decade*" as it will cause "*a cataclysmic change to the user experience*" and he expects "*there are going to be many companies built that are only voice*" (cnbc.com). Given this, it's not surprising that **Facebook** is developing its own voice assistant. Apparently, Facebook's augmented reality and virtual reality hardware team has been working on the voice assistant since early 2018. This is a strategic move as it would enable Facebook to leverage its existing structural capital in the form of its Oculus headsets and its Facebook Portal tablet-like video chat device it launched in November 2018, which is currently integrated with Alexa (cnbc.com). However, we believe Facebook could face significant privacy and trust concerns from consumers that might be wary of its ulterior motives. Meanwhile, to validate the ability of developers to build, test and publish Amazon Alexa skills, Amazon is introducing its first certification program. To achieve the AWS Certified Alexa Skill Builder — Specialty certification — you need to pass the 170-minute multiple-choice online exam, with the recommended prerequisite of proficiency with a programming language, six months of hands-on experience building Alexa skills and publishing an actual Alexa skill (aws.amazon.com/certification).

Alphabet's Wing receives first FAA certification for drone delivery

Alphabet's Wing Aviation just received the first FAA certification in the U.S. for commercial carriage of goods by drone. Wing plans to pilot its drone delivery service in Virginia later this year (techcrunch.com). We note Wing just launched its drone delivery service in Australia a few weeks ago, delivering small goods such as medicine, coffee and groceries from a range of local businesses to 100 homes outside of Canberra and is preparing to launch a trial service in Helsinki, Finland. If you don't feel comfortable having Amazon deliver packages into your home or your car, you now have a third option — your garage. Amazon's new Key for Garage program is now available to Prime members in 50 cities across the U.S. who purchase a Chamberlain or LiftMaster myQ garage door for $180 or affix their existing door opener with an $80 hub. In addition to receiving an alert when the package is delivered, you can also set up a camera to watch the delivery process remotely on your phone (fortune.com). In addition to fighting porch piracy, Amazon is now tackling delivery driver identity fraud. Amazon is using facial recognition to reduce identify fraud, making its Amazon Flex delivery drivers take selfies (theverge.com).

Store brands gaining share in the mass retail channel

Not surprisingly, store brands are gaining share from national brands in the mass retail channel. According to a new study from the Private Label Manufacturers Association, since 2013, store brands have seen their sales rise at a 5-year CAGR of 7.1% (from $43.1 billion to $60.8 billion) versus only 1.4% for national brands (from $236.1 billion to $253.6 billion), resulting in the share of store brands increasing from 15% to 19% (prnewswire.com).

Airbnb faces rising competition as Selina raises $100 million and Sonder looks to raise $200 million

Selina, a hospitality brand for Millennial digital nomads, just raised a $100 million Series C round to further advance its mission to help travelers live, work and explore anywhere in the world. This follows closely behind the venture rounds of $150 million it raised in December and $95 million last April. Since December, Selina has expanded its footprint of hostel-like lodging combined with co-working spaces from 31 to 47 properties across Mexico, Latin America and South America, and it now plans to expand to 400 properties by 2023. Selina will also use the funding to improve its booking and algorithmic recommendations (techcrunch.com). Meanwhile, Sonder, a tech-driven hospitality company launched in San Francisco in 2014, is close to raising a $200 million investment that would value it at $1 billion. Sonder competes against Airbnb as it offers short-term home rentals but its business model is more like WeWork as it leases, furnishes and maintains its properties, as well as providing guests with toiletries and clean sheets and towels ((wsj.com). Although this creates a more asset-intensive business model, it provides Sonder with greater control over the guest experience.

As I read about the Westfield Garden State Plaza mall in New Jersey getting a massive makeover, it made me think about how disillusioned I felt as I walked through Hudson Yards on Sunday. The five-storey mall — albeit new and shiny — was really just a mall and walking through it paled in comparison to the rich experience of strolling down Madison Avenue or browsing through Soho. The mall itself offered nothing really new in terms of experiences and seems a bit risky with Neiman Marcus as its anchor department store tenant. The reality is that Instagram is becoming the new mall as it transforms into a social e-commerce platform and retailers will soon find it harder to compete with Amazon as it starts to offer 1-day Prime shipping. And the retail apocalypse seems to have gotten worse since I was in NYC in September as it seemed like every block I walked down had at least one to two vacant retail spaces "for lease".

The one brilliant retail concept I visited is Made By We, WeWork's new retail/co-working space on Broadway which offers a very California hippie surf vibe. In addition to selling a curated selection of 50 products made by WeWork members, it hosts fascinating events offering a unique experience, like the upcoming conversation with Tim Ferriss next Monday. And in speaking with one of the staff, I learned that WeWork plans to have 25 Made By We locations by the end of this year. On that note, I can't wait to read through WeWork's upcoming S-1 as it just confidentially filed to IPO. It looks like Airbnb is waiting to IPO next year as it deals with rising regulatory issues as well as new competitors as Marriott recently entered the luxury home rental space. And although I've been a fan of Airbnb since my first stay in NYC five years ago, I have to admit that I booked a hotel this time as I've become increasingly frustrated with the experience of having to struggle with lockboxes and keys that don't work and Airbnb's own poor customer service.

The Experience: May 2, 2019

Uber Freight partners with SAP while Amazon enters the freight brokerage space

Disruptive new entrants into the $72 billion U.S. freight brokerage market like Uber Freight and **Amazon** are raising the structural disruption risk for legacy North American freight brokers like **C.H. Robinson Worldwide**, Total Quality Logistics, **XPO Logistics**, **Echo Global Logistics**, Coyote Logistics (**UPS**) and DHL (**Deutsche Post**). Uber Freight, which generated $359 million in revenue last year, just entered a strategic partnership with **SAP**. Uber Freight is integrating its Uber Freight API into the SAP Logistics Business Network, enabling SAP's customers to optimize their logistics by accessing Uber Freight's instant, real-time pricing data and national network of freight capacity (news.sap.com). This strategic partnership could be a significant growth catalyst for Uber Freight, whose on-demand trucking brokerage platform has grown to 36,000 carriers with 400,000 drivers and 1,000 shippers since launching two years ago.

And we just learned that Amazon is also entering the freight brokerage space. Amazon, which is licensed as a freight broker, has been internally testing a new online service to match truck drivers with shippers since last year so it can better manage its existing network of carriers and expedite the cargo matching process. Amazon has been beta testing the service, which allows shippers to get instant quotes on shipping packages between warehouses in five states (Connecticut, Maryland, New Jersey, New York, Pennsylvania), with hundreds of approved carriers (cnbc.com). The digitization of trucking and logistics is attracting venture capital globally. For example, in India, BlackBuck, an on-demand freight trucking brokerage platform launched in 2015, just raised a $150 million Series D round. BlackBuck currently has 300,000 trucks and 10,000 shippers on its platform, including **Coca-Cola**, **Unilever** and **Tata Motors** (techcrunch.com).

Amazon raises convenience bar for retailers as it moves to 1-day Prime shipping

Amazon is pushing the edges of the convenience frontier with its announcement in its Q119 results that it is evolving Prime from 2-day to 1-day shipping, starting in North America in Q2 and then going global. We have no doubt this will raise the bar further for retailers, placing them at a further competitive disadvantage to Amazon on the e-commerce layer. Amazon also disclosed that Amazon Day has been adopted by millions of its U.S. Prime members, which could help offset shipping costs. Interestingly, Amazon's shipping cost delta remained unchanged from a year ago at -$3.0 billion, as the $1.3 billion increase in its subscription revenue to $7.3 billion was offset by the $1.3 billion increase in its shipping costs to $4.3 billion.

Boundaries are blurring in the hospitality space

New developments on the hospitality front point to an increasing blurring of the boundaries between hotels and home rentals. For example, **Marriott International** is launching Homes & Villas, a curated collection of 2,000 luxury homes in 100 markets across the U.S., Europe, Caribbean and Latin America offering an elevated travel experience (forbes.com). Although Marriott's new home rental platform represents less than 0.2% of its inventory of 1.3 million guest rooms globally, this strategic move is significant as it highlights the increasing importance of connecting with guests on an emotional level by offering authentic experiences. Meanwhile, Airbnb is partnering with RXR Realty to convert one-third of Rockefeller Plaza, a Class A office building in Midtown Manhattan, into Airbnb lodgings. RXR Realty is redeveloping the top 10 floors of the 32-storey office tower into 200 luxury Airbnb suites which will be staffed by unionized labour to comply with NYC regulations (wsj.com). OYO, India's largest hotel network, is expanding into home vacation rentals in Europe with its acquisition of @LeisureGroup from Axel Springer for $415 million. Since launching in India in 2013, OYO has grown to 8,500 budget hotels across 230 cities in India and raised $1.7 billion, with strategic investors such as **SoftBank**, Grab, Didi and Airbnb (techcrunch.com). We note that as Uber owns equity stakes of 23.2% in Grab and 15.4% in Didi, it is also an indirect investor in OYO and the travel hospitality space.

Amazon ventures into hospitality space — through AWS

In the past few months, AWS has signed new clients such as **Korean Air Lines**, **Ryanair Holdings** and **Choice Hotels** and, more importantly, has been advertising for positions such as Global Business Development Leader, Solutions Architect and Global Travel Senior Consultant for its new Hospitality and Travel Industry Solutions vertical. Given this, it seems like AWS is moving beyond being a cloud storage vendor for airline, cruise lines, hotels and restaurants to providing industry-specific subject matter expertise and actively advising them how to transition to a cloud-first infrastructure (skift.com). AWS has also opened its managed blockchain-as-a-service for general availability. This enables its customers, which include **AT&T** Business, **Nestle** and **Singapore Exchange**, to get a functioning blockchain network set up quickly and easily (techcrunch.com).

Top U.S. mall gets a massive makeover — but Instagram is becoming the new mall

The 61-year old Westfield Garden State Plaza mall, which attracts over 20 million visitors a year and is one of the highest revenue-producing malls in the U.S., is getting a massive makeover. **Unibail-Radamco-Westfield** is redeveloping the mall into a modern-day town centre, diversifying into office, residential and hotel space, as well as improving the customer experience by adding open green space, more food options, and health and wellness spaces (cnbc.com). However, investors in retail REITs need to be aware that Instagram (**Facebook**) is becoming the new mall as it transforms into a social e-commerce platform. Instagram is starting to empower creators/influencers to tag specific products in their photos to sell directly to people viewing their posts and stories. Instagram is launching the beta tests with 23 brands and 55 influencers. Although creators will not see a cut of the sales, they will gain access to a shared analytics platform that will provide them with valuable data to give them leverage when they are negotiating with brands (theatlantic.com).

Walmart tests shoppable ads through Vudu

Walmart is testing shoppable ads through its Vudu on-demand movie streaming service that would enable you to purchase featured products through a pop-up window. Vudu is also launching several interactive shows later this year that it is creating through its joint venture with Eko, an interactive content start-up (techcrunch.com). However, the downside to e-commerce is that 15–40% of online purchases are returned, which is creating a challenge for online and even omnichannel retailers. This is creating an opportunity for retail start-ups like Happy Returns, which operates over 350 Return Bars in convenient locations such as malls and college campuses. To advance its efforts, Happy Returns just raised an $11 million round led by **PayPal** Ventures, bringing its funding since it launched in Santa Monica in 2015 to $25 million (cnbc.com).

Amazon's net sales rise 17% to $57.9 billion while Alexa reaches over 90,000 skills

Amazon's net sales in Q119 rose 17% to $59.7 billion and it beat on the bottom line, reporting a record quarterly EPS of $7.09 versus $3.27 a year ago. The big driver continues to be its high-margin AWS division, where net sales rose 41% to a record $7.7 billion and operating margin rose 320 bp to 28.9%. The company's overall operating margin increased 360 bp to 7.4% as its operating margin in North America, which accounts for 60% of its net sales, rose 260 bp to 6.4%, and its International operating margin improved 360 bp to -0.6%. On the grocery front, Amazon now offers Prime Now two-hour delivery from Whole Foods in 75 U.S. metros and grocery pick-up in 30 metros. And Alexa is now at over 90,000 skills (seekingalpha.com). Amazon is also rebranding Souq, which it acquired for $580 million in March 2017, to Amazon.ae as it launches a new marketplace in the Middle East. Amazon.ae, which is available in Arabic language, will offer over 30 million products, including 25 million available on Souq and 5 million from Amazon U.S. (cnbc.com).

Pets.com déjà vu as PetSmart files to IPO Chewy.com

Pets.com déjà vu? PetSmart, which acquired Chewy.com for $3.4 billion two years ago, is looking to capitalize on the unicorn IPO stampede and spin off Chewy.com. On April 29, Chewy.com, which calls itself the largest pure-play pet e-tailer in the U.S., filed its S-1. Like many unicorns, Chewy.com is fast growing (its net sales rose 67% last year to $3.5 billion) but unprofitable (Chewy.com lost $268 million last year, equating to a negative net margin of 7.6%) (cnbc.com).

Chapter Ten: The Naked Unicorn

The rules of the game are changing — fast. Last week, Warren Buffett disclosed that Berkshire Hathaway has been buying shares in Amazon, and this week we are about to witness the IPO of Uber — one of the largest tech IPOs in history. Just like companies need to realize they can no longer function as non-tech businesses and evolve up the value pyramid, investors need to realize the lines between growth and value investing are blurring and they can no longer rely on traditional valuation metrics like P/E and P/BV. For by just looking at the numbers, they risk drinking the "blue Kool-Aid" and being seduced into the value traps of companies that still operate at the base of the value pyramid.

They also miss out on companies that are building defensive moats by playing the long game — like Amazon and Uber — who are sacrificing short-term profits by investing in intangibles higher up the capital pyramids like customer relationships, R&D and platform ecosystems. For example, as I write in my April 29 research report, "Take a Once-In-A-Lifetime Ride On An UBERcorn", I believe Uber is uniquely positioned to evolve beyond being a global transportation and delivery platform and expand its total addressable market by capitalizing on the convergence of its higher forms of capital to potentially create new blue oceans in industries like financial services, travel, healthcare, restaurants and staffing.

The Rules: May 7, 2019

Lines between value & growth investing blur as Warren Buffett's Berkshire buys Amazon stock

The acceleration in structural disruption is changing the rules for investors as it blurs the lines between value and growth investing, as Warren Buffett disclosed to CNBC that for the first time ever **Berkshire Hathaway** has been buying shares of **Amazon** (cnbc.com). Given Amazon is trading at over 50 times forward earnings and 20 times 12-month trailing book value, this is changing the rules of the game for traditional value investors who assess companies primarily on their valuation metrics. At Berkshire Hathaway's AGM this weekend, Buffett argued that value isn't tied solely to valuation metrics like P/E and P/BV as all investing is focused on value, effectively "*putting out money now to get more later on*" (marketwatch.com). We note that back in January 2018, Berkshire Hathaway partnered with Amazon and **JPMorgan Chase** to launch a not-for-profit healthcare venture, now named Haven.

Intu Properties' warning of drop in rental income is a red flag for retail REITs

As a red flag for retail REITs, in the U.K., **Intu Properties** just warned of a bigger drop in rental income this year as a result of a higher-than-expected level of CVAs and a slowdown in new lettings as tenants delay their decisions owing to the uncertain retail and political environment. Debenhams, which launched its CVA last week, accounts for 3% of its rental income and Arcadia Group accounts for another 4% (ft.com). Arcadia Group, the owner of apparel retail chains Topshop and Dorothy Perkins, which saw its sales decline 15% over the holidays, is involved in tense negotiations with landlords and pension regulators over plans to cut rents and close stores as it works toward a CVA (Company Voluntary Arrangement) (ft.com). In London, over 20,000 commercial units have been vacant for at least six months, with over half of these, or 11,000, vacant for over two years (theguardian.com). We continue to believe the future of retail is stores that function more as showrooms than selling goods. For example, **Nordstrom** is bringing its Nordstrom Local boutique concept to the West Village and UES in NYC. Nordstrom Local, which is a fraction of the size of a typical Nordstrom department store at only 2,000–3,000 square feet, does not actually sell anything as it serves instead as a neighbourhood service hub, offering online order pick-up, alterations and personal styling (prnewswire.com). We note that Nordstrom opened its first Nordstrom Local store in West Hollywood in October 2017 and two more in LA in July 2018.

Facecoin is coming to Facebook!

Facebook is creating a digital coin as party of a new cryptocurrency-based payment system. Apparently, Facebook has been working on this secret initiative, code-named Project Libra, for over a year, which coincides with the timing last August of David Marcus stepping down from the board of Coinbase to avoid any conflict of interest as he set up a new group at Facebook around blockchain. As we mentioned back in December, Facebook was developing a way to use a stablcoin to transfer money on WhatsApp in India. Users will be able to send Facecoin, which will be underpinned by blockchain technology and pinned to the U.S. dollar, to each other and make purchases on Facebook as well as across the Internet. Most importantly, this would enable Facebook to monetize its 1.56 billion daily active users (wsj.com). This validates our thesis that those companies best positioned to transition up to the new crypto-economy, creating new ways to extract value, are not new ICOs but existing marketplace companies. On that note, according to Dead Coins, the number of ICOs that have joined the cryptocoin graveyard since we last reported on it in July has nearly doubled from 868 to now 1,614 (deadcoins.com).

Target expands its media network as NBC launches ShoppableTV thru QR codes

Target is rebranding Target Media Network to Roundel as part of its strategy to expand beyond display ads on Target.com to leverage its customer data through creating personalized campaigns and content for clients (techcrunch.com). Meanwhile, NBCUniversal (**Comcast**) is launching a new feature called ShoppableTV. Although NBC claims this will increase advertising conversion rates by driving direct sales, I think it risks turning shows into infomercials by displaying QR codes on the screen which it hopes viewers will scan to then be taken directly to a retailer's e-commerce site (techcrunch.com). What makes more sense is what Google (**Alphabet)** is doing — leveraging its YouTube platform by testing embedding Google Shopping links below YouTube videos (pymnts.com). In addition, Google is rebranding Google Express, which has positioned itself as the go-to online shopping mall for retailers looking to compete with Amazon, to Google Shopping. We believe this name change reflects the expansion of its offering beyond home delivery to voice-based ordering (androidpolice.com).

As I sat on my parent's couch on Mother's Day reading aloud one of my favourite childhood books to my 5-year-old, I couldn't help but think about Lyft and Uber. I feel a bit like the child who innocently cried out, "But he isn't wearing anything at all" in "The Emperor's New Clothes" for as I wrote in my May 8 research note, "Why I'm

Still Not Drinking the LYFT Kool-Aid", none of the analysts on Lyft's Q119 conference call (of which 10 of the 11 had Buy recommendations, with target prices ranging from $72 to $95) dared to speak the truth and ask hard questions. While I'm still questioning whether the LYFT unicorn is wearing any clothes (i.e., has a sustainable business platform), I think investors are being myopic when it comes to Uber. Although the UBERcorn may also seem naked at a distance, it is actually wearing multiple layers of clothing that should result in long-term value creation through its geographic diversification, synergistic multi-platform model, blue ocean growth opportunities, equity in Uber ATG and equity in international ridesharing firms Didi, Grab and Yandex Taxi. As Dara Khosrowshahi wrote in his email to staff on Monday morning: "Today is another tough day in the market, and I expect the same as it relates to our stock. But it is essential for us to keep our eye on the long-term value of Uber for our customers, partners, drivers and investors" (bloomberg.com).

The Naked Unicorn: May 14, 2019

Nike Fit enables you to scan your feet using your smartphone

Nike is launching Nike Fit, enabling you to use your smartphone to scan your feet to determine the right shoe size. Nike Fit is built on technology developed by Invertex, the Israel-based computer vision firm it acquired last April. Nike expects Nike Fit will enable it to reduce its return rate, better manage its inventory and increase conversion rate at stores. More importantly, Nike Fit should help it increase its emotional connection with customers by increasing its membership base, which currently stands at 150 million customers globally, driving its DTC sales channel, which represented 30% of sales in 2018, up from 28% in 2017. And the bigger vision for Nike Fit is to help it make better shoes (cnbc.com).

SEC approves a new Silicon Valley exchange

Ironically, the same day that Uber went public, the SEC approved the formation of a new Silicon Valley exchange. The Long-Term Stock Exchange, which was conceived by Eric Ries in his 2011 book, *The Lean Startup*, is backed by heavy-weight tech titans like Marc Andreessen who are concerned about the Street's focus on short-term profits. The Long-Term Stock Exchange seeks to prioritize long-term value creation by aligning companies with long-term investors that share the goal of value creation; its key features include banning the tying of executive pay to short-term financial performance as well as scaled voting power (cnbc.com).

Fifth Avenue vacancy rate at 25%, HBC pursues strategic alternatives for Lord & Taylor

It felt like the retail apocalypse was deepening as when I visited NYC a few weeks ago every block I walked down had at least 1–2 vacant retail spaces "for lease". My suspicions were correct as according to Cushman Wakefield, the availability rate (i.e., vacancies and expiring leases) for the luxury stretch on Fifth Avenue from 49th to 60th street reached 25% in Q1, up from 17% a year ago. This is leading to a decline in rental rates, with the average rent down 11% from its peak two years ago to $2,779 per square foot (wsj.com). **Hudson's Bay Company**, which recently closed Home Outfitters and is conducting a fleet review of Saks OFF 5th, is now pursuing strategic alternatives for Lord & Taylor, including a possible sale or merger (financialpost.com). We note that last June, HBC announced it would be closing up to 10 of its 48 Lord & Taylor stores, including its flagship Manhattan store that it sold to WeWork in October 2017. We also wonder what this implies for **Walmart**, which strategically partnered with Lord & Taylor a year ago to feature over 125 of its premium brands on its online mall. Amazon continues to capitalize on the retail apocalypse, opening its Amazon Go store at Brookfield Place in lower Manhattan — its first in NYC and 12th in the U.S. Although the 1,400-square-foot store will still be cashierless, it will have an employee on site with a mobile device to accept cash (cnbc.com).

Tempur-Pedic goes DTC to upscale buyers with Tempur-Cloud

As a new red flag for **Sleep Country Canada**, whose same-store-sales declined 3.4% in Q119, Tempur-Pedic (**Tempur Sealy International**) is going DTC to upscale buyers with the launch of Tempur-Cloud, its first high-end bed-in-the-box mattress. The Tempur-Cloud, which retails for $1,799, is being tested first in Seattle. Tempur-Pedic is also testing two new innovative products: the Tempur Active Breeze which employs cooling technology as well as a sleep tracker and monitor (furnituretoday.com).

Edgewell Personal Care acquires Harry's for $1.37 billion

Edgewell Personal Care is following in the footsteps of **Unilever**, which acquired Dollar Shave Club for $1 billion in 2016, with its $1.37 billion acquisition of Harry's. Harry's, the DTC subscription shaving company that has raised $375 million since launching in NYC in 2011, has gone omnichannel, with half of its sales coming from Walmart and **Target**, and expanded into women's razors as well as shower and face products. Edgewell, whose portfolio of personal care brands includes Schick and Wilkinson Sword (razors), Banana Boat (sunscreen) and Wet Ones (moist wipes), is going on the defensive with this strategic acquisition as its Q2 sales declined 8.9%. In addition, as the acquisition is 79% cash and 21% stock, it is adding $1.1 billion of debt to its balance sheet, which is significant given its own market cap is only $1.8 billion (cnbc.com).

Walmart expands in-store vet clinics as Petco launches first-ever pet food kitchen

In advance of PetSmart's IPO of Chewy.com, Walmart is making strategic moves into the pet space. In addition to launching WalmartPetRX.com, its new online pet pharmacy that offers low-cost prescriptions from over 300 brands for dogs, cats, horses and livestock, Walmart is expanding its in-store veterinary clinic footprint from 21 to 100 stores over the next 12 months (cnbc.com). Petco is also taking experiential retail to a new level for pet parents — launching its first-ever pet food kitchen in its flagship store in NYC. Petco is partnering with JustFoodForDogs, a natural pet food start-up that has raised $11 million since launching in LA in 2010. The pet kitchen will feature trained chefs that will prepare 2,000 pounds daily of veterinarian-designed recipes to sell in-store and distribute to other Petco locations (forbes.com). According to the American Pet Products Association, Americans spent $72.5 billion on pet products last year, with just under one-half spent on food and one-quarter on vet care

Alexa triples devices to 60,000 as Google starts to close off its smart home ecosystem

Amazon's Alexa now works on 60,000 devices from 7,400 unique brands, up from 20,000 devices from 3,500 brands in September (forbes.com). This is twice as many as **Alphabet**'s Google Assistant, which works on over 30,000 devices from 3,500 brands. Interestingly, it looks like Google is making the strategic move to gain greater control over its smart home ecosystem. In addition to integrating Nest into its overall line of Google Home products and re-branding them as Google

Nest, Google is shutting down the Works with Nest program as it moves to a single integrated platform based on Google Assistant. The problem is that this will dismantle the set of controls that allow other device manufacturer and service providers to integrate with the Nest ecosystem, which has grown to thousands of devices since Works with Nest was launched in 2014. This move will force these companies to support Google Assistant as well as force customers to get a Google account (theverge.com).

Google brings Driving Mode to Google Assistant and partners with Qualcomm

Google is making moves outside the home as well. It is bringing Driving Mode to Google Assistant. The voice-enabled driving mode will feature driving-relevant activities, top contacts and personalized recommendations. In addition, you will soon be able to use Google Assistant with Waze, which will make it much safer for reporting crashes, stalled traffic and obstacles on the road (theverge.com). And **Qualcomm** has partnered with Google to create the Qualcomm Bluetooth Headset Development Kit, a reference design and development kit for building Google Assistant-enabled Bluetooth headphones (techcrunch.com). We note that back in October, Qualcomm partnered with Amazon to offer a pre-made chip integrated with Alexa that headphone manufacturers could drop into their headsets, reducing their costs and leading to an increased supply of Alexa-enabled headphones.

Amazon incentivizes its employees to quit to join its Amazon Delivery Service Partner program

Amazon looks to be accelerating its Amazon Delivery Service Partner program as it shifts to one-day delivery. Amazon is leveraging its employee capital by incentivizing its existing employees to quit to work as entrepreneurs for its new local delivery program, offering them as much as $10,000 for start-up costs and the equivalent of three months' gross salary (wsj.com). Perhaps Amazon is hoping some of its warehouse employees will take it up on its offer as it continues its drive for automation to improve safety, speed up delivery times and improve efficiency across its network. Amazon is rolling out packing machines to automate boxing up customer orders that it has been piloting in a handful of warehouses. The CartonWrap machines, which are manufactured by Italian firm CMC Srl, are 8–10 times as efficient as a single machine can pack 600–700 boxes per hour, which is 4–5 times faster than the manual rate, which requires two employees (cnbc.com).

USPS plays hardball with Stamps.com causing its stock price to plummet over 50%

Stamps.com's stock price plummeted over 50% on May 8 after it disclosed in its Q119 results that the USPS is renegotiating the NSAs (Negotiated Service Agreement) of several of its reseller partners and cut its EPS guidance 35% for this year, warning it expects margins for its resellers to start declining in the second half and continue through to 2021 (cnbc.com). This follows the 50% plunge in Stamps.com's stock price on February 15 after it disclosed during its Q418 results that it was ending its long-standing exclusive partnership with the USPS. We note that Stamps.com's stock price has declined 86% since peaking at over $280 last June.

Amazon launches Lending Referral Program in China

Amazon has launched a new Lending Referral Program in China to connect pre-qualified sellers with a local lender to help the merchants purchase inventory and grow their business. According to Marketplace Pulse, over 40% of Amazon's best-selling merchants are in China so it makes sense for it to bring Amazon Lending, which currently operates in the U.S., U.K. and India, to China. Amazon's local lending partner is Shanghai Fuyou Commercial Factoring (cnbc.com).

I love watching my boys draw as they aren't afraid to colour outside the lines. And when you think about it, the key to corporate survival these days is the willingness for management to innovate and colour outside industry lines. For example, we are seeing an increasing blurring of lines in real estate, with The We Company launching a $2.9 billion real estate investment fund, the upscale fitness operator Equinox partnering with Industrious to offer co-working space above its new lifestyle hotel in NYC, Accor expanding beyond hospitality with the launch of its new co-working brand and Taco Bell opening a "taco oasis" pop-up hotel in Palm Springs.

Lines are blurring in logistics as well: Amazon just broke ground on a $1.5 billion new air hub and led the $575 million round for restaurant delivery start-up Deliveroo in the U.K. while Ola, the ridesharing leader in India, expanded into financial services. And Amazon is blurring even more industry lines as it just partnered with a leading online travel agency in India to offer domestic flights and also filed a trademark application for FireTube, a YouTube competitor.

As I advised two years ago in my June 6, 2017 research note: "As industry lines blur, investors will discover they can no longer rely on research that analyzes companies through a rear-view mirror."

The Lines: May 22, 2019

Walmart launches next-day delivery as Amazon invests $1.5 billion in new Prime Air hub

Walmart will start to offer next-day delivery for 220,000 items on its website in Phoenix, Las Vegas and Southern California with the goal to reach 75% of U.S. households by the end of this year (cnbc.com). This is clearly a defensive move as it follows less than three weeks after **Amazon** announced it is evolving Prime from two-day to one-day delivery. Although Walmart is meeting Amazon's functional value proposition in terms of convenience, Walmart still falls short in terms of variety of choice and pricing as the service is only free for orders over $35. And Amazon continues to invest in air logistics infrastructure. On May 14, Jeff Bezos tweeted: "*We're investing $1.5 billion in our new air hub to get you your packages faster. Three million square feet, and it's going to create 2,000 jobs. And if you're guessing that driving a front loader was fun, you're right! #amazon #prime*". The new air hub, which is located near Cincinnati/Northern Kentucky International Airport, is scheduled to open in 2021. Meanwhile, TuSimple, an autonomous driving technology company, was awarded a contract for a two-week pilot with the USPS. TuSimple will do five round trips, with a safety engineer and pilot onboard, hauling USPS' trailers the over 1,000 miles between its distribution centres in Phoenix and Dallas (techcrunch.com). Interestingly, Amazon was recently rumoured to be in talks to acquire TuSimple, which has raised $178 million since launching in San Diego in 2015.

Ascena closing Dress Barn, LVMH develops blockchain platform for luxury goods

Ascena Retail Group plans to wind down its Dress Barn

women's value fashion brand and close all 650 stores (cnbc.com). We note that last month Ascena Retail Group sold its majority interest in Maurices, its women's apparel chain of 943 stores, for $300 million to a London-based private equity firm. On the luxury side of the retail spectrum, **LVMH** has developed a blockchain system for authenticating luxury goods in partnership with **Microsoft** and ConsenSys. The AURA platform will help consumers track the lifecycle of goods, including design, raw materials, manufacturing and distribution. In addition, it will also help LVMH safeguard its IP and curb advertising fraud (retaildive.com). And **Farfetch** is entering the online luxury handbag reseller market with the launch of its new "Second Life" service. Farfetch is offering its customers in the U.K. and Europe the opportunity to trade in their luxury handbag from 27 designers, including **Christian Dior**, Gucci and Balenciaga (**Kering**), Celine (LVMH), Chloe (**Richemont**) and Chanel, for Farfetch credits. Similar to Rebag in the U.S., customers just need to upload photos of their handbag on its app to receive a free quote and then ship it to the company's headquarters to receive immediate payment (vogue.co.uk).

Kohl's bets on Amazon Returns to drive traffic as its SSS declines 3.4% in Q1

Kohl's stock price tumbled 12% on May 21 after reporting a surprising 3.4% decline in Q119 comparable-store sales. As a further red flag, management would not disclose on the call whether this was driven by a decline in traffic or pricing (cnbc.com). We're guessing it was traffic, as just a few weeks ago Kohl's announced it will be rolling out the Amazon Returns service nationwide to all its 1,155 stores in July, with its top strategic priority being to drive traffic. In the U.K., Amazon is strategically partnering with **Next Plc** to roll out its new click-

and-collect Amazon Counter service across the U.K. Next Plc, the U.K.-based retailer of apparel, footwear, accessories and home goods, is hoping to gain customer traffic by offering over 500 of its stores across the U.K. to serve as collection hubs for customer to pick-up Amazon parcels. Amazon is apparently also working on a returns option (pymnts.com). This makes us wonder if Amazon will expand its Amazon Counter service with Next Plc in the U.K. to include returns, as apparently it is working on a returns option — and also whether Amazon will expand its Amazon Returns service with Kohl's in the U.S. to include pick-ups.

Alexa is now a security guard, LG develops AI chip to power smart appliances

Alexa is now a home security guard. Amazon is rolling out Alexa Guard to all Echo owners in the U.S. that enables your Echo device to function as a home security device when you're out. You just need to say "*Alexa, I'm leaving*" and your Echo device will active "Smart Alerts" and listen for key sounds such as breaking glass or smoke/carbon dioxide alarms and then send you an alert with the audio recording (techcrunch.com). Meanwhile, Google (**Alphabet**) quickly reversed course on its decision to shut down its Works with Nest program on August 31, much to the relief of its customers and developers. Google still plans to move to a single integrated platform based on Google Assistant but the smart home set-up for Nest customers will not be interrupted — customers just won't be able to add any new devices and their Nest accounts will be moved to maintenance mode. In addition, Google is working with Amazon so Alexa and Nest can continue to work together (cnet.com). Speaking of the smart home, **LG** has developed its own AI chip to power its smart home appliances. The chip, which is embedded with the LG Neural

Engine, uses deep learning algorithms to enable its smart home devices to identify places, locations, objects and people in videos. It also helps the smart devices differentiate between speakers, noises and sounds, and analyzes physical and chemical changes to optimize the devices themselves (zdnet.com).

Amex acquires Resy restaurant booking platform, Luckin Coffee IPOs on Nasdaq

American Express is acquiring Resy, a restaurant booking platform that has raised $45 million since launching in NYC in 2014. Although Resy will provide American Express with valuable structural capital on the digital layer, it contributes very little in terms of supplier capital as it only has 4,000 restaurants in 154 U.S. cities on its platform, less than 10% of the over 51,000 restaurants on Open Table's (**Booking Holdings**) platform (fastcompany.com). We wonder what this means for Airbnb, a strategic investor in Resy, which has been using Resy to power its restaurant booking platform within its app since May 2017. **Luckin Coffee**, the new aggressive disruptive entrant in China to **Starbucks**, which was founded less than two years ago, went public on NASDAQ on May 17. Luckin Coffee priced its shares at the high end of its expected range, at $17, raising $561 million, which is on top of the $150 million Series B+ round it just raised and its $200 million Series B round in December. Although the stock opened at $25, nearly 50% above its IPO price, it closed the day at $20.38, up 20%, and has since traded down, close to its $17 IPO price (wsj.com). Like many young unicorns, Luckin Coffee is controversial with investors as it is more focused on growth than profitability, with a negative operating margin of 110% in Q119. Postmates, which is prepping to IPO, is coming under criticism for making changes to its pay structure. In addition to eliminating its $4 minimum job guarantee, it has lowered the base rate per job as well as the per-mile rate for drivers in some markets (techcrunch.com).

Bowery Farming disrupts the physical field with its AI-powered warehouse farms

Farming is moving up the structural capital side of the value pyramid. Bowery Farming is disrupting the physical field through its warehouse farms which leverage the digital and AI layers (e.g., LED lighting, robotics, data analytics) to grow leafy greens indoors. In addition to being more environmentally sustainable, using only 5% the amount of water and no pesticides, the warehouse farms are 100 times more productive per square foot than traditional farms and face no weather risk (cnbc.com). We note that Bowery Farming has raised $118 million since launching in NYC in 2015.

Amazon enters the travel space in India

Amazon is entering the travel space. It has partnered with Cleartrip, a leading online travel company in India, to start offering domestic flights in India to Prime members (techcrunch.com). It's interesting as last April, Cleartrip launched an Alexa skill to enable people to find the cheapest flight in India (gadgets.ndtv.com).

Is Amazon developing a YouTube competitor?

In January, Amazon filed a trademark application for FireTube, which seems similar to YouTube, as it would provide *"online network services that enable users to share content, photos, videos, text, data, images and other electronic works"* and deliver "*non-downloadable pre-recorded audio, visual and audiovisual works via wireless networks on a variety of topics".* Interestingly, this description seems very similar to the two trademarks Amazon filed back in 2017 for Amazontube and Opentube, when it also registered the domains AlexaOpenTube.com, AmazonAlexaTube.com and AmazonOpenTube.com (mediapost.com).

Chapter Eleven: The Road Not Taken

As I gaze wistfully at the cappuccino maker, yearning for it to come back to life, I can't help but think of the famous American Express slogan from the 1990s: "Membership has its privileges". And for me, one of the biggest privileges of being a member of WeWork is the experience of savouring a cup of cappuccino as I work away. It's interesting as more and more companies are embracing the membership subscription model as a means to deepen the emotional connection with their customers, increase loyalty and increase switching costs. For example, Uber is looking at launching an Uber Eats Pass which it could potentially bundle together with its Ride Pass ridesharing discount subscription. Urban Outfitters is copying Rent the Runway and launching an apparel rental monthly subscription service. Loop is launching its circular economy shopping platform which could provide opportunities for CPGs to introduce subscription models on the e-commerce layer. Life Time Fitness is looking to leverage its membership model with the introduction of Life Time Village, which offers Millennials the opportunity to live, work and work out under the same roof. Amazon keeps investing in promoting its Amazon Prime membership, this time with an interactive billboard in Times Square that uses augmented reality to showcase its upcoming "Good Omens" Prime Video show. And Facebook is trying to monetize its 2.4 billion members by launching its own "Global Coin" cryptocurrency next year.

As evidenced by these new strategic developments in the past week by Uber, Urban Outfitters, CPGs, Life Time Fitness, Amazon and Facebook, the convergence of societal, technological and economic factors is leading to the rise of the membership economy. And the winners in the new membership economy will be those companies that can keep offering us the best privileges while coming up with new ways to capture and extract value.

The Membership Economy: May 28, 2019

Facebook plans to launch "Global Coin" in early 2020

Facebook is planning to launch its own cryptocurrency in early 2020. This will enable Facebook to monetize its customer capital by empowering its 2.4 billion monthly active users to convert dollars and other international currencies into its "Global Coin" to use to buy things on Facebook and across the Internet, as well as transfer money without needing a bank account (theguardian.com). Mark Zuckerberg has apparently also been in talks about "Global Coin" with his Harvard classmate rivals, the Winklevoss twins, who founded the Gemini Trust bitcoin exchange in 2015 (cnbc.com). As we previously mentioned, this totally validates our thesis that those companies best positioned to transition up to the new crypto-economy, creating new ways to extract value, are not new ICOs but existing platform economy companies. On that note, according to Dead Coins, the number of ICOs that have joined the cryptocoin graveyard since we last reported on it in July has nearly doubled from 868 to now 1,647 (deadcoins.com).

Circular economy shopping platform Loop launches in Paris & NE U.S.

Loop, a new circular economy shopping platform developed by

TerraCycle in partnership with **UPS**, has just launched its pilot program in Paris and select zip codes in the Northeast U.S. states of D.C., Maryland, New Jersey, New York and Pennsylvania. To acquire customers, Loop is partnering with grocery retailers like **Carrefour** in Paris, **Kroger** and **Walgreens** in the U.S. and it will be partnering with **Tesco** when it launches in London later this year. This has the potential to introduce a subscription model on the e-commerce layer for CPG companies as it features hundreds of products in re-usable packaging from a wide coalition of CPG companies that customers can schedule to be picked up to send back when they are empty. The exciting part is that it enables CPG companies to design innovative re-usable containers and packaging, improving the functional and aesthetic features on the physical layer. Loop plans to launch in California, Tokyo and Toronto next year (supplychaindive.com).

Google adds food delivery button, DoorDash raises $600 million, Uber looking at Uber Eats Pass

You can now order food delivery directly through Google (**Alphabet**). Google has added a new "Order Online" button that appears when you search either Google Search or Google Maps for a supported restaurant. You can also order food delivery from a restaurant using Google Assistant. The ordering interface and payment are through Google and it has partnered with privately held DoorDash, Postmates, Delivery.com, Slice and ChowNow for the actual delivery. For now, Google does not support food delivery from privately held Deliveroo or leading publicly traded players like **Uber** Eats, **GrubHub** or **Just Eat** (techcrunch.com). Speaking of DoorDash, it just raised a $600 million Series G round only three months after raising a $400 million Series F round. DoorDash is achieving impressive growth as its annualized gross bookings reached $7.5 billion, up 280% from $2.0

billion a year ago. DoorDash now delivers for over 340,000 stores and restaurants in 3,950+ cities across the U.S. and 50 cities in Canada (techcrunch.com). If we assume a 20% commission, this implies DoorDash is generating $1.5 billion in revenue, which at its new valuation of $12.6 billion would equate to a valuation to revenue ratio of 8.4 times, which seems quite optimistic. **Ford** is partnering with Agility Robotics on a research project to test how two-legged robots can work together with self-driving vehicles to solve the curb-to-door problem (techcrunch.com). We note Agility Robotics has raised $8 million since being spun out of the Dynamic Robotics Laboratory of Oregon State University in late 2015.

Uber has an advantage over pure-play food delivery companies as it can leverage its ridesharing platform. For example, Uber is apparently looking to launch an Uber Eats Pass. For a monthly subscription fee of $9.99, Uber would waive its service fee, which equates to 15% of the order cost (techcrunch.com). It's interesting as Uber could potentially bundle this with its newly launched Ride Pass ridesharing discount subscription service to create an Uber Prime-like offering, which would increase switching costs and customer loyalty and position it to gain a greater share of wallet. The other growth option for Uber Eats is cloud kitchens. It recently started piloting a program in Paris where it rents out fully equipped commercial-grade kitchen space to restaurants selling food through Uber Eats. Interestingly, as a result of intense competition from Zomato and Swiggy on the food delivery front in India, Ola is pivoting Foodpanda, the Indian food delivery business it acquired from **Delivery Hero** only eighteen months ago. Instead of delivering food from third-party restaurants, Ola will only deliver curated food offerings from its own portfolio of private-label food brands and over fifty cloud kitchens (techcrunch.com).

Urban Outfitters launches an apparel rental subscription service

Urban Outfitters is trying to copy Rent the Runway, launching an apparel rental subscription service called Nuuly. Nuuly offers consumers a unique functional value proposition in terms of:

- *Price*: For $88 per month, you can pick six items, up to a combined value of $800, equating to a rental cost of $15 per item.
- *Variety of Choice*: Over 3,000 styles from Urban Outfitters' own brands (i.e., Urban Outfitters, Free People, Anthropologie), as well as outside labels like Reebok (**adidas**) and vintage pieces sourced from flea markets and dealers).
- *Convenience*: Order items online and return them in a reusable bag with a prepaid postage label with the option to purchase items you want to keep.

We expect more apparel brands to embrace rental subscription models as a means of increasing the switching costs and deepening the emotional connection with their customers, which are becoming both more cost and social conscious. For example, according to thredUP's *2019 Resale Report*, the number of women in the U.S. shopping second-hand rose 27% last year, from 44 million to 56 million.

Amazon encourages its warehouse workers to play video games on the job

Amazon is looking to improve the productivity of its pickers and packers by gamifying monotonous and repetitive tasks through video games on screens attached to workstations. Amazon is piloting this at five of its warehouses (digitaltrends.com).

Amazon is also gamifying Times Square in NYC with its new interactive experience to promote its upcoming Prime Video "*Good Omens*" show that uses billboards with augmented reality to show octopus tentacles, flying UFOs and raining fish descending upon the crowd (thedrum.com). We note that Amazon brought the "*Good Omens*" apocalypse to SXSW with its interactive "*Good Omens Garden of Earthly Delights*" interactive experience. And a month after closing all of its 87 mall-based pop-up stores, Amazon has quietly launched "Presented by Amazon" kiosks in four high-traffic malls (businessinsider.com).

The Avon lady has made her last call

Avon Products, whose physical door-to-door sales model has been disrupted by the rise of online DTC beauty companies, is being acquired by **Natura Cosmeticos**. Natura, which is Brazil's largest cosmetics company, is acquiring Avon via a share swap that values Avon at $2 billion and creates the world's fourth-largest pure-play beauty company (wsj.com).

Target is in preliminary talks to acquire Triad Retail Media from WPP

Target is reported to be in preliminary talks to acquire Triad Retail Media from WPP. Just like Walmart, which bought advertising tech company Polymorph Labs last month, Target is likely looking to capitalize on its supplier capital (i.e., long-standing relationships with big brands) and customer capital through expanding its in-house advertising business. Interestingly, Walmart, which was one of Triad's largest clients, is winding down its relationship with Triad as Walmart brings its digital ad business in-house (wsj.com).

Amazon is making strategic moves all over the map: going after Google and Facebook with its acquisition of Sizmek's ad tech plat-

form, extending its reach to hospitals and stadiums through its Alexa Smart Properties team, looking at breaking into the wireless space through the potential purchase of Boost Mobile from T-Mobile and Sprint, and enabling its AWS clients to extract text and structured data from millions of document pages in just hours with its new Textract platform.

And just days after the retail apocalypse wreaks total havoc on the stock prices of mall-based retailers Abercrombie & Fitch, PVH, J. Jill and Gap, Amazon further raises the structural risk for all retailers and retail REITs as it starts to roll out one-day delivery to U.S. Prime members. Even Walmart, which has been the most aggressive retailer in terms of moving up the structural capital side of the value pyramid, is threatened by this as its new next-day delivery service offers much less variety of choice (220,000 items versus 10 million for Amazon) and its goal is to reach only 75% of U.S. households by the end of this year. But Walmart knows it needs to pick up the pace and has just hired a 15-year Amazon veteran as its new CTO and CDO.

Adding to this chaos and uncertainty comes the depressing news from Merrill Lynch that the mighty P/E ratio, the top metric used by investors, no longer works as low P/E stocks have underperformed since 2010. And although Merrill blames market efficiencies and the rise in growth investing, I think the simple truth lies in my value pyramid: the acceleration in structural disruption has led to value flowing up the three capital sides of the value pyramid, changing the rules of the game for investors.

And on that final note, I'm excited to share with you the tagline I've come up with for the cover of my new book: the finale of the "Secrets of the Amazon" trilogy:

"A strategic map for investors & CEOs to survive & conquer the new disruptive era"

The Strategic Map: June 4, 2019

Deloitte calls for U.S. warehouse market to cool as supply outpaces demand growth

Our contrarian thesis on industrial REITs seems to be gaining support as the Deloitte Center for Financial Services warned in a report published on May 30 that the U.S. warehouse market will cool down as new supply outpaces demand growth. As you will recall, in our February 26 research report, *The Alpha Playbook to the Sensual Revolution*, we reversed our bullish stance on industrial REITs from being an emerging structural opportunity to having a moderate level of structural risk. Our thesis was that structural tailwinds from the race for the last mile will be offset by the following supply-side developments: 1) increased efficiency from growth in smart warehouses; 2) increased space utilization as warehouses expand vertically; 3) utilization of stores as distribution centres; and 4) conversion of retail into industrial space. Deloitte believes that warehouse demand peaked last year at 227 million square feet and expects it to drop to 129 million square feet by 2023, a reduction of 43%. At the same time, the growth in supply of warehouse space is expected to climb from 7.0% last year to 10.3% by 2023 (wsj.com). Interestingly, Singapore-based GLP, which was planning to spin off its portfolio of U.S. industrial warehouses in an IPO just two months ago at an expected valuation of over $20 billion (wsj.com), has decided instead to sell it to **Blackstone Group** for $18.7 billion. The U.S. real estate portfolio comprises 1,300 industrial warehouses totalling 180 million square feet, equating to an average value of over $14 million per warehouse, or $104 per square foot (wsj.com).

P/E ratio is still the most popular investor metric — but it is

a value trap

On June 1, CNBC published a fascinating article, *Everyone still relies on a stock's P-E ratio to invest, but a study shows it's bunk*, discussing the new quant study by Bank of America Merrill Lynch that found nearly 80% of investors rely on a company's P/E ratio, making it the most popular metric for the 14th consecutive year. However, this metric is not working as low P/E stocks have underperformed the market since 2010 while high P/E stocks, like the FANGs, have contributed to the majority of the market's gains. Merrill blames this on efficient markets already pricing the ratio into the market as well as the rise in growth investing (cnbc.com). However, we believe the real reason lies in our value pyramid: the acceleration in structural disruption has led to value flowing up the three capital sides of the value pyramid, changing the rules of the game for investors.

Retail apocalypse wreaks havoc on mall-based retailers

On June 3, **Amazon** started to roll out free one-day delivery for over 10 million products to Prime members in the U.S. (cnbc.com), raising the convenience bar and structural risk for all retailers and retail REITs. Ironically, this comes just days after the retail apocalypse wreaked havoc upon mall-based retailers. On Wednesday, shares of **Abercrombie & Fitch** plummeted 26%, the most since it went public, while shares of **PVH** declined 10%. On Thursday, **J. Jill** crashed 53% and on Friday, **Gap** dropped 9% (wsj.com). The bankruptcies and stores closures continue as **Arcadia Group**, the U.K.-based multi-national retailer, is closing all 11 of its Topshop stores in the U.S. as it files for Chapter 15 bankruptcy protection in the U.S. Arcadia Group plans to exit its U.S. operations and begin liquidating inventory in its U.S. stores (wsj.com). As we noted a few weeks ago, Arcadia Group, which saw its sales decline 15% over the holidays, has been involved in tense negotiations with landlords and pension regulators over plans to cut rents and close stores as it works toward a CVA (Company Voluntary Arrangement) in the U.K. And in the U.K., Amazon is opening ten "Clicks & Mortar" pop-up shops. Amazon is partnering on a year-long pilot with **Square**, Enterprise Nation and Direct Line for Business to provide 100 small online businesses with a physical presence (theguardian.com).

Amazon goes after Google and Facebook with Sizmek ad tech platform acquisition

Amazon is going after the digital ad duopoly of Google (**Alphabet**) and **Facebook** with its acquisition of part of Sizmek's ad tech platform — its ad server and dynamic creative optimization platform. This will give Amazon the second-largest ad serve footprint after Google, and provide it with a tool to help personalize ads using data, enabling it to expand its advertising market to companies that don't sell products on Amazon, like restaurants and airlines (cnbc.com). We note that Sizmek declared bankruptcy on March 30.

AWS rolls out Textract to enable clients to extract text and data from documents

AWS just announced it is rolling out Textract, its cloud-based fully-managed service that enables its clients to extract text and structured data from any document. Textract, which requires no machine learning experience, can process millions of document pages in just a few hours and is already being used by data-intensive organizations like the Globe & Mail, U.K. national weather service and PwC (venturebeat.com).

Alexa Smart Properties team extends reach to hospitals and stadiums

Amazon's Alexa Smart Properties team is empowering homebuilders and property managers and hoteliers with new ways to save time and costs, as well as harvest and manage data. For example, Alexa-fying rental apartments with smart locks and pre-installed Echo devices saves property managers time and costs by simplifying the ability to change door locks and grant access to contractors as well as reduce heating/AC costs in vacant units. More importantly, as evidenced by Alexa Smart Properties' new "*Sr. Manager of Business Development*" job posting, Amazon is looking to extend Alexa's reach in hotels, multi-family homes, master-planned communities, as well as new domains like hospitals and stadiums (wsj.com).

Amazon could be looking to break into wireless space

On May 30, Reuters reported that Amazon is interested in buying prepaid cellphone wireless service Boost Mobile from **T-Mobile** and **Sprint**. In advance of their planned $26 billion merger, T-Mobile and Sprint have agreed to sell Boost Mobile to reduce market share as one of the concessions to the Department of Justice. Acquiring Boost Mobile would allow Amazon to break into the wireless space, giving it access to T-Mobile's wireless network for at least the next six years and the potential to offer discounted cellphone service to its Prime members. In addition, Amazon has started to offer phone calls through Echo Connect (reuters.com).

Walmart hires Amazon veteran as new CTO & CDO

"The technology of today and tomorrow enables us to serve customers and associates in ways that weren't previously possible. We have started a significant digital transformation in our business, but we have a long way to go. We want to pick up the pace and increase the magnitude of change, so we're creating a new role, reporting directly to me, of Chief Technology Officer (CTO) and Chief Development Officer (CDO)". This statement by **Walmart**'s CEO,

Doug McMillon, in his May 28 internal memo underlines how aggressively Walmart is moving up the structural capital side of the value pyramid as it looks to take on Amazon (techcrunch.com). Interestingly, Walmart's new CTO and CDO is Suresh Kumar, a 15-year Amazon veteran, who, according to his LinkedIn profile, was "*responsible for technology that powers core retail functions such as pricing, promotions, catalog and vendor management for all Amazon properties worldwide*" when he was VP, Worldwide Retail Systems and Services from 2008 to 2014.

IKEA will finally let us shop online, iRobot's new cleaning robots work with each other

IKEA is launching a new app that will finally let its customers shop online, eliminating the need to trek out to the big blue box. IKEA is rolling out the app in France and the Netherlands and then to its next top eight markets, which includes Germany, China and the U.S. The app, which features AR, will help you find the ideal piece of furniture for your home as you will be able to enter your room dimensions and select from different styles as well as life stages (reuters.com). And **iRobot** wants to help you keep the floors in your rooms clean. It has unveiled its two newest cleaning robots, which can communicate with each other to take turns cleaning your floor. The new Roomba s9+ mop and Braava m6 vacuum use iRobot's new Imprint Link Technology and Home App (techcrunch.com).

Nike publishes sustainability manual for brands

Nike is publishing a guide to sustainability for brands, essentially a manual for designers that outlines the 10 principles of circular design and features case studies from its experiences as well as other brands such as Patagonia (fastcompany.com).

TheRealReal files for IPO, pink unicorns become less of a rarity, UN warns Alexa is sexist

TheRealReal, the world's largest online marketplace for consigned luxury goods, has filed to IPO on NASDAQ (ticker: REAL). TheRealReal raised a $115 million Series G round in July, bringing its total funding since it launched its luxury closet sharing platform in San Francisco in 2011 to $288 million and providing it with a $745 million pre-IPO valuation. Although TheRealReal does not yet qualify for unicorn status, it shares many of the same characteristics, exhibiting high growth (it sold $711 million in gross merchandise last year, up 45% from $492 million last year) but being unprofitable (its net loss widened from $52 million to $76 million last year) (cnbc.com). The one differing characteristic is that TheRealReal was founded by a female. But pink unicorns may become less of a rarity. Since March, three retail DTC brands founded by females have gained unicorn status: Away (suitcases), Glossier (beauty products) and Rent the Runway (apparel rental) (retaildive.com). Despite these advances by female founders, the tech industry remains quite sexist, as evidenced by Amazon's Alexa, **Apple**'s Siri and **Microsoft**'s Cortana all being female. As the United Nations warns in the 146-page research report from UNESCO, these voice assistants reinforce gender biases that women are subservient and tools of the patriarchy (wsj.com).

Airbnb starts to add hotels from HotelTonight to its platform

Airbnb is starting to transition to a hotel platform just months following its $400 million acquisition of HotelTonight, a last-minute hotel booking app. In addition to starting to integrate a limited number of HotelTonight hotel partners onto its Airbnb platform, Airbnb is moving toward the industry standard by eliminating the guest booking fee for hotels on its platform (skift.com). Although this will provide its guests with a greater variety of choice, it seems like a further red flag that Airbnb is trying to ramp up supply before going public and straying away from its community-driven social mission "*to belong anywhere*".

Two roads diverged in a wood, and I—
I took the one less traveled by,
And that has made all the difference.

Robert Frost – The Road Not Taken

As I watched Adam skip along the forest trail with his kindergarten friends, proudly wearing his birthday crown, I couldn't help but wonder where time has gone. It seems like only yesterday that I published my first research report as an independent analyst, just weeks after the birth of my first son, Brady, who is now 8½. And as you'll discover in my soon to-be-published finale of the "Secrets of the Amazon" trilogy, it was this research report, "Social Media: An Exposing Disruptive Force — Look for Companies with 'Heart' and 'Soul' But Beware of 'Empty Shells'" which I published back in January 2011 that formed the foundation of the first side of my Value Pyramid — customer capital. Although my new Value Pyramid seems simple, it is actually the product of my nearly decade-long intellectual journey down "the road not taken", researching the convergence of emerging societal, technological and economic forces.

The Road Not Taken: June 11, 2019

Big developments on transportation & logistics front from Amazon, FedEx & Walmart

Amazon debuted its new Prime Air delivery drone at its

re:MARS conference in Las Vegas on June 5. The drone, which can carry up to 5 pounds and fly up to 15 miles in half an hour, features a hexagonal hybrid design that allows it to take off and land vertically like a helicopter but fly horizontally like an airplane. Amazon designed virtually all of the drone's software and hardware stack in-house and has invested heavily in AI to ensure safety when flying and dropping off packages. The FAA just issued Amazon Prime Air a Special Airworthiness Certificate, giving it approval for the next year to operate its drone for R&D and testing purposes, but not commercial deliveries. However, Amazon expects to use the drone to start delivering packages to Prime members in a country likely outside the U.S. within months (cnbc.com).

As a sign of Amazon's increasing competitive threat in air freight and logistics, **FedEx** has decided not to renew its FedEx Express U.S. air service shipping contract with Amazon. However, FedEx will continue to serve as Amazon's carrier and last-mile delivery partner (cnbc.com). This defensive move comes only weeks after Bezos tweeted, "*We're investing $1.5 billion in our new air hub to get you your packages faster*" as he broke ground on Amazon's new air hub near Cincinnati/North Kentucky International Airport. As Amazon accounted for less than 1.3% of FedEx's total revenue last year, this move seems more of a signal to retailers that FedEx is focused on serving the broader e-commerce market. For example, back in in January, FedEx launched its Extra Hours delivery service to empower traditional retailers to compete with Amazon Prime by picking up the ordered products directly from the retailers' stores instead of from their regional distribution centres, thus reducing the shipping process by 2–3 days.

Walmart will soon start delivering groceries right inside your fridge. It is rolling out a pilot launch of its new InHome Delivery service this fall, making it available to nearly a million people living in Kansas City, Missouri and Vero Beach. Walmart is wisely controlling the customer experience by using its own employees to do both the grocery shopping and delivery, wearing Walmart-branded uniforms and driving Walmart-owned and branded cars. To alleviate privacy and security concerns, Walmart's employees will enter a one-time code on a smart lock to access the home while wearing a body camera device so homeowners can watch the delivery remotely (cnbc.com). We note Walmart first trialed an in-home delivery service with August Home back in September 2017.

Value stocks trading at deepest discount to market in the past 30 years

The rules of the game for investors are changing. According to JP Morgan's chief U.S. equity strategist, value stocks are trading at the deepest discount to the market in the past 30 years, on both a P/E and P/BV basis (marketwatch.com).

Alarms bells ring on U.K. high street, Hudson's Bay Company receives bid to go private

Alarm bells are ringing on the U.K. high street, warning of a fresh wave of store closures and job losses after the British Retail Consortium reported sales declined 2.7% in May, the weakest performance since it started the monthly survey in 1995 (theguardian.com). Meanwhile, Richard Baker, Chairman of **Hudson's Bay Company**, is leading a bid to take the struggling retailer private in an all-cash deal valued at $1.74 billion, offering C$9.45 per share, a 48% premium to Friday's closing price. The deal includes other shareholders, including Rhone Capital LLC and WeWork Property Advisors, which together control a combined 57% of the shares (wsj.com).

Amazon brings new innovations to fashion & beauty with The Drop, StyleSnap, & "try on"

Amazon is moving to the emotional level in fashion with its new shopping concept called The Drop. It is collaborating with a rotating roster of fashion influencers to create limited edition capsule wardrobes that it will drop every few weeks for only a 30-hour window. Interestingly, all products will be made on demand and shipped within 10 days (businessinsider.com). Interestingly, this new concept is looking to create demand through scarcity, which is the opposite of Amazon's traditional functional value proposition of an abundance of variety of choice. To help you shop for clothes, Amazon just launched StyleSnap, a new AI feature in the Amazon app. StyleSnap allows you to upload a photo of a fashion look you like and then it uses computer vision and deep learning to identify apparel pieces that are the closest match (techcrunch.com).

Amazon is also bringing **L'Oreal**'s AI-powered beauty technology to its site, enabling you to virtually try on lipstick. To use the AR "try on" feature you just need to take or upload a photo of your face or you can select from one of nine models that has your skin tone. And if you're on an Android, you can actually use Live Mode (allure.com). We're thinking this partnership might be deeper as L'Oreal is making this technology available for over 400 lipsticks listed on Amazon, not just its own brands. We note L'Oreal acquired this technology back in March 2018, with the acquisition of AR beauty start-up ModiFace, and last August it partnered with Facebook to develop AR experiences on its platform so its customers can see how they would look with different lipsticks, foundation shades or eye shadows. This illustrates how personal products companies like L'Oreal are ideally positioned to use the AI layers to enhance the customer experience and increase e-commerce conversion rates.

eMarketer expects digital ad spending to overtake traditional in the U.S. this year

eMarketer expects digital will pass traditional ad spending in the U.S. for the first time this year. It forecasts U.S. digital ad spending to increase 19% this year to $129 billion, accounting for 51% of total ad spending, up from 46% last year. In terms of players, eMarketer expects Amazon's share of the U.S. digital ad market to more than double from 4.0% last year to 8.8% this year. Interestingly, Amazon's share gains are expected to come mostly at the expense of smaller players as Google's (**Alphabet**) share is expected to only decline by 100 bp to 37.2% and **Facebook**'s by 30 bp to 21.8% (adage.com).

Voice payments to represent a new era of commerce, Alexa & Siri becoming more human

According to Amazon Pay VP, Patrick Gauthier, voice payments will represent a new era of commerce and it is "*akin to what happened with mobile maybe 10 years ago or even with e-commerce 20 years ago*". Amazon's latest research shows that one in four consumers in Europe are currently ready to buy with their voice. But, more importantly, he said Amazon still needs to understand how to use voice commerce to augment the customer experience before, during and after the purchase (cnbc.com). One way Amazon is improving the v-commerce experience is by enabling you to have a more normal conversation with Alexa and not have to constantly say her name. At its re:MARs conference, Amazon disclosed that it has developed a new dialogue system for Alexa that will predict next actions and switch between different Alexa skills which will go live to users in the coming months. It has also developed a new dialogue tool for developers called Alexa Conversations (techcrunch.com). Apple is also making talking to

Siri more natural as her voice will now be entirely generated by neural text-to-speech technology rather than a human-based recording. At Apple's WWDC 2019, Apple also announced that Siri will be able to read incoming messages to AirPod wearers and let them respond. And in the car, Siri will be compatible with more third-party apps like Waze and Pandora (**Sirius XM Holdings**). Apple also announced that iTunes will be divided into three separate apps for music, podcasts and TV (theverge.com).

Amazon launches credit card in U.S. for underbanked, sets up kiosks in U.K. train stations

In the U.S., Amazon is targeting the underbanked that have bad credit. It is partnering with **Synchrony Financial** to launch the "Amazon Credit Builder", which provides financial literacy tools and tips to let users build up credit through a secured credit card and then eventually graduate to an unsecured Amazon credit card (cnbc.com). This enables Amazon to expand its total addressable market to non-customers that shop at Walmart and the dollar stores, as it can now offer this card to people that aren't approved for an Amazon credit card. In the U.K., Amazon is setting up physical kiosks in train stations, offering passerbys a rotating selection of exclusive limited-edition products or cheap deals. Amazon is looking to offer a similar experience to its Amazon's Treasure Truck fleet of carnival-looking trucks that have been touring the country since December 2017 (techcrunch.com).

Google acquires Looker for $2.6 billion, Google reveals details for Stadia game platform

Google is looking to accelerate the growth of its cloud business through the $2.6 billion acquisition of Looker, a data analytics company launched in 2011 in Santa Cruz. According to Canalys, Google had a 7.6% cloud market share at the end of 2018, lagging **Microsoft** (13.7%) and Amazon (32%) (cnbc.com). Interestingly,

Alphabet's growth equity fund, CapitalG, is a strategic investor in Looker, having led its $82 million Series D round back in March 2017 and participated in its $103 million Series E round in December 2018. Google is looking to leverage its cloud through its new streaming game platform. Google will be launching Stadia in November in 14 different countries, including the U.S., U.K. and Canada. The initial "Founder's Edition", which costs $130, includes the hardware starter kit, a single game (*Destiny* 2) and a three-month subscription. Next year, Stadia will be coming to Android phones and eventually to all devices so you won't need to purchase a console — just pay the monthly $10 fee. But Stadia seems more like Amazon than **Netflix**, as you will need to buy the games from its cloud game marketplace, which will initially feature a selection of at least 31 games from 21 different publishers (theverge.com).

Bumble dating app opening first cafe

Bumble, the dating app which has grown to 60 million users since launching in Austin in 2014, is moving down the structural capital side of the value pyramid to the physical layer with the opening of its first cafe. Bumble is hoping its new Soho all-day café and wine bar, which will be yellow with hive branding, will serve as a meeting spot for its members in NYC as well as a venue for networking events (ny.eater.com). Interestingly, Bumble is not looking to make money from the café, but views it more as an investment to offer a unique experience to enhance the emotional connection with and between its members.

Chapter Twelve: Dr. Alexa

Although Alexa is at the age when most kids enter kindergarten, she just graduated from medical school. She is obviously gifted as since I first met her in February 2017, her learning has grown exponentially, from 10,000 to over 90,000 skills. And in May 2019, she earned her MD – becoming HIPPA-compliant. As you'll discover, Amazon has been making strategic moves into the healthcare space with the establishment of its not-for-profit healthcare venture Haven and acquisition of PillPack — but I believe Bezos' secret weapon for invading the $3.5-trillion healthcare space is a little girl not yet five years old – Dr. Alexa.

The Product: October 16, 2018

Dr. Alexa: Bezos' secret weapon for invading healthcare & advertising

Dr. Alexa? As further evidence of how Alexa is Bezos' secret weapon for invading the healthcare space, **Amazon** was just granted a patent it filed in March 2017 for a "*voice-based determination of physical and emotional characteristics of users*" that will enable Alexa to detect illness by analyzing your speech and voice data. In addition, the patent suggests that Amazon wants Alexa to be able to detect additional data, such as your emotional state, location, accent, age and gender, which Amazon could then use to send targeted ads, also advancing its push into the emerging frontier of advertising (thenextweb.com).

The Narrative: October 30, 2018

Amazon launches home health brand for people with diabetes and hypertension

Amazon has partnered with Arcadia Group, a health brand consultancy, to launch an exclusive brand of home health products. The Choice brand includes glucose monitors, targeting the 30 million Americans with diabetes, as well as blood pressure cuffs, for the one in three people diagnosed with high blood pressure. More importantly, Arcadia Group is looking to incorporate Alexa functionality into these devices in the near future (cnbc.com). We note that back in July 2017, Amazon hosted the $125,000 Alexa Diabetes Challenge in partnership with **Merck** to encourage innovators to experiment with creating voice-enabled solutions to empower those with type 2 diabetes to change their habits and improve their well-being.

The Amazon Man: November 14, 2018

Is Amazon using AWS to push deeper into healthcare?

Amazon is looking to push deeper into healthcare with AWS which just made its Translate, Transcribe and Comprehend services HIPPA eligible. This means that companies in the healthcare ecosystem can now use AWS to perform tasks like transcribing text from audio files, interpreting foreign languages and extracting insights from unstructured tasks (venturebeat.com). Faced with the threat of Amazon's upcoming launch of PillPack, **CVS Health** has made a desperate defensive move to lock in customers, piloting a membership program at 350 stores in the Boston area called CarePass. CarePass enhances the functional value proposition for customers through both convenience (i.e., free delivery on most prescriptions and online purchases and access to a pharmacist helpline) and pricing (i.e., a 20% discount on all CVS-branded products and a monthly $10 coupon) (cnbc.com). However, it seems like CVS is paying customers to become members as the membership fee is only $48 per year or $5 per month.

Below the Red Tide: November 27, 2018

Walgreens and Humana exploring to take stakes in each other

In June, **Walgreens** partnered with health insurer **Humana** to open senior primary care centres, opening two pilot centres inside Walgreen stores. Now the two companies are reportedly in preliminary talks to take stakes in each other and expand their partnership (cnbc.com). This could be highly strategic as it would enable Humana to leverage Walgreens' structural capital (i.e., its drugstores) and Humana's customer capital (i.e., it is the second-largest provider of private Medicare in the U.S. to seniors) to deepen their relationships with seniors. Interestingly, it was only back in April that **Walmart** was in early talks to acquire Humana. We believe augmented hearing devices and hearables could represent an opportunity on the healthcare front for Amazon, who just made the Alexa Mobile Accessory Kit, which it started to roll out in January, widely available to developers. This enables wearable devices (e.g., hearables, headphones, smartwatches, fitness trackers) to connect to Alexa by pairing with Bluetooth to the Amazon Alexa app (theverge.com). We note that just a few weeks ago, **Qualcomm** started to offer a pre-made chip integrated with Alexa for headphone manufacturers to drop into their headsets.

The Disappearance: December 4, 2018

Quip, the first-to-market DTC oral care subscription company that started selling its electric toothbrush starter kits in **Target** in October, has raised $40 million in equity and debt financing. More importantly, it looks like Quip is trying to move up the economic capital pyramid to the online marketplace layer as it is looking to build the supply side by launching a program for dental service providers to offer Quip's products to their patients (techcrunch.com). On the topic of healthcare, at the Forbes Health conference, John Doerr stated he is convinced that Amazon will roll out a Prime Health service (cnbc.com)

The Existential Threat: December 11, 2018

Peloton's Digital Membership could extend its disruption beyond SoulCycle

Ever since Equinox hosted a Lunch 'n Learn a week ago at WeWork, I've been thinking of re-joining as I used to love working out at Equinox when I lived in NYC. But I'm re-considering after learning how Peloton, which has raised $995 million since launching in NYC in 2012, has more than doubled its customer base in the past year and now has 4% more customers than SoulCycle (owned by Equinox), which actually saw a 10% decline in customers in the past year (recode.net). Like SoulCycle, Peloton has attracted a cult-like following by operating at the peak of the customer capital pyramid through its accessibility-focused social mission "*to use technology and design to connect the world through fitness, empowering people to be the best version of themselves anywhere, anytime*". Peloton is expensive as you need to purchase upfront a Peloton Bike, which starts at $2,950, and then pay $40 in monthly membership fees. But Peloton's disruptive power comes from its ability to leverage the physical object (i.e., the Peloton Bike) through the digital layer to offer customers a superior fundamental value proposition in terms of convenience (can work out anytime) and variety of choice (can virtually participate in up to 14 live studio spinning classes per day as well as access its growing library of now over 10,000 on-demand online classes). More importantly, the recent introduction of its $20 monthly Peloton Digital Membership, along with the addition of outdoor and indoor fitness classes, further enhances its variety of choice and, most importantly, offers an appealing price point to a much wider market, which could extend its disruption to health clubs.

Uber and Lyft expand into medical transport

To expand their total addressable market, both Uber and Lyft are making key strategic hires as they advance their medical transport efforts. Uber, which launched Uber Health in March, a HIPAA-compliant B2B ride-hailing platform for healthcare providers such as hospitals and clinics to assign rides for their patients and clinics from a centralized dashboard, has brought on health consultant Aaron Crowell and Dan Trigub from Lyft. Meanwhile, Lyft has hired Megan Callahan, a former **McKesson Corporation** executive to help expand its health transportation offering (cnbc.com). We note that in May 2017, Blue Cross Shield partnered with Lyft to offer free transportation to doctor appointments to its base of 106 million members in the fall while **Allscripts Healthcare Solutions** partnered with Lyft in March.

The next frontier for wearables: hearables

According to Gartner, the next frontier for wearables is hearables, defined as "ear-worn devices". The main use for hearable products such as **Apple** AirPods, **Samsung**'s Gear IconX and **Plantronics**' BackBeat FIT is communications, entertainment, and fitness and health coaching. However, as evidenced by Bose Hearphones, which are hearphones that enhance conversations, hearables are starting to extend into hearing aids and medical devices (scmp.com). To compete against Amazon's upcoming launch of Pillpack, **Walgreens** is partnering with **FedEx** to offer nationwide next-day delivery service for prescription drugs at a cost of $4.99 (wsj.com). This is the same rate that **CVS Health** started charging back in June when it rolled out its delivery program with the USPS. However, as we cautioned back then, just like the rise in grocery delivery is starting to reduce spending on impulse snack items at the check-out counter, we are concerned that the rise in prescription drug delivery could negatively impact front-of-store sales at drug retailers.

The Letter: December 18, 2018

Bad news for U.S. dollar stores: Lyft & Sun Basket seek to bring oasis to food deserts

To provide low-income consumers with limited transportation options access to healthier foods, Lyft is partnering with a non-profit in D.C. to give local families living in food deserts shared rides for only $2.50 to and from grocery stores such as Safeway and Giant (**Ahold Delhaize**). Lyft is running the pilot from January to June with 500 families in D.C. (theverge.com). The online healthy meal kit service Sun Basket is also targeting Americans living in food deserts — many of whom are struggling with pre-diabetes, hypertension and high cholesterol. Sun Basket, which has raised $113 million since launching in San Francisco in 2014, has partnered with the American Heart Association, American Diabetes Association and American Cancer Society to design some of its customizable meal plans for specific health problems. It also just appointed Dr. David Katz, the founding director of Yale University Prevention Research Centre, as its Chief Science Advisor and has partnered with a major insurer to conduct two pilot programs providing discounted meal boxes in California and a clinical trial measuring biomarkers in Louisiana diabetics (forbes.com). We believe these two initiatives foreshadow a rising threat of competition for dollar stores such as **Dollar General** and **Dollar Tree**, which prey on low-income consumers living in food deserts, selling them mainly shelf-stable processed foods.

Amazon partners with OMRON to develop the first Alexa-integrated blood pressure monitor

Amazon teamed up with Omron Healthcare (**OMRON**) to develop the first blood pressure monitor integrated with Alexa. By pairing the Omron cuff to Omron's mobile app and connecting to the Alexa skill, you can then ask Alexa to read your blood pressure, calculate your average reading, compare levels throughout different times of the day and even have Alexa remind you to take your blood pressure. As a foreshadowing of Amazon's intention to partner with health care companies, Omron Healthcare CEO Ranndy Kellogg, stated: "*My team here who wrote the skill worked hand-in-hand with Amazon's Alexa and Echo teams to build the skill, test it, and even add new features as Amazon makes them available to health care companies*" (cnbc.com). Interestingly, Amazon launched its own exclusive Choice brand of glucose monitors and blood pressure cuffs in October, stating its intent to incorporate

Alexa functionality into them in the near future. Amazon has also been exploring entering the consumer health diagnostics space, posing a competitive threat to testing giants like **Quest Diagnostics** and **Laboratory Corporation of America Holdings**. Apparently, Amazon was in discussions this year to buy Confer Health, a start-up that has raised $10 million since launching in Boston in 2015, which develops clinical-grade hardware for at-home tests for fertility and strep throat (cnbc.com). Apple is also making stealth moves into the healthcare space as CNBC has discovered that **Apple** has hired nearly 50 medical doctors in secrecy in recent years. The doctors are working across a number of different teams, including Apple Watch, health records and AC Wellness primary care (cnbc.com). Meanwhile, Walmart has extended its prescription services agreement with **Express Scripts** for three years. In addition, Walmart will participate in Express Scripts' pharmacy-savings program, InsideRx, which provides an average 40% discount to uninsured Americans using brand-name prescription drugs (wsj.com).

The Smart Toilet: January 8, 2019

Omron receives FDA clearance for its HeartGuide watch

Omron has received FDA clearance for its HeartGuide watch, which is able to take oscillometric blood pressure readings from the wrist. The watch, which will start shipping in January, costs $499. Omron is looking to start creating a personal baseline of health for people so it will be able to predict days or weeks ahead when a heart attack or stroke is imminent (wareable.com).

The Community: January 16, 2019

Walgreens partners with Microsoft while CVS looks to open health concept store

As a defensive move against **Amazon**, **Walgreens** has entered into a seven-year partnership with **Microsoft** to create "*new transformational platforms in retail, pharmacy and business services*". As part of the partnership, Walgreens will migrate the majority of its IT infrastructure to Microsoft's Azure cloud service and roll out Microsoft 365 to its 380,000 employees and its stores (theverge.com). At the JP Morgan Healthcare conference, **CVS Health** announced it will open its first retail health concept store focused on chronic disease next month in Houston. The store will feature care concierge services, enhanced screening for chronic disease, phlebotomy services and personalized prescription support. CVS Health is taking a patient-concentric approach as it starts to integrate its newly acquired healthcare insurer Aetna. CVS Health is launching a specialized support program for Aetna members to help prevent avoidable hospital re-admissions, as well as piloting a program that leverages its pharmacists to educate members on available care management programs (chainstoreage.com).

The Obsession: January 22, 2019

Could Apple's greatest contribution to mankind be about health?

Tim Cook believes **Apple**'s greatest contribution to mankind will be about health. Given this, it isn't surprising that Apple is in talks with private Medicare plans to discuss how to bring its Apple Watch to at-risk seniors to use a health tracker. With the latest version including fall detection and cardiac arrhythmia monitoring, it could be a valuable preventative device (cnbc.com). To validate the effectiveness of its technology, Apple is collaborating with **Johnson & Johnson** on a multi-year research study of seniors to analyze the impact of the Apple Watch on the early detection and diagnosis of atrial fibrillation. By accelerating the diagnosis of atrial fibrillation, they hope to be able to improve the health outcomes of the 33 million people worldwide living with the atrial fibrillation, which in the U.S. alone impacts 2.7 million people, resulting in 130,000 deaths and 750,000 hospitalizations annually (jnj.com).

What If?: January 29, 2019

Google gains FDA clearance for EKG smartwatch feature

Verily, **Alphabet**'s life sciences arm, has achieved FDA clearance for the electrocardiogram (EKG) feature in its smartwatch that allows healthcare researchers to study cardiovascular conditions. It doesn't sell its Study Watch, which it launched in April 2017 as a tool to improve clinical studies, to consumers as it is instead focused on building research partnerships with health firms. However, Verily could share its EKG technology with Google to launch an EKG-equipped smartwatch (businessinsider.com). We note that Google just paid $40 million to **Fossil Group** for its smartwatch IP, who it is collaborating with to create a new product line within its Wear OS family. This could provide competition on the healthcare front for the Apple Watch. Speaking of Apple, **Apple** Pay is adding 14,000 new stores to its U.S. retail footprint, including 1,850 **Target** stores, over 7,000 Taco Bells (**Yum! Brands**), Speedway (**Marathon Petroleum**) convenience stores, **Jack in the Box** restaurants and Hy-Vee supermarkets. Apple Pay is now supported by 74 of the top 100 merchants in the U.S., which translates to 65% of all retail locations (fortune.com).

The Empowerment: February 13, 2019

U.S. dollar stores could face rising threat of substitutes from health insurers

U.S. dollar stores like **Dollar Tree** and **Dollar General** will soon face a rising threat of substitutes as health insurers are starting to pilot subsidized meal delivery service programs to low-income consumers living in food deserts as a preventative health care measure. Health Care Service Corp., the fourth-largest health insurer in the U.S. serving 16 million members, is launching a new meal delivery service called foodQ targeting "food deserts" in 25 Chicago zip codes with plans to expand to 15 zip codes in Dallas in April. By providing convenient access to affordable but nutritious food, Health Care Service Corp. hopes to address the root causes of obesity and diabetes which lead to high healthcare costs. If the program is successful, Health Care Service Corp., which operates Blue Cross plans in five states, plans to scale it and potentially offer it to Blue Cross clients (forbes.com).

Amazon has started to sell smart hospital rooms

Amazon continues to expand its portfolio of medical supplies: it is now selling prefab hospital rooms. EIR Healthcare, a health care construction innovation firm, is selling its MedModular smart hospital room for $285,000 through Amazon Business, targeting hospitals and health care systems (cnbc.com). Drug retailers continue to go on the defense and are now experimenting with adding dental services to their stores to make healthcare more accessible and enhance their convenience value proposition. **CVS Health** is running a pilot program with SmileDirectClub, opening SmileShopExpress stores inside six of its drugstores which will offer 3D scans to create invisible braces. **Walgreens** just opened its first Aspen Dental location in Florida and plans to open a second in Q2 (cnbc.com). Even **Kohl's** is getting into the health and wellness game as it is partnering with **WW** (formerly known as Weight Watchers) on a series of wellness initiatives. Kohl's is providing WW with structural capital (it will open a WW-branded 1,800-square-foot studio in one of its stores in Chicago) and customer capital (Kohl's employees will receive access to a subsidized WW membership) while WW is providing Kohl's with supplier capital in the form of select WW kitchen products for Kohl's to sell in its stores and online starting in June (cnbc.com).

Aetna partners with Apple on health-tracking app

Aetna is partnering with **Apple** on a new health-tracking and motivation app called Attain. By providing rewards such as gift cards and Apple Watches, Aetna is hoping it will be able to incentivize its members to engage in healthy behaviours such as regular exercise, getting enough sleep, and remembering to take their medication and flu shot (cnbc.com). We note that Aetna, one of the largest U.S. health insurers with 22.1 million medical members, was acquired by **CVS Health** in November. Meanwhile, Verily, **Alphabet**'s life sciences arm, is pitching a prototype of a smart shoe with sensors to detect health-related issues by monitoring a person's weight, movement and even detect falls (cnbc.com). And to empower the deaf and those hard of hearing, Google just launched a new Live Transcribe feature for Android. By transcribing audio in real time, Live Transcribe, which will be available in 70 languages, lets deaf people read the text on the screen and carry on a conversation with others (techcrunch.com).

Smart?: February 19, 2019

Apple wants its greatest contribution to mankind to be about health

Tim Cook's aspirations for **Apple**'s greatest contribution to mankind to be about health are starting to take shape as Apple just hosted its first health-focused event at an Apple Store. Apple hosted a panel discussion on heart health at its Union Square Apple Store in San Francisco and demonstrated features on the Apple Watch. In support of Heart Month, Apple has scheduled three more events this month to also take place in Chicago and New York (cnbc.com). To increase convenience for Chinese tourists, **Walgreens** is more than doubling the number of U.S. locations accepting Alipay (**Alibaba**) from 3,000 to 7,000 by April. According to Nielsen, over two-thirds of Chinese tourists use their smartphones to pay while traveling abroad (pymnts.com).

$USTAINABILITY: March 5, 2019

Amazon appoints head for Pillpack, Cedars-Sinai hospital pilots Alexa in patient rooms

Amazon has taken a step closer to rolling out PillPack, which it acquired in September for $753 million, with the appointment of Nader Kabbani to run its new pharmacy business. Although Kabbani has no medical background, he is a 14-year Amazon veteran who helped build the Kindle self-publishing platform and was most recently in charge of Amazon Flex and other parts of its last-mile strategy (cnbc.com). Further to our thesis that

Alexa will be Amazon's secret weapon for healthcare, Cedars-Sinai hospital in LA is leveraging Alexa to empower its patients to control their TV and call the nurse. The hospital is piloting Aiva, which founded its voice-powered healthcare assistant for patient care in LA in 2016 (fortune.com). Interestingly, Amazon invested in Aiva's venture round in September through its Alexa Fund alongside Google. Amazon also announced it is launching its third Alexa Accelerator, which is part of its $200 million Alexa Fund (venturebeat.com). The not-for-profit healthcare venture between Amazon, **Berkshire Hathaway** and **JPMorgan Chase** is focusing on helping their 1.2 million employees by looking at how to redesign health insurance and is planning to deploy smaller-scale tests to improve access to primary care and reduce the costs of maintenance drugs. They are also looking to bring transparency to healthcare costs, although there are no current plans to compete with PBMs. These details were revealed by newly unsealed court testimony from one of its executives during the trial of a lawsuit filed by **UnitedHealth Group**'s Optum health-services to stop its former employee, David Smith, from working for the venture as it claims he is bound by a non-compete agreement (wsj.com). And Cult boutique fitness brand, Orangetheory Fitness, which operates 700 locations across the U.S. and another 300 internationally, hinted it is looking to partner with **Apple** on an initiative involving the Apple Watch. The partnership makes sense as one-third of Orangetheory's members already have Apple Watches and the concept behind Orangetheory is to get your heart rate past the maximum threshold, or "orange zone", for 12–20 minutes during the 60-minute class (businessinsider.com).

The Scooters: March 13, 2019

Amazon finally reveals the name of its new healthcare venture

The not-for-profit healthcare venture between **Amazon**, **Berkshire Hathaway** and **JPMorgan Chase** now has a name —Haven — which as its new website states: "*reflects our goal to be a partner to individuals and families and help them get the care they need, while also working with clinicians and others to make the overall system better for all*". Haven's vision seems to be based on an accessibility-focused social mission: "*we believe it is possible to deliver simplified, high-quality, and transparent health care at a reasonable cost. We are focused on leveraging the power of data and technology to drive better incentives, a better patient experience, and a better system*" (havenhealthcare.com). As evidence of how Amazon is already leveraging the power of data and technology, it is working with a Harvard-affiliated teaching hospital in Boston to test how AI can simplify medical care to improve operating efficiencies and reduce costs. For example, it is using Amazon's technology to better book operating time, help find important paperwork before surgery and predict when patients are likely to miss appointments with high-demand specialists (healthdatamanagement.com). On the hearables front, **Apple** is apparently working on an AR headset that would sync with your iPhone. The AR headset could be available as early as a year from now (techcrunch.com).

The Ubernomics Quake: March 19, 2019

Amazon now accepts HSA/FSA for OTC healthcare products

Amazon is moving deeper into the healthcare space. Americans now can use their HSA (health savings accounts) and FSA (flexible savings accounts) debit cards to pay for a wide range of eligible OTC products on Amazon. In addition to providing Amazon with valuable data to learn more about consumers' purchasing behaviour of healthcare products, it could be its first step into expanding into pharmacy and employer benefits (cnbc.com).

Dr. Alexa: April 9, 2019

Amazon positions to invade healthcare as Alexa becomes a MD

Alexa is now HIPPA-compliant, solidifying our thesis that Alexa is Amazon's secret weapon for invading the $3.5 trillion healthcare space. **Amazon** has launched an invite-only program in the U.S. for select developers from covered entities subject to HIPPA to create HIPPA-compliant skills for Alexa (cnbc.com). We note this follows Amazon's announcement back in November that AWS made its Translate, Transcribe and Comprehend services HIPPA eligible. To showcase the potential of Alexa's new medical capabilities, Amazon announced the launch of the following new Alexa skills:

1. ***Cigna***: Allows eligible employees to manage their health improvement goals and earn wellness incentives
2. ***Express Scripts (Cigna)***: Check status of home delivery prescription
3. ***Livongo***: Ask for last blood sugar reading
4. ***Boston Children's Hospital***: Its KidsMD skill enables the families of children dismissed from the hospital to ask specific questions from the care team and the doctor to remotely check in on the child's recovery process
5. ***Providence St. Joseph and Atrium Health***: Find an urgent

care centre or schedule an appointment

Eargo, a DTC hearing aid company, just raised a $52 million Series D round to advance its accessibility-driven mission "*to empower the world to hear life to the fullest*". On the hearables front, Eargo, which has now raised $135 million since it was launched in Mountain View, California in 2013, just launched Neo for $2,550, a small and virtually invisible hearing aid with Bluetooth connectivity that comes in an AirPods-style chargeable case (techcrunch.com).

A Different Species?: April 16, 2019

CVS Health partners with Target's Shipt to offer same-day prescription delivery

Faced with the new threat of Dr. Alexa, **CVS Health** is enhancing its convenience value proposition as it partners with **Target**'s Shipt to offer same-day prescription delivery for $7.99 from 6,000 U.S. locations, including 1,200 of the 1,600 CVS Pharmacy locations inside Target stores (digitalcommerce360.com). Interestingly, last June, CVS Health partnered with the USPS to offer one- or two-day prescription delivery for $4.99. In Australia, **Alphabet**'s Wing division is launching a pilot-drone delivery service. The drones will deliver small goods such as medicine, coffee and groceries from a range of local businesses to 100 homes outside of Canberra. Wing is now preparing to launch a trial service in Helsinki, Finland (engadget.com).

The Red Flag: April 25, 2019

Best Buy ventures deeper into healthcare with new partnership with TytoCare

Best Buy, which partnered with **Amazon** in April to become its exclusive brick-and-mortar seller for its new line of smart TVs, is looking to compete with it on the healthcare front. After acquiring connected health company Great Call Inc. for $800 million in August, Best Buy is venturing deeper into the healthcare space with its new partnership with TytoCare, an Israel-based mobile health platform and device start-up. Best Buy is now the official retailer for TytoCare's all-in-one digital diagnostics kit, which retails for $299.99 and is available online and at its stores in California, Ohio, Minnesota and the Dakotas (techcrunch.com). TytoCare will provide Best Buy with valuable supplier capital to offer Great Call's existing 900,000 senior customers and expand its portfolio of connected healthcare offerings. Interestingly, **Walgreens** was a strategic investor in TytoCare's $27 million Series C round last January.

The Lines: May 22, 2019

Google's Verily partners with pharmaceutical companies on clinical trials

Verily, **Alphabet**'s life sciences arm, is joining forces with pharmaceutical companies on clinical trials. Verily just announced strategic alliances with **Novartis**, **Otsuka**, **Pfizer** and **Sanofi** as they look to leverage Google's technology to reach patients in more targeted ways and to aggregate data across a variety of sources, including electronic medical records and health-tracking wearable devices. For example, Verily's clinical patient registry, Baseline, uses Google ads to find patients based on health-based searches (cnbc.com).

The Membership Economy: May 28, 2019

Amazon is working on a Dr. Alexa wearable that could read your emotions

As further evidence of how Dr. Alexa is Bezos' secret weapon for invading the healthcare space, **Amazon** is working on a voice-activated wearable capable of reading human emotions. The project, codenamed "Dylan", is a collaboration between Amazon's hardware R&D group Lab126 and its Alexa team (cnbc.com). We wonder if this is related to the patent Amazon was granted in October 2018 for a "*voice-based determination of physical and emotional characteristics of users*" that would enable Alexa to detect illness by analyzing your speech and voice data. In addition, the patent suggests that Amazon wants Alexa to be able to detect additional data, such as your emotional state, location, accent, age and gender, which Amazon could then use to send targeted ads, advancing its push into the emerging frontier of advertising. **Comcast** is also venturing into healthcare as it looks to capitalize on its unique access to people's homes through its cable service technicians. Comcast is working on an in-home device to monitor health metrics for at-risk individuals, such as seniors and those with disabilities, using ambient sensors, and is also building tools for detecting falls. Comcast plans to experiment with pilots at the end of the year and potentially release the devices commercially next year (cnbc.com). We note this is similar to **Best Buy**, which is venturing into healthcare to leverage its Geek Squad through its recent acquisitions of Great Call Inc. and TytoCare.

The Road Not Taken: June 11, 2019

CVS expands HealthHUB, fitness studios = new anchors, Peloton confidentially files for IPO

CVS Health is looking to compete against **Amazon** by providing "*convenient, personalized and integrated access to local healthcare*" by rolling its new HealthHUB concept to 1,500 stores by 2021. CVS is remodeling its drugstores to carve out at least 20% of the space for healthcare products and services, including an expanded health clinic staffed by experts such as dieticians and respiratory specialists which includes a lab for blood testing and health screening, and wellness rooms to host yoga classes and seminars for customers. The HealthHUB concept seems to be working as the first three stores that CVS opened in Houston in February have seen higher volume in terms of MinuteClinic traffic, prescription sales and front-of-the-store sales (cnbc.com). As evidence of the health and wellness trend, the new anchor tenants in urban neighbourhoods are fitness studios, like SoulCycle, Equinox and Orangetheory Fitness. According to CBRE, the number of fitness outlets in D.C. more than doubled from 80 in January 2014 to over 160. In turn, they are attracting healthy restaurants like Sweetgreen and juice bars like Juice Press, looking to capitalize on the traffic of health-conscious consumers, creating an ecosystem of health and wellness related businesses (wsj.com). Speaking of fitness, Peloton, the connected bike which has raised $995 million since launching in NYC in 2012, has confidentially filed for an IPO (techcrunch.com). Peloton has attracted a cult-like following by operating at the peak of the customer capital pyramid through its accessibility-focused social mission "*to use technology and design to connect the world through fitness, empowering people to* *be the best version of themselves anywhere, anytime"*.

Chapter Thirteen: A New Automotive Era

I remember first hearing about the automotive legend Bob Lutz when I joined Deutsche Bank's global auto research team in NYC in 2000. So when I came across the article he penned for Automotive News in November 2017, "Kiss the good times goodbye", I paid close attention. Like me, he believes value in the auto space will flow to the top of the Value Pyramid: "The era of the human-driven automobile, its repair facilities, its dealerships, the media surrounding it — all will be gone in 20 years... The value is going to be captured by the companies with the fully autonomous fleets...Automakers, if they are smart, may be able to adapt".

The Unicorn Stampede: October 23, 2018

Amazon partners with Sirius XM as Walmart partners with Advance Auto Parts

Amazon continues to drive faster into the auto space. Just after launching the $50 Echo Auto, it is now joining forces with **Sirius XM Holdings**, which recently acquired Pandora Media. As part of the partnership, Amazon will give customers that purchase an Echo device on its website a free three-month subscription to Sirius XM while Sirius XM will give away Echo Dots to customers that sign up for a subscription through Sirius XM's website. More significantly, Amazon stated it is looking to integrate Sirius XM with Alexa later this year (fastcompany.com). **Walmart** is also putting its foot on the gas pedal. It is partnering with **Advance Auto Parts** to create a specialty auto parts store next year on Walmart.com and offer home delivery and same-day pick-up at both of their stores. Although this partnership will basically just deepen Walmart's variety of choice of auto parts products and give Advance Auto Parts access to Walmart's customers, it is negative for auto parts companies as it will likely put downward pressure on prices (cnbc.com).

The Amazon Man: November 14, 2018

Alexa is driving deeper into the vehicles space

Alexa is investing in an on-demand parking service platform. The **Amazon** Alexa Fund is the lead investor in ParkWhiz's $5 million Series D round, which follows only two months after its first $20 million Series D raise. ParkWhiz, an on-demand parking spot platform that has been used by 40 million customers, recently created an Alexa skill to let people find and reserve parking spaces using their voice (techcrunch.com).

The Letter: December 18, 2018

Hertz debuts biometric scanners as it continues to lose share to Uber & Lyft

Hertz has debuted an airport gate that uses biometric scanners to speed up the car rental process. Hertz just opened its "*Hertz Fast Lane powered by CLEAR*" at the Atlanta airport which reduces the time to collect a car by 75% by enabling travelers to use fingerprint scanners and facial technology instead of showing their physical ID. Interestingly, the technology was developed by CLEAR, a biometrics company, which partnered with **Delta Air Lines** back in March. The service is available to Hertz Gold Plus Rewards members and the company plans to roll it out across 40+ locations next year (cnbc.com). Although it is positive that Hertz is moving up the structural capital pyramid to the AI layer, it continues to lose share to Uber and Lyft. For example, since we published our highly controversial research report on February 17, 2017, *Driving into the Abyss: How the Auto Fault Line is Creating Deep Structural Cracks for Avis Budget and Hertz*, ride-sharing companies have gained 15 percentage points on the U.S. ground transportation market as their share has risen from 56% to 71%, with two-thirds of this being at the expense of rental car companies whose share has declined from 33% to 23%.

As a foreshadowing of how automobile manufacturers may be able to use the AI layer to increase the speed and efficiency of the manufacturing process, **Tesla** has filed a new patent titled "*augmented reality application for manufacturing*" with the World Property Organization office (zdnet.com). Also on the transportation front, Google (**Alphabet**) just acquired Sigmoid Labs, the maker of one of the most popular train-tracking apps in India, for a reported $30 to $40 million. The *Where is My Train* app, which claims to have 10 million registered users, helps commuters track arrivals and departures and buy tickets for the 14,000 trains that run in India (techcrunch.com).

SoftBank-backed parking real estate tech firm acquires Impark

Most strategic acquisitions involve traditional firms buying start-ups, but not in this case. ParkJockey, a parking real estate tech firm launched in Miami in 2013, has received a strategic investment from **SoftBank** to fund the acquisition of two of the largest parking operators in North America. ParkJockey is acquiring Vancouver-based Impark, which operates 3,600 facilities in 330 cities, from Ontario Teachers' Pension Plan, as well as Citizens Parking, which operates 1,100 locations in over 20 cities. As James E. Hyman, CEO of Citizens Parking, states: "*ParkJockey is applying the latest technologies in online booking, consumer insights, and data analytics to maximize the value of parking spaces*" (businesswire.com).

The Community: January 16, 2019

Autos: The new voice battleground for Amazon and Google

As you need to be hands-free when you're driving, autos seem to be one of best-use cases for voice technology. In fact, according to a new survey from Voicebot.ai, the number of U.S. adults that use voice assistants on their smartphones is 90.1 million, in their car 77.0 million and via smart speakers 45.7 million (recode.net). We expect the usage of voice assistants in cars to continue to accelerate as **Amazon** has begun shipping Echo Auto, which it has received over 1 million pre-order requests for since it debuted the device in September. The Echo Auto is available on an invitation-only basis on Amazon's website for an introductory offer price of $25, half off its $50 list price (techcrunch.com).

Amazon is driving deeper into the auto space, entering into strategic partnerships with two navigation providers. **Telenav**, a Santa Clara-based connected car and location-based services provider, will be integrating Alexa directly into its in-car navigation system. Amazon is also partnering with HERE Technologies, a mapping data and GPS navigation software provider that is majority-owned by a consortium of German automobile companies (**Audi**, **BMW, Daimler**). Amazon will bring its Alexa voice-first in-car navigation system into the over 100 million vehicles equipped with HERE (techcrunch.com). **Alphabet**'s Google Assistant is following Alexa into the vehicle. At CES, Anker and JBL (**Samsung Electronics**) unveiled their new car chargers that bring Google Assistant into your vehicle. The $50 Anker Roav Bolt and the $60 JBL Link Drive plug into the 12-volt adapter in your car and then connect to your vehicle through Bluetooth or an auxiliary cable (theverge.com). Google Assistant is also now available on Google Maps, enabling you to use your voice to control navigation, reply to texts and play music (techcrunch.com).

The Obsession: January 22, 2019

Outdoorsy P2P RV marketplace raises $50 million

Outdoorsy, a peer-to-peer recreational vehicle (RV) marketplace founded in Austin in 2014, has raised a $50 million Series C round. Outdoorsy is looking to increase the utilization of RVs, which are an expensive asset and sit idle 97% of the time, disrupting the $32 billion RV market. Outdoorsy currently has 35,000 listings of RVs and campervans in eight countries and booked over 650,000 travel days last year. It plans to use the funds to nearly double its supply-side of listings to 65,000, expand internationally, and diversify its platform with the addition of campsites and outdoor travel experiences (statesman.com).

The Empowerment: February 13, 2019

Amazon makes strategic investment in self-driving start-up Aurora

Amazon just made a strategic investment in Aurora, the secret stealth self-driving start-up which was founded in December 2016 by autonomous vehicle veterans from **Alphabet**, **Tesla** and Uber. Aurora, which had previously raised a $90 million Series A round a year ago, just raised a $530 million Series B round (techcrunch.com). Speaking of Tesla, it is embracing Amazon as a new distribution channel. After only selling Tesla-branded merchandise on its own website, Tesla has opened a store on Amazon and has started selling a limited selection of its Tesla-branded merchandise, such as iPhone cases, hoodies, hats, coffee mugs and Tesla diecast model cars (businessinsider.com). Somewhat auto-related, AutoCamp, a glamping hospitality start-up launched in San Francisco in 2013, just raised its first round of capital: a massive $115 million venture round to advance its mission "*to connect people to the environment and each other*". AutoCamp, which currently operates three glamping sites in California (Russian River, Yosemite), will use the funds to buy land, outfit customized Airstream trailers and expand to up to 20 new markets. Interestingly, back in December, AutoCamp partnered with **Thor Industries**, the maker of the iconic Airstream, to be the exclusive developer of Airstream hotels (fastcompany.com).

Smart?: February 19, 2019

Amazon invests in electric pick-up truck start-up while Ford trials last mile delivery

Only a week after investing in the stealth self-driving start-up Aurora, **Amazon** has led a $700 million investment in Rivian Automotive, an electric pick-up truck manufacturer start-up. It was rumoured that **GM** would also invest but this is still unknown. Rivian plans to sell its R1T pick-up truck in fall

2020, which will feature a 400-mile range, hit 60 mph in three seconds and tow up to 11,000 pounds (cnbc.com). Interestingly, **Tesla** also has its sights on the electric pick-up truck market as Elon Musk alluded in his December 11 tweet: "*I'm dying to make a pickup truck so bad ... we might have a prototype to unveil next year*". We also note Rivian had only raised $201 million in debt financing since it launched in Detroit in 2009. Meanwhile, **Ford** is partnering with Gnewt, a zero-emission urban parcel courier, to trial last-mile delivery in London. The concept is to use delivery vans like those made by Ford as "*warehouses on wheels*" to serve as dynamic delivery hubs and drop off packages at strategic locations to for last-mile delivery by more nimble, efficient and cost-effective modes of transport like pedestrian couriers — and one-day bicycle couriers, drones or autonomous delivery robots. The parcel delivery process will be managed by Ford's cloud-based, multi-modal routing and logistics software MoDe:Link (logisticsmanager.com).

$USTAINABILITY: March 5, 2019

Tesla and Lyft signal the end of the line for the traditional auto ecosystem

"*The era of the human driven automobile, its repair facilities, its dealerships, the media surrounding it — all will be gone in 20 years...*" Investors would be wise to re-read automotive legend Bob Lutz's dire prediction for the entire auto ecosystem in his article, *Kiss the good times goodbye*, which I shared in my November 14, 2017 research note, *The End of the Line*, as it started to play out last week with Elon Musk's announcement he will be closing nearly all Tesla retail stores and Lyft's filing of its S-1. On February 28, Elon Musk announced the launch of **Tesla**'s long-awaited standard Model 3 electric vehicle for $35,000, achieving the ambitious vision he set out back in 2006 in *The Secret Tesla Motors Master Plan (just between you and me)* to create "*affordably priced family cars*". We believe this will be hugely disruptive to the entire auto ecosystem. In addition to disrupting the pricing equation for vehicles, he is also disrupting the industry's distribution channel cost structure with his decision to shift all global sales online. By closing nearly all of Tesla's retail stores, with the exception of a small number of stores in high-traffic locations that it will turn into showrooms, Elon Musk will be able to reduce its fixed cost structure and lower the average price of its vehicles by 6% (cnbc.com). However, we don't believe most automobile manufacturers, especially the Big Three (**GM**, **Ford**, **Fiat Chrysler**), will be able to follow this strategy as: 1) companies with social missions like Tesla are uniquely positioned to leverage their cult-like followings to drive DTC e-commerce sales as evidenced by the fact it already sells 78% of its vehicles online and 82% of its customers bought a Tesla without taking a test drive; 2) Tesla only has four different models of vehicles; and 3) Tesla is vertically integrated whereas The Big Three don't own their car dealerships. In addition to the auto ecosystem, the closure of Tesla retail stores will lead to vacancies for some Class A retail REITs.

The Ubernomics Quake: March 19, 2019

Amazon is creating Echo Auto skills

Amazon is looking for developers to build skills specifically for the Echo Auto. In its newly released guide, *Best Practices for Designing Alexa Skills for Automotive*, it advises developers to design for the driver and on-the-go situations, be succinct and limit phone and app interaction, enable a continuity of experiences and be location-aware.

The Two Flavours of Kool-Aid: April 2, 2019

Volkswagen partners with AWS to transform manufacturing & logistics processes

Volkswagen has entered into a multi-year agreement with Amazon's AWS to transform its manufacturing and logistics processes through machine learning, IOT and analytics. Volkswagen it looking to increase production flexibility, improve plant efficiency and increase vehicle quality by using AWS' technology to track and leverage real-time data from 122 manufacturing plants with the goal to eventually integrate over 30,000 facilities and 1,500 suppliers (cnbc.com). Meanwhile, **Daimler** Trucks, the world's largest truck manufacturer, is acquiring a majority stake in Torc Robotics to collaborate on the development of Level 4 self-driving trucks. Torc Robotics was founded in Virginia in 2005.

Dr. Alexa: April 9, 2019

BMW partners with Microsoft as VW introduces its first U.K. vehicle subscription service

Automobile firms are joining forces with tech companies to transform their manufacturing processes. A week after **Volkswagen** partnered with **Amazon**'s AWS, **BMW** is teaming up with **Microsoft** to create an Open Manufacturing Platform built on the Azure cloud platform with the goal to add 4–6 partners by year end. BMW, which already has 3,000 machines, robots and autonomous transport systems connected through its own IoT platform built on Azure, is looking to accelerate the development of smart factories and stimulate innovation (ca.reuters.com). Volkswagen is introducing its first vehicle monthly subscription service in the U.K. The service is available for three vehicle models — Golf, Passat, Tiguan — and offers a high level of convenience as it can be completed online in 48 hours and covers everything but fuel (fleeteurope.com).

The Red Flag: April 25, 2019

Ford becomes a co-investor with Amazon in Rivian Automotive and partners with AWS

Ford is making a $500 million strategic investment in Rivian Automotive, only two months after **Amazon** made a $700 million investment in the electric pickup manufacturer start-up. It's interesting as at the time, it was rumoured that **GM** would also invest. Ford plans to develop a new vehicle using Rivian's skateboard platform (cnbc.com). In addition to co-investing with Amazon in Rivian, Ford is partnering with AWS to create "*innovative mobility services and differentiated customer experiences*". As part of the deal, AWS will host the Transportation Mobility Cloud created by Ford's Automatic LLC which is designed to "*connect vehicles, mass transit, pedestrians, city infrastructure and service providers*" (siliconangle.com). We note this follows less than a month after **Volkswagen** partnered with AWS to transform its manufacturing and logistics processes and **BMW** teamed up with **Microsoft** to create an Open Manufacturing Platform built on the Azure cloud platform.

The Experience: May 2, 2019

Enterprise launching subscription car rental service as Ford joins Amazon Key In-Car

Enterprise Holdings plans to launch a monthly subscription car rental service in the next few weeks. This follows just weeks after **Volkswagen** announced it will be introducing its first monthly vehicle subscription service in the U.K. While automobile manufacturers like Volkswagen will be offering customers a reduced lease duration, car rental companies like Enterprise Holdings will actually be offering a longer lease duration. Enterprise Holdings is looking to offer a wide variety of choice, allowing customers to swap up to four times a month from of over 20 different makes and models from 6 different vehicle classes. The monthly fee, which it hasn't yet announced, will also cover expenses like maintenance, registration, insurance and Sirius (**Sirius XM Holdings**) radio (theverge.com). Meanwhile, **Ford** is joining **Amazon**'s Key In-Car service, which Amazon rolled out a year ago in partnership with **GM** and **Volvo** to deliver packages to the trunk of your car when it is parked in your driveway or at your office. Eligible Ford vehicles include Ford model 2017 or newer with FordPass Connect and Lincoln model 2018 or newer with Lincoln Way. The in-car delivery service will be available for Prime members in 50 cities across the U.S. (techcrunch.com).

The Rules: May 7, 2019

Toyota launches its 2nd $100 million AI Venture Fund as Maersk invests in FreightHub

Since **Toyota** launched the $100 million Toyota AI Ventures fund in July 2017, it has made 16 investments in early-stage robotics and autonomous technology start-ups. It is now launching a second $100 million fund focused on the unbundling of mobility in areas such as ridehailing and micromobility (techcrunch.com). The digitization of logistics is accelerating, with participation from industry players. For example, Maersk Growth, the corporate venture arm of container shipping giant **A.P. Moeller Maersk**, is a strategic investor in the $30 million Series B round for FreightHub. FreightHub, which was launched in Berlin in 2016, offers digitized transport services for sea, air and rail freight. The digitized services include booking, communications, data exchange, document management and supply chain optimization (techcrunch.com).

The Naked Unicorn: May 14, 2019

GM's Cruise raises $1.15 billion as Amazon is in talks to acquire TuSimple

Cruise, the autonomous driving start-up which **GM** acquired for $1 billion in March 2016, has just raised a $1.15 billion corporate round. This values Cruise at $19 billion, which represents over one-third of GM's current market capitalization of $52 billion. Cruise's new round included existing strategic investors like **Honda**, **SoftBank** Vision Fund, and its parent company GM. To achieve its goal of deploying its commercial robo-taxi service in San Francisco by the end of the year, Cruise is looking to double its talent base to 2,000 employees (wsj.com). We note that only three weeks prior, SoftBank Vision Fund invested in the $1 billion round for Uber ATG along with strategic investors **Toyota** and **Denso**, valuing it as a separate corporate entity at $7.5 billion.

According to a Chinese media post, **Amazon** is in talks to acquire TuSimple, an autonomous driving technology company. TuSimple has raised $178 million since launching in San Diego in 2015, with NVIDIA participating as a strategic investor. TuSimple, which operates in Beijing, San Diego and Arizona has 12 customers and is expanding its on-road fleet to 50 autonomous trucks (siliconangle.com). We note that Amazon has been making strategic moves into trucking and logistics with its investments in February in Aurora (self-driving start-up) and Rivian Automotive (electric pickup truck manufacturer start-up). In addition, in early May, we learned that Amazon is entering the freight brokerage space as it has been internally testing a new online service to match truck drivers with shippers.

The Strategic Map: June 4, 2019

Waymo brings its self-driving trucks back to Phoenix

Waymo (**Alphabet**), which started testing its self-driving trucks in Arizona, California and Georgia in 2017, is now bringing its self-driving trucks back to the Phoenix area. Interestingly, Waymo's in-house development system is designed to be used by any type of vehicle (autonews.com).

The Road Not Taken: June 11, 2019

Mercedes' & Hertz's new subscription car rental service signals the end of car ownership

The death of a car salesman is the ominous title of the article in the FT that explores how the shift from car ownership to car sharing via subscriptions threatens to upend the century-old automobile business model. **Volvo** — whose exhibit at the Los Angeles Auto Show stood out as it had no cars on display just a website to promote its new subscription service —

predicts that half of its cars will be diverted to its subscription product line by 2025 (ft.com). It's not just Volvo — Mercedes-Benz (**Daimler**) is expanding its "Mercedes-Benz Collection" subscription service to Atlanta based on the success of its year-long pilot in Nashville and Philadelphia, where 82% of its subscribers were new customers. Its luxury vehicle subscription service, which is available with three tiers of pricing, ranging from $1,095 to $2,995 per month, offers customers a superior value proposition in terms of variety of choice, with unlimited access to over 50 different models. Most importantly, it offers a new level of convenience with on-demand access to swap vehicles via the app, after which a concierge from Mercedes will deliver the customer the new vehicle, with a tank full of gas, and take back the old one. The service also comes with insurance, 24/7 roadside assistance, vehicle maintenance and unlimited mileage (techcrunch.com).

While automobile manufacturers like Mercedes-Benz offer customers a reduced lease duration, car rental companies like Enterprise Holdings — and now Hertz — are offering a longer lease duration. **Hertz** plans to launch a monthly subscription vehicle rental service called Hertz My Car. Although Hertz is pricing its monthly subscription below Enterprise Holdings ($999 for basic and $1,399 for luxury versus $1,499 for Enterprise), it offers less variety of choice as customers are only allowed to swap vehicles two times a month versus four times for Enterprise. In terms of convenience, they both cover expenses like maintenance, registration, insurance and roadside assistance (engadget.com).

Apple looks to acquire Drive.ai as Fiat Chrysler partners with Aurora

Apple is rumoured to be looking at acquiring Drive.ai, a start-up specializing in deep learning-based driving software that has raised $77 million since being founded in 2015 by two young researchers from Stanford's AI Lab (cnbc.com). Meanwhile, **Fiat Chrysler** is strategically partnering with Aurora, a self-driving start-up founded in December 2016 by autonomous vehicle veterans from Google (**Alphabet**), **Tesla** and **Uber.** Fiat Chrysler is integrating Aurora's technology into its Ram Truck commercial vehicles, including its cargo vans and trucks (techcrunch.com). We note that **Amazon** made a strategic investment in Aurora in February 2019 when it raised a $530 million Series B round.

Chapter Fourteen: The UBERcorn

I still remember taking my first Uber ride — I was visiting NYC with my husband and then one-year-old. I was so inspired by that experience that I wrote the LinkedIn article, "Social Capital: The Secret Behind Airbnb and Uber", which, as you know, motivated me to start researching the sharing/on-demand economy and led to the creation of my Ubernomics book two years later. It has been a long wait as my baby is now in kindergarten. I was excited to read through Lyft's S-1 prospectus on the flight to the SXSW conference in Austin in mid-March but as I wrote in my "Why I'm Not Drinking the LYFT Kool-Aid" which I published on March 26 (pre-IPO), I was concerned about the five dashboard warning lights that were flashing red. In contrast, after digging into Uber's S-1, I realized that Uber was a different species of unicorn than Lyft, and on April 29 (also pre-IPO) I recommended investors "Take A Once-In-A-Lifetime Ride On An UBERcorn".

The Unicorn Stampede: October 23, 2018

Uber looking to IPO early next year at astronomical valuation of up to $120 billion

We have a few updates on Uber, which is preparing an IPO for early next year — at an astronomical valuation of up to $120 billion! Uber is apparently developing Uber Works, a short-term staffing platform for events and corporate functions (techcrunch.com). This is a brilliant strategy as in addition to adding diversification to Uber's operations, Uber Works would enable Uber to leverage its existing supplier capital (i.e., its millions of Uber drivers that might want to earn extra income working as a waiter or security guard), its existing customer capital (i.e., its corporate customers) and its structural capital (i.e., its infrastructure and technology). And looking to the future, it would provide alternative employment opportunities for its drivers as it starts to displace them with autonomous vehicles. Flying burgers? Uber is looking at launching food delivery drones as early as 2021. UberExpress, the drone delivery operations unit within Uber Eats, posted a job listing for a drone executive to "*enable safe, legal, efficient and scalable flight operations*" (wsj.com). This isn't too sci-fi as back in June, **Alibaba**'s Ele.me received regulatory approval to start delivering restaurant meals by drone in Shanghai's Jinshan Industrial Park. The deliveries will take 20 minutes and will be dropped off by drones at two fixed locations within the 58-square-kilometre industrial area.

The Existential Threat: December 11, 2018

Uber and Lyft file to IPO next year at reported valuations of $120 billion and $15 billion+

Late last week, Uber and Lyft filed confidential paperwork with the SEC, setting the stage for two of the most anticipated IPOs (wsj.com). With Uber looking at a valuation of $120 billion and Lyft $15 billion+, this provides real evidence that value in the auto space is flowing to the top of the customer capital pyramid (i.e., they have built cult-like followings through their respective social missions), to the top of the structural capital pyramid (i.e., they operate on the digital and AI layers) and to the middle of the economic capital pyramid (i.e., they are both online ride-sharing platforms).

Lyft is targeting to hit the market in March or April while Uber was looking to IPO in the second half but may move to the first half if market conditions worsen. Lyft, which has raised $4.9 billion since launching in San Francisco in 2012, actually evolved out of Zimride, a ride-sharing company founded back in 2007. Despite its sustainability-focused mission "*to take cars off the road*", Lyft has brought on board **GM** and **Magna International** as strategic investors. In the third quarter, Lyft's revenue rose 88% to $563 million but it lost $254 million. Uber has raised $24.2 billion since launching in San Francisco in 2009 with the accessibility-focused mission "*to bring transportation as reliable as running water to everyone, everywhere*". Uber is over five times the size of Lyft, with its revenue in the third quarter rising 38% to $2.95 billion with a loss of $1.07 billion (wsj.com).

However, Uber and Lyft could face rising labour risks on the supplier side. For example, the NYC Taxi and Limousine Commission just ruled that starting in mid-January 2019 ride-sharing platforms like Uber and Lyft must pay drivers a minimum hourly rate of $17.22 after expenses, which equates to a gross rate of $28/hour (fortune.com). Based on the Commission's estimate of an average increase of $10,000/year for 96% of the 80,000 ride-sharing drivers in NYC, this will result in a total increase of over $750 million in labour costs for ride-sharing firms.

The Letter: December 18, 2018

Uber testing Uber Eats Pool

According to Stephen Chau, Head of Products for Uber Eats, Uber intends to become a marketing platform for restaurants. One way Uber Eats is looking to gain influence with customers is through testing a new concept called Uber Eats Pool. Just like Uber Pool saves you money by sharing a ride, Uber Eats Pool will save you money by allowing your food to share a ride (techcrunch.com). Careem, a Dubai-based ride-sharing company founded in 2012, is also expanding into food delivery as it believes the opportunity for deliveries is even bigger than ride-hailing. Careem, which is trying to close a massive $500 million funding round, is looking to invest over $150 million to build Careem Now, its food delivery service that will have its own app and operate independently (techcrunch.com).

The Smart Toilet: January 8, 2019

Didi Chuxing expanding into financial/insurance services – could Uber be next?

Financial services companies could face the threat of new entrants such as ride-sharing companies that are ideally positioned to leverage their transaction data to gain valuable insights into personal spending and risk profiles. Didi Chuxing, China's largest ride-hailing company, is expanding into financial and insurance services. This comes as ride-hailing companies operating in China face tighter driver regulation with all drivers required to hold a local residency permit as well as a commercial driving license as of January 1. Didi will start to offer auto loans, as well as health and auto insurance to its drivers, and then offer credit and wealth management services to drivers and passengers (techcrunch.com).

The Obsession: January 22, 2019

Lyft files VR & AR patents

Lyft is exploring ways to integrate virtual reality (VR) and augmented reality (AR) into Lyft rides. In July 2017, Lyft filed two patents: one for a VR transportation experience and one that would overlay virtual objects on a passenger's real-world surroundings to help with the pick-up or drop-off process (techcrunch.com). Interestingly, in October 2018, Lyft acquired Blue Vision Labs, a London-based AR start-up that had raised $17 million since launching in 2016.

The Empowerment: February 13, 2019

Uber Freight continues to raise the bar for trucking brokerage firms

Uber Freight is introducing a new Yelp-like feature on its app called Facility Ratings to create a new level of transparency into shipping and receiving facilities for its drivers. This follows just two months after it debuted Lane Explorer to introduce a new level of price transparency for its shippers. With Facility Ratings, Uber Freight hopes to empower drivers by enabling them to rate their experience at shipping and receiving facilities from 1 to 5 and leave written comments. Since Uber Freight piloted Facility Ratings two months ago, it has gathered ratings on over 10,000 facilities, enabling it to provide drivers with valuable crowdsourced intelligence as well as amenities information such as the availability of restrooms, overnight parking and online scales. In addition to improving the driver experience, Uber Freight hopes to increase efficiency and safety. For example, according to the U.S. Department of Transportation the annual loss from time wasted idling at facilities ranges from $1,300 to $1,500 per driver, totaling $1.1–$1.3 billion for the industry and for every 15 minutes drivers spend at the facility beyond the 2-hour detention window, the probability of a crash increases 6.2%.

$USTAINABILITY: March 5, 2019

Lyft files its long-awaited S-1

On March 1, Lyft filed its long-awaited S-1. Lyft is looking to go public on NASDAQ under the ticker "LYFT" at an expected valuation of $20–$25 billion. We note this would be 32–66% higher than the $15.1 billion valuation reached last June from its $600 million Series I round which was led by Fidelity. Lyft has raised $4.9 billion since it evolved in May 2012 out of Zimride, a ride-sharing company founded back in 2007. Lyft is staying true to its sustainability-focused mission "*to take cars off the road*" as it states in its S-1 how Lyft is at the forefront of the massive societal change from car ownership to Transportation-as-a-Service (TaaS) as: 1) an estimated +300,000 Lyft riders have given up their personal cars; 2) almost half of Lyft riders use their cars less; and 3) 22% report owning a car has become less important. Lyft has been gaining share of the U.S. ride-sharing market from Uber, as it reached 39% market share at the end of the year, up from 22% two years ago. In 2018, Lyft's revenue doubled to $2.2 billion, driven by the combination of a 76% increase in its bookings and a 370-bp improvement in its revenue cut to 26.8%, but it is not profitable as it reported a net loss of $911 million. Lyft's revenue rose 95% to $670 million in Q418, resulting from a 48% increase in the number of active riders to 18.6 million and a 32% increase in revenue per rider to $36.04. Lyft's key strategic stakeholders are **Rakuten** (13%), **GM** (8%) and **Alphabet** (5%).

The Scooters: March 13, 2019

Lyft starts its IPO roadshow a month ahead of Uber

Lyft started its IPO roadshow on March 18 and is targeting to start trading on NASDAQ as early as March 29. Lyft plans to sell 30.77 million shares, at a price ranging between $62 and $68 per share, raising between $1.9 billion and $2.1 billion. This would imply a valuation of $21–$23 billion. In addition to being highly unprofitable, losing $911 million last year on revenue of $2.1 billion, Lyft has a high level of corporate governance risk as its two co-founders have nearly 50% voting control, despite owning only 7% of the stock (wsj.com). Uber is following close behind, apparently planning to release its S-1 and start its IPO road show in April. Uber is looking to go public at an expected valuation of $120 billion (cnbc.com). In preparation for its IPO, Uber is in talks with a consortium of investors, including **SoftBank**, to raise $1 billion for its autonomous vehicle unit, valuing the unit at between $5 billion and $10 billion (wsj.com).

Scooters will accelerate the shift from car ownership to Transportation-as-a-Service

In addition to investing in autonomous vehicles, both Uber and Lyft are investing in a nearer-term solution that will accelerate the shift from car ownership to TAAS by helping to solve the first and last-mile challenge: scooters. In fact, I counted that Lyft actually mentions the word "*scooter*" 158 times in its newly filed S-1. Uber launched its first Jump scooter in Santa Monica in October, only six months after acquiring Jump, a bike-share start-up, for $200 million. Since then, Uber has expanded its Jump scooter-sharing platform to 17 cities in North America, as well as Berlin and Lisbon, with plans to launch in Montreal as early as this spring (cbc.ca). Importantly, Uber is rolling out a custom electric dockless scooter later this year that promises to be more comfortable, durable and difficult to vandalize (fortune.com).

The Unicorns are Coming: March 26, 2019

Ford bringing its Spin scooters to 100 cities as WeWork launches "future cities" initiative

The scooter wars are heating up. **Ford**, which acquired Spin for $100 million in November, will be launching Spin scooters in 100 cities by the end of this year (techcrunch.com).

The Two Flavours of Kool-Aid: April 2, 2019

Five new major strategic developments add toxicity to the LYFT Kool-Aid

Since I published my March 25 research report, *Why I'm Not Drinking the LYFT Kool-Aid & New Insights from SXSW*, there have been five major new strategic developments that add to the toxicity of the **LYFT** Kool-Aid:

1. **Limited Ability to Take Increasing Cut of Bookings from Drivers**: On March 25, hundreds of Uber and Lyft drivers in LA held a 25-year strike, protesting Uber's recent announcement it will be cutting drivers' pay per mile by 25%

in LA and parts of the OC. The strike was organized by Rideshare Drivers United, which is calling for minimum pay that matches NYC's new legislation mandating a $28 per hour salary for ridesharing drivers before expenses (nbcnews.com). This protest highlights our concern that while Lyft has been able to take a greater cut of the bookings from its drivers (from under 20% in 2016 to 28.7% in Q418), its ability to take an increasing cut is limited.

2. **Uber Making Aggressive Moves to Gain Share from Lyft**: Uber is expanding its Ride Pass discount subscription service, which it has been piloting for the past five months in 5 U.S. cities, to an additional 17 cities across the U.S. At a monthly cost of $15–$25, Ride Pass offers a compelling value proposition for frequent riders as it offers savings of up to 15% for UberX and UberPool and eliminates surge pricing. With Ride Pass, Uber is looking to increase both the number of rides per rider and switching costs and customer loyalty (digitaltrends.com).
3. **Lyft's Valuation Discount to Uber Should Widen as Uber Expands Geographically:** Uber is acquiring its Middle East rival, Careem, for $3.1 billion, comprising $1.7 billion in convertible notes and $1.4 billion in cash. Careem, which currently serves over 30 million customers in 120 cities in 15 countries in the Greater Middle East, launched in Dubai in 2012. Uber is looking to close the acquisition of Careem by Q120, pending regulatory approval. Uber intends to operate Careem as a stand-alone operation, led by its founders, to maintain its homegrown brand appeal (techcrunch.com).
4. **Lyft's Valuation Discount to Uber Should Widen as Uber Expands Uber Freight**: Uber is bringing Uber Freight to Europe, launching first in the Netherlands with plans to access

other parts of Europe in the near future. The $400 billion European truckload marketplace is the third largest in the world, behind China and the U.S. (uber.com/newsroom).

5. **New ride-sharing Entrant in China Challenges Assumption of Lyft/Uber Duopoly in U.S.**: Could the Lyft-Uber ride-sharing duopoly in the U.S. ever be challenged by a new entrant? What would happen to the astronomical valuation of Lyft, and, to a lesser extent, Uber, if the Big Three (**GM**, **Ford**, **Fiat Chrysler**) decided to strategically join forces with tech giants like Google (**Alphabet**), **Apple** and **Amazon** to build a ride-sharing and autonomous driving platform? This is exactly what is happening in China... Didi, the Chinese ride-sharing giant that has raised $21 billion since launching in Beijing in 2012, will soon face the threat of a new entrant called t3. A consortium of a dozen Chinese retail, automobile manufacturing and tech companies is forming the t3 joint venture, investing $1.45 billion with the mission to build a "*smart mobility system*" by developing "*car-sharing services powered by renewable energy*". They plan to start running a fleet of 5,000 cars in late May or early June. Retail giant **Suning** is the largest shareholder, with 17% equity, followed by three state-owned Chinese automobile manufacturers (FAW Group, Donfeng Motor Corporation, Changan Automobile) which each have 16% equity, and the remaining 35% is split between tech giants **Alibaba** and **Tencent Holdings** and six smaller firms. Ironically, Alibaba and Tencent Holdings are both investors in Didi. Interestingly, the three automobile manufacturing firms signed an agreement to work together back in December 2017, and in July 2018 they created a new entity called T3 Mobile Travel Service to explore ride-

sharing and autonomous driving (techcrunch.com).

A Different Species?: April 16, 2019

Lyft's stock price falls 22% below its IPO price

Investors are no longer drinking the Kool-Aid on **Lyft** as its stock price has fallen 22% below its IPO price and 35% below its $87 opening price on March 26. Lyft is now facing operational challenges with its electric bikes as it is temporarily pulling its fleet of 3,000 electric bikes from its bike-share programs in NYC, D.C. and San Francisco owing to a braking problem. To prevent service interruptions, Lyft is working to replace the electric bikes with traditional bikes. Electric bikes currently represent 15% of Lyft's fleet of 20,000 shared bikes in these three cities (cnbc.com).

Uber offers a global platform play on the future of transportation and delivery

Investors might want to take a closer look at Uber. In addition to being one of the rare publicly traded companies to operate at the peak of all three sides of the value pyramid, it offers a global platform play on the future of transportation and delivery. Based on my initial review of its S-1, here are my insights:

- **Uber's Revenue Growth Trajectory Is Slowing**: Uber grew its platform bookings last year 45% to $50 billion as its number of active riders rose 34% to 91 million. But its core platform adjusted revenue only rose 39% as its cut of bookings declined 80 bp to 20.1% as a result of competitive pressures and negative mix shift (Uber Eats has grown from 9% to 16% of bookings). However, Uber's number of active riders added each quarter has been on an upward trend the past three quarters.

- **Uber Loses Money on Each Ride But Its Operating Loss is Narrowing as It Gains Operating Leverage:** Uber is still unprofitable but its operating loss narrowed last year from $4.1 billion to $3.0 billion. However, it is gaining operating leverage as all of its line expense items have declined on a per-ride basis, resulting in its operating loss per ride declining 47% to $0.58 in 2018.
- **Uber Is the Leading Global Ride-sharing Player:** Uber operates in 63 countries around the world and offers upside on the growth in ride-sharing in China, Russia and Southeast Asia through its equity ownership in Didi (15.4%), Yandex Taxi (38.0%) and Grab (23.2%).
- **Uber Is Leveraging Its Platform through Uber Eats and Uber Freight:** Uber is capitalizing on its customer, structural and supplier capital by expanding into food delivery (Uber Eats) and trucking logistics (Uber Freight) which results in network effects and operating leverage.
- **Uber Is a Play on the Future of Autonomous Vehicles:** Uber's Advanced Technologies Group, which has grown to 1,000 employees, spent $457 million last year on R&D and Uber has entered into strategic partnerships with Volvo, Daimler and Toyota to deploy their autonomous vehicles onto its platform.

Uber continues to innovate its platforms. For example, it is expanding its total addressable market with Uber for Business' launch of Uber Vouchers, which enables businesses to cover the cost of an Uber ride for their customers or employees (travelandleisure.com). Uber is also bringing a new level of transparency to Uber Eats. It now sends you real-time updates, including the ETA, enabling you to visually track the Uber driver's route to the restaurant, the restaurant preparing your order and the Uber driver's route to your location (engadget.com).

The Red Flag: April 25, 2019

The red flag we raised on Lyft's market share is now playing out in court

One of the red flags we raised on **Lyft** in our March 26 research report, *Why I'm Not Drinking the Lyft Kool-Aid*, is now playing out in court as investors have filed two separate class-action complaints against Lyft claiming it exaggerated its U.S. market share at 39% in its prospectus (bloomberg.com). As you will remember, in our report, we expressed our concern about the lack of disclosure in Lyft's S-1 in terms of its U.S. ride-sharing market share. Specifically, we stated:

Lyft reports that, according to Rakuten Intelligence, its share of the U.S. ride-sharing market rose from 22% in December 2016 to 39% in December 2018. This raises three red flags:

- ***Potential conflict of interest**: Rakuten Intelligence's parent company, **Rakuten**, holds over a 5% equity stake in Lyft.*
- ***Accuracy of data**: Second Measure reports that Lyft's market share stood at 28.9% in January 2019, up from 18.0% in January 2017 and 25.9% in January 2018.*
- ***Missing data points**: Why did Lyft not provide us with its historical quarterly market share?*

The Experience: May 2, 2019

Uber offers public transport data in London & expands driver loyalty program in U.S.

Uber has integrated public transport data from Transport for London into its app, providing real-time information on public transportation options (e.g., tube, bus, rail, train, river boat) in the city of London (theguardian.com). This more collaborative approach seems to be part of its global strategy to rebuild goodwill with stakeholders, and especially in London where Uber was granted a provisional 15-month operating license back in June 2018. It also might be a step toward launching a subscription service in London, like it is doing in the U.S. with its Ride Pass discount subscription service which aims to increase customer loyalty and improve retention on the demand side. On the supply side, to attract and retain high-quality drivers, Uber is expanding its Uber Pro driver loyalty program which rewards high ratings and low cancellation rates. Uber, which it has been testing Uber Pro in 10 cities since it launched in November, is rolling it out nationwide across the U.S. to 20 more cities and will start testing it in Mexico. Rewards include cash back on fuel purchases, discounts on vehicle maintenance and free roadside assistance with the highest perk being free college tuition at Arizona State University (theverge.com).

Lyft expands subsidized shared ride program for low-income consumers in food deserts

Lyft is also working to build goodwill with cities. It is launching the Grocery Access Program to provide low-income consumers living in food deserts with subsidized shared rides so they can have access to healthier foods. Lyft will give local families living in food deserts shared rides for an average flat fare of only $2.50

to and from partner grocery stores. Lyft, which started to pilot the program in December in D.C. and expanded it to Atlanta, is rolling it out to a dozen cities in the U.S., and to Toronto and Ottawa in Canada (engadget.com). As we've previously mentioned, this could be negative for U.S. dollar stores, like **Dollar Tree** and **Dollar General**.

The Naked Unicorn: May 14, 2019

Uber's IPO gets hit by the perfect storm as its stock price tumbles 18%

Uber ended up pricing its IPO at $45 per share, equating to a valuation of $82.4 billion, or 6.8 times revenue, right in line with Lyft, but down considerably from its initial targeted valuation of $120 billion, or 10.6 times revenue. However, Uber was hit by the perfect storm — in addition to rising negative investor sentiment on Lyft, President Trump's decision to impose higher tariffs on $200 billion in Chinese imports led the market to tumble over 300 points just as it started trading on Friday, causing Uber to open at $42 and close the day at $41.55. On Monday, China retaliated and raised tariffs on $60 billion in U.S. goods to as high as 25%, sending the market down over 600 points and Uber's stock price plummeting a further 11% to $37.10, down 18% from its IPO price. Uber is now valued at $68 billion, a discount to Lyft (at 6.0 times versus 6.4 times revenue) despite Uber's superior geographic diversification, multiple platforms and greater growth opportunities, plus its equity in Uber ATG, Didi, Grab and Yandex Taxi. Uber's IPO does not bode well for Postmates, which is preparing to IPO in June or July. Postmates raised a $100 million Series F round in January, bringing its total funding since it launched in San Francisco in 2011 to $678 million and valuing it at $1.85 billion. Postmates is less than one-third the size of Uber Eats, generating $400 million in revenue last year versus $1.46 billion for Uber Eats, and operates only in the U.S. whereas Uber Eats operates globally (wsj.com).

Gett B2B ride-hailing start-up raises $200 million while Lyft might have to upgrade its scooter fleet

Gett, the Israeli B2B ride-hailing start-up founded in 2010, just raised a $200 million Series E round, including a strategic investment from **Volkswagen**. Gett, which operates in Israel, U.K. Russia and NYC, only lost $3.5 million on revenue of $1 billion last year as it focuses on the higher-margin business market with 20,000 corporate clients. Gett, which is now valued at $1.5 billion, is targeting to IPO next year (telegraph.co.uk). As another red flag for **Lyft**, it might soon have to upgrade its scooter fleet to commercial-grade, increasing its future scooter capex. For example, Bird is migrating its fleet of shared e-scooters from consumer-grade scooters made by **Xiaomi** and Segway-Ninebot to commercial-grade. The new Bird One, which it is also selling directly to consumers for $1,299, offers superior functionality with a battery that lasts twice as long and a longer range of 30 miles per charge. Most importantly, it improves the expected economics as the company expects it will last over four times longer (verge.com). As we explored in our March 25 research report, *Why I'm Not Drinking the LYFT Kool-Aid & Insights from SXSW*, Bird was losing nearly $300 per scooter based on an average RLI of 2.5 months. Based on the longer RLI of 10 months, we calculate the scooter would need to cost Bird less than $1,050 for it to breakeven; however, this doesn't take into account the many scooters that are vandalized or stolen. Meanwhile, in India, Uber is partnering with Yulu on a pilot project to offer shared bikes on its app in the city of Bengaluru. However, Yulu is a small player in the micromobility space as it has only raised $7 million since launching in India in 2017 and only has 4,500 bikes and e-bikes on its platform (techcrunch.com).

The Lines: May 22, 2019

New developments lower Uber's risk in U.S. and raise it slightly in U.K.

In the past week, we have seen three developments, which reduce Uber's risk profile in the U.S. and raise it slightly in the U.K.:

- **Driver reclassification risk reduced in the U.S.:** One of **Uber** and **Lyft**'s biggest supply-side risks was just lowered as the U.S. National Labor Relations Board issued an advisory memo stating that Uber drivers are independent contractors, not employees: "*Drivers' virtually complete control of their cars, work schedules, and log-in locations, together with their freedom to work for competitors of Uber, provided them with significant entrepreneurial opportunity*" (theverge.com). Interestingly, this is similar to what we wrote in our April 29 Uber research report regarding Driver Reclassification risk: "*However, the taxi industry sets precedence for companies such as Uber since most taxi drivers are deemed independent contractors in that they lease the vehicles from the taxicab company itself and pay for all associated costs such as gas and maintenance. Uber could also argue it provides even more freedom for its drivers as they are free to set their own timetables, drive their own vehicles and drive for other companies*".
- **GM Maven is no longer a future threat in North America:** **GM** is scaling down Maven, its vehicle-sharing platform,

with plans to exit 8 of 17 North American cities over the next few months, including Boston and Chicago (wsj.com). We note that GM launched Maven in January 2016 to meet the shifting demand for Millennials opting for on-demand transportation alternatives in cities where car ownership is expensive. This could be negative on the supply side for ridesharing and gig economy companies whose drivers rented vehicles through Maven Gig, but in the long term, it is a positive for Uber, and moreso for Lyft, as it eliminates the threat of future competition from Maven.

- **Competition increases for Uber Eats in the U.K. as Amazon invests in Deliveroo:** Amazon is getting back into restaurant delivery in the U.K. — it just led the $575 million Series G round for Deliveroo (bbc.com). It's interesting as Amazon retreated from the U.K. in November as it quietly closed Amazon Restaurants U.K. after finding it too difficult to compete against Deliveroo, Uber Eats and **Just Eats**. Deliveroo, which was launched in London in 2012, delivers food from over 80,000 restaurants in 500+ cities and towns across 14 countries, including the U.K. Australia, Hong Kong and the UAE. Although the re-entry of Amazon into restaurant delivery poses a competitive threat to Uber, its Uber Eats business only accounts for 13% of its core platform revenue and Deliveroo does not operate in North America, which accounts for over one-half of Uber's revenue. Interestingly, back in September, Uber was apparently looking to acquire Deliveroo.

New developments enhance Uber's growth profile

In the past week, we have seen the following four developments, which enhance Uber's growth profile:

- **Uber's potential to enter financial services rises**: Our thesis that Uber is uniquely positioned to create new blue oceans in financial services just strengthened on the news that Ola, the ridesharing leader in India, is following the recent moves by Didi and Grab into financial services. Ola is capitalizing on its customer and structural capital (i.e., relationship and data on its 150 million users) to expand into financial services. Ola is partnering with **Visa** and SBI Bank to issue as many as 10 million credit cards over the next 3 1/2 years which can be managed digitally through the Ola app (techcrunch.com).
- **Uber Eats looking to expand into grocery**. As we noted back in December, Uber Eats was hiring a head of grocery product in Toronto with the goal to "*build the organization and globally scale a brand new product offering which will fundamentally evolve how people purchase their groceries*". Now, Uber has announced it is opening a new engineering hub in Toronto, which it expects to grow to 400 employees, to focus on new products such as Uber Grocery, as well as Uber Marketplace health and Uber Fintech tools (mobilesyrup.com).
- **Enhances experience for Uber Black customers**: If you don't want to talk with your Uber driver, you can now select "Quiet Mode". Uber is introducing "Rider Preference" features for its Uber Black customers, enhancing the customer experience by enabling them to advise their driver if they have bags with them as well as select their desired temperature in the car (warm or cold) and their desired level of conversation (yes or no). Uber is hoping this will shift customers toward its premium and higher-margin Uber Black product as well as further differentiate it from Lyft (techcrunch.com).
- **Potential to improve pick-up efficiency at airports**: Do you

remember the old days when you used to have to stand in line at the airport to wait your turn for a taxi? Uber is piloting a new way to match passengers with drivers at the Portland Airport — instead of getting matched directly to a driver, passengers will receive a 6-digit PIN numeric code and then wait their turn in a line where they will be matched in turn to the line of drivers. Interestingly, Uber developed this PIN-matching solution back in 2016 to serve high-volume, high-density event venues and has used it at over 60 events globally since. This could reduce wait times and improve pick-up efficiency for Uber at locations like airports where many people want to depart from a single destination, which could be significant given rides to or from airports generated 15%, or $6.2 billion, of Uber's ridesharing bookings last year (techcrunch.com). We note that last month Lyft started to pilot a similar 4-digit PIN code at San Diego airport.

The Membership Economy: May 28, 2019

Uber brings Jump e-bikes to London & scUber submarine rides to Great Barrier Reef

First, **Uber** integrated public transport into its app in London and now, it is bringing its Jump electric bikes to the city. These goodwill gestures are not surprising given Uber's provisional ridesharing license in the city of London is set to expire in September. Uber is trialing 350 Jump bikes in the borough of Islington but no scooters as they are still illegal in London (techcrunch.com). We note that since Uber brought its Jump electric bikes to Europe in November, it has rolled them out in Lisbon, Paris and Brussels, and has rolled out is electric scooters to Paris and Madrid. In Australia, Uber is partnering with Queensland to launch the scUber — the world's first ridesharing submarine. Travelers can now use their Uber app to book a one-hour ride on a submersible to explore the Great Barrier Reef in Australia. The cost for the one-hour ride for two people is $2,060, which includes a helicopter ride to the scUber (travelandleisure.com). And **Lyft** is looking to making ridesharing more affordable with its Shared Saver option, which is targeted at those who want to save money by sharing their ride and don't mind walking a few blocks to a more general pick-up/drop-off location. Lyft is expanding Shared Saver from NYC, Denver and San Jose to six more large U.S. cities (engadget.com).

The Strategic Map: June 4, 2019

Uber makes strategic moves to restore its brand equity

Uber is making a number of strategic moves to restore its brand equity, which is important as management disclosed on its Q1 2019 conference call that "*signs of competition is becoming more focused on brand and products versus incentives*". For example, Uber is now holding riders accountable for their behaviour with the announcement that it will start de-activating riders in the U.S. and Canada with low ratings. This comes as Uber releases its new Community Guidelines which promote "Safety and Respect for All" with three principles: 1) treat everyone with respect; 2) help keep one another safe; and 3) follow the law (techcrunch.com). Uber is also taking a more collaborative approach with cities, as evidenced by its new partnerships with public transit bodies such as Denver's Regional Transit District. In January, Uber integrated real-time public transport data into its app, providing real-time information on public transportation options in the city of Denver, like it just did with the city of London last month. Now Uber is taking the integration in Denver one step further, enabling people to buy public transit tickets directly on the Uber app (forbes.com). Although this may cannibalize some of Uber's ridesharing sales, it is part of its bigger play to build a multimodal transportation network. In addition, it may enable it to expand its total addressable market by bringing those that take public transit into its Ridesharing and Uber Eats platform ecosystem. And Uber is bringing its Jump dockless electric bikes to Canada, starting with the launch of hundreds of Jump bikes in Montreal's city centre this month (cbc.ca).

The Road Not Taken: June 11, 2019

Uber merging Uber Eats into main Uber app, Uber launches Uber Copter in NYC

Uber is starting to capitalize on its multi-platform ridesharing and food delivery model by merging Uber Eats into its main Uber ridesharing app. This will enable Uber to do cross-promotions, reducing its customer acquisition costs on each platform, providing it with a significant competitive advantage against pure-play ridesharing platforms like **Lyft** and pure-play food delivery platforms like DoorDash. The merged app is currently available in iOS in all cities where Uber doesn't offer micromobility transportation options (i.e., shared e-bikes and e-scooters) (techcrunch.com). Uber is offering a new transportation offer — entering the urban air mobility market with the launch of its new pilot helicopter service in NYC. Interestingly, Uber is leveraging Uber Copter to promote its Uber ridesharing loyalty program, as access is only available to members of the two top-tier levels of its loyalty program (fortune.com).

Chapter Fifteen: Secrets of WeWork

It didn't take long for me to start drinking the WeWork Kool-Aid after I joined the tribe in October 2017. But I had no clue that I was becoming part of a fast-growing cult that would grow from 168 to over 650 locations worldwide. In 2009, Adam Neumann and Miguel McKelvey planted the seeds for their WeWork movement, inspired by their community-based social mission to empower people to "Make a Life. Not Just a Living". A decade later, in January 2019, guided by their original vision, they re-branded WeWork to The We Company, signaling their intent for global domination as they advance with the new highly aspirational mission "to elevate the world's consciousness". It's fascinating as Adam Neumann shared a slide from the pitch deck he put together for "The we brand companies" back in 2009 which included not just we work and weLive, but also weSleep, weConnect and weBank, confirming my thesis that WeWork has always been more of a human capital play than a real estate play.

The Curator: October 2, 2018

WeWork brings WeWork Labs to Toronto

WeWork, which partnered with the City of Toronto in June to launch Toronto Start-up Passport, is now bringing WeWork Labs to Toronto. This will be the first Canadian location for

WeWork Labs, which has grown to 12 cities since launching early this year (betakit.com). Speaking of Toronto, **Shopify** is aggressively planning to expand its headcount in Toronto, which currently stands at 700 employees, and its office footprint. In addition to leasing 178,000 square feet at King Street West in early 2019, Shopify is in the final stages of negotiation to sign a 15-year lease for 254,000 square feet at The Well for $384 million (bloomberg.com). As we discussed in last week's research note, Spaces (**IWG**) also just signed a lease for 127,158 square feet in The Well at 460 Front Street West being developed by **Allied Properties REIT** and **Riocan REIT**, which is set to open in 2022.

The Offense: October 10, 2018

Boundaries blurring between co-working and retail

Just like **Amazon** is building a physical foundation with Amazon 4-star and Amazon Go to enhance its emotional connections with its Prime members, it seems to be following the same game plan to enhance its emotional connections with its AWS customers. Ironically, although Amazon is a member of WeWork, it is also starting to build its own network of co-working spaces called AWS Loft, which is available for free to its AWS customers. Amazon, which operates permanent AWS Loft locations in San Francisco, New York and Tokyo, also operates pop-ups in major cities such as London and Tel Aviv. In addition to providing a place for start-ups and developers to meet, Amazon offers free technical sessions, technical bootcamps and walk-in appointments with AWS technical experts (geekwire.com). The boundaries between co-working and retail seem to be blurring as WeWork, which debuted its new retail concept, WeMRKT, in June inside its WeWork at 205 Hudson, has expanded WeMRKT to three more locations in NYC with plans to open 500 more WeMRKT stores over the next few years along with an e-commerce store (digiday.com). As we observed in our July 4 note *The One-Two-Three Punch*: "*WeMRKT is a brilliant concept — by creating a small shop featuring curated merchandise of snacks, office supplies and WeWork-branded apparel from select member firms, it enables it to create a physical marketplace "by our members, for our members", leveraging both its customer and structural capital*".

The Product: October 16, 2018

WeWork in talks to raise $15–$20 billion from SoftBank

SoftBank is in discussions to take a majority stake in WeWork, making an investment of between $15 billion and $20 billion from its $92 billion Vision Fund, resulting in a pre-IPO valuation of up to $40 billion (techcrunch.com). We note that WeWork raised $1 billion from SoftBank in the form of a convertible bond in August and $4.4 billion from SoftBank in a private equity round in August 2017. Further to our thesis that WeWork will be more of a human capital play than a real estate play, WeWork is launching the WeWork Creator Fund, a venture fund to invest in social impact start-ups and "future of work" technology start-ups focused on HR, recruitment, training and education, employee experience and real estate. The venture fund will also house the existing 50 investments WeWork has made through its $20 million Creator Awards initiative (wsj.com). We believe this is a brilliant strategy as it enables WeWork to leverage its structural capital (i.e., it is the home for tens of thousands of start-ups around the world) and its customer capital (i.e., its community managers interact with the members of start-ups on a daily basis). We note that in June, WeWork Labs partnered with

Mercer International (**Marsh & McLennan**) to launch an eight-week accelerator program to incubate, support and grow the next generation of start-ups focused on workplace innovation.

The Unicorn Stampede: October 23, 2018

WeWork expanding in Japan & NYC as it partners with Rent the Runway

WeWork, which opened its first location in Japan in February, is planning to expand to 11 locations in four cities by the end of the year and reach 10,000 members. WeWork's alliance with **SoftBank** (a 50/50 joint-venture partner in WeWork Japan) is a competitive advantage as it provides it with credibility with both companies and property developers as it looks to attract enterprises such as **Kawasaki Heavy Industries**, which moved six members of its innovation team into WeWork in May. Co-working is gaining popularity in Japan; according to CBRE, co-working space now accounts for 7.9% of office space in Tokyo, up from only 0.5% in 2009 (ft.com). WeWork also continues to aggressively expand in NYC and has leased all 11 office floors of 609 Fifth Avenue in Midtown Manhattan from **SL Green Realty**, totaling 139,000 square feet. **Puma** has leased the bottom two retail floors (commercialobserver.com).

As office real estate becomes more consumerized, office building owners and landlords will need to figure out how to move up the customer and structural capital pyramids in order meet the rising expectations of tenants. On this note, Convene, which recently raised a $152 million Series D round from strategic partners such as **Brookfield Asset Management**, has launched a turnkey solution to help Class A office landlords and building owners design, build and/or manage flexible work and amenity spaces (techcrunch.com). By providing them with control over the space, design and branding, Convene will help landlords compete against WeWork, which is gaining an increasing share of the enterprise market though initiatives such as its recently launched Powered by We office-space-as-a-service and its new HQ by WeWork, a WeWork-lite offering for small and medium companies.

But unlike Convene, WeWork is more of human capital play than a real estate play. For example, Rent the Runway, the online designer apparel and accessories subscription rental company that has raised $196 million since launching in NYC in 2009, wants to bring high-end fashion to the office. Rent the Runway is partnering with WeWork, setting up drop boxes at 15 WeWork locations in NYC, San Francisco, LA, Chicago, D.C. and Miami, and promoting the launch with temporary pop-up shops showcasing its clothes for rent at a few of the WeWork locations. This will provide Rent the Runway with valuable physical structural capital, enabling it to scale beyond its five current physical locations, as well as increase its convenience value proposition for customers, especially those with an unlimited subscription plan that currently need to return items via mail (cnbc.com). More importantly, it will provide Rent the Runway with access to WeWork's valuable membership base.

The Amazon Man: November 14, 2018

CBRE enters flexible office space market

CBRE Group, the world's largest real estate service firm, expects flex space to rise from 1% to 10% of the global office real estate market over the next few years. According to Knight Frank LLP's new survey of global companies with 3.5 million employees, this could be even higher as over half of them expect flexible space to account for at least 20% of their total office space versus 5% now (theedgemarkets.com). To meet this shift in demand, CBRE, which leases 1 billion square feet of office space for landlords, announced on October 31 that it is launching a new wholly owned subsidiary — Hana. Unlike WeWork, which leases office space from landlords and then sub-leases it to individuals and enterprises, Hana plans to partner directly with landlords to help them meet the demand from their enterprise tenants for flex space (ft.com).

WeWork raises another $3 billion from SoftBank — Could it be too big to fail?

Could WeWork be too big to fail? That's the interesting premise put forth by Andrew Ross Sorkin, the co-creator of *Billions*, one of my favourite shows, as well as the author of *Too Big to Fail.* In the event of an economic downturn, WeWork might have more bargaining power than its landlords as it has grown to the size where it holds so many leases in so many cities so they may be compelled to just renegotiate WeWork's lease agreements on more favourable terms or let WeWork act as a property manager (nytimes.com). And WeWork is set to become even bigger as it just raised $3 billion from **SoftBank** in the form of a warrant, providing it with a pre-IPO valuation of $42 billion. The warrant, which SoftBank will pay in two installments ($1.5 billion on January 15 and $1.5 billion on April 15) gives SoftBank the option to buy WeWork shares at a price of $110 before September 2019 (businessinsider.com). We note WeWork raised $1 billion from SoftBank in the form of a convertible bond in August and $4.4 billion in a private equity round in August 2017 that valued the company at $20 billion. Meanwhile, Ucommune, WeWork's main rival in China, has raised a $200 million Series D round, bringing its total funding since it was launched in Beijing in 2015 to $650 million. Ucommune operates 200 locations in 37 cities, mostly in China, but it also has an international presence in Hong Kong, NYC, Singapore and Taipei. Ucommune plans to use the proceeds to accelerate its international expansion growth to 350 cities in 40 countries (techcrunch.com).

The New Forms: November 20, 2018

WeWork partners with Arianna Huffington to create Rise and Thrive

WeWork is partnering with Arianna Huffington to create Rise and Thrive. The first step of the partnership is an immersive, all-day experience at WeWork's Rise by We in NYC on January 19 focused on how to keep well-being top of mind during the workday (wellandgood.com).

The Disappearance: December 4, 2018

WeWork reaches 500 locations in 96 cities around the world

WeWork, which now operates 500 locations in 96 cities around the world, is enhancing the functional value proposition for its members through strategic partnerships with start-ups such as Rent the Runway and now Sweetgreen to offer its members free delivery of healthy salads. This provides Sweetgreen with valuable structural capital (in the form of the 50 WeWork locations in seven cities that will be adding Sweetgreen at WeWork outposts) that will enable it to scale beyond its 89 physical restaurant locations as well as valuable customer capital in the form of WeWork's members which are looking for convenient healthy meal options (techcrunch.com). We note that Sweetgreen, which launched in DC in 2007, raised a $200 million Series H round in May.

Upscale co-working firms Second Home & NeueHouse raise the competitive bar

The emergence of upscale co-working firms like Second Home and NeueHouse is likely to raise the competitive bar for WeWork. Second Home, the creative workspace company, just raised £20 million, bringing its total funding since it was founded in London in 2014 to £61 million. Second Home is upping the game for co-working firms, by featuring luxury locations with gorgeous biophilic architecture and design that function as both leading cultural venues as well as workspaces with curated communities. Although Second Home only currently operates two locations in London and one in Lisbon, it is close to opening another two locations in London, one in Lisbon and two in LA, and it is likely to use the proceeds to expand further (techcrunch.com). Likewise, NeueHouse, an upscale co-working firm that describes itself as a "*private cultural and collaborative space for prominent creatives, artists and entrepreneurs*", just raised a $30 million venture round. NeueHouse also brought on a new CEO, Josh Wyatt, who was previously heading up the new boutique hotel business for upscale health club Equinox. NeueHouse plans to use the funds to expand from its current two locations in NYC and LA to two more locations in LA and is looking at San Francisco and Toronto, as well as medium-sized cities like Nashville and Texas (wsj.com).

Co-living spaces: the next big disruptor in hospitality

According to Ian Schrager, who pioneered the boutique hotel concept in 1984, the next big disruptor in hospitality is co-living spaces. Co-living spaces, which blur the distinction between residences and hotels, are being embraced as communes for digital nomads while critics label them as "dorms for adults" (skift.com). It's interesting as I actually experienced both worlds during my trip to NYC in September as I stayed for three nights at WeWork's WeLive and then spent the weekend at Ian Schrager's boutique Hudson Hotel. While I loved the complimentary social amenities offered by WeLive (happy hour, comedy night, round table dinner) and the communal environment, I have to admit I preferred the more luxurious ambience of the Hudson Hotel to the "dorm-like" feel of WeLive.

The Existential Threat: December 11, 2018

WeWork partners with American Express to drive its enterprise share

As further evidence of WeWork's intent to drive its enterprise share, WeWork has partnered with **American Express**. Starting in February 2019, Amex Business Platinum cardholders in the U.S. will receive a complimentary year of WeWork's Global Access membership. This virtual passport, which will give them unlimited access to WeWork's network of now over 500 locations in 96 cities around the world, has a value of $2,700 (businessinsider.com). We are starting to see the blurring of hospitality and co-working with the emergence of hospitality brands for Millennial digital nomads like Selina, which just raised $150 million to advance its mission to help travelers live, work and explore anywhere in the world. Selina operates 31 properties in Panama, Costa Rica, Columbia, Mexico, Guatemala, Nicaragua, Peru, Bolivia, Ecuador and Portugal that offer hostel-like lodging combined with co-working spaces. Interestingly, Adam Neumann, the co-founder of WeWork, participated in Sienna's $95 million venture round earlier this year in April.

Selina plans to use the proceeds to open 15 locations in the U.S. by the end of 2020 (skift.com).

The Letter: December 18, 2018

Could co-living be the next hot trend?

Just like co-working is transforming the office market, could co-living transform the residential real estate market? Medici Living Group, a PropTech company launched in Berlin in 2012, has received a €1 billion investment commitment over the next five years from **Corestate Capital Holding SA**. The proceeds will go toward developing 35 co-living properties across Europe with a combined 6,000 units under its QUARTERS brand, which currently operates three co-living properties in Chicago, New York and Berlin. Interestingly, Medici Group aspires to become the WeWork of co-living; however, WeWork launched its co-working arm, WeLive, in 2016 and currently operates two WeLive locations in NYC and D.C. (venturebeat.com). The bottom line is that just as office REITS are shifting toward space-as-a-service, residential REITs will need to figure out how to move up the customer and structural capital pyramids.

Riveter, Company and Life Time Work embracing new co-working models

Riveter, a co-working space exclusively for women launched in Seattle in 2017, has raised a $15 million Series A round. Riveter plans to use the proceeds to open eight new locations next year, more than doubling its physical footprint from its existing five locations in Seattle and LA, with the ambitious plans to reach 100 locations by 2022 (fastcompany.com). Company is introducing a new co-working model in which it brings together a curated base of tenants, whereby enterprises will pay a premium to be in close proximity to start-ups. The Milstein real estate family is backing Company's project, investing $150 million to redevelop its $1 billion office building at 335 Madison in Midtown Manhattan. To create a communal environment, 150,000 square feet is being allocated to shared amenities (e.g., restaurant, bar, 150-square-foot theatre, pop-up retail shops), 250,000 square feet will be leased to start-ups like Palantir at a subsidized rent of $65/square foot and 700,000 square feet will be leased to enterprises like **Facebook** at a premium rent of $100/square foot. In addition, Company is launching a $50 million venture fund to invest in the start-ups in its building (forbes.com). Since Bahram Akradi founded Life Time Fitness in Minneapolis in 1990, he has grown the company to 139 premier health clubs across the U.S with revenue expected to top $2 billion next year. In this fascinating interview with Gregg Schoenberg, he shares his vision to expand into co-working (Life Time Work) and co-living (Life Time Living) and bring everything together under one roof called Life Time Village. He has opened three Life Time Work locations this year, which include the added benefit of a health membership, and is looking to expand to 50–60 co-working locations (techcrunch.com). As evidence of how mainstream co-working has become, the Canadian government is apparently now exploring the concept of co-working spaces for its public service employees (cbc.ca).

The Smart Toilet: January 8, 2019

WeWork's disruptive threat to office ecosystem is finally being recognized

WeWork's disruptive threat to the office ecosystem is finally being recognized by the industry. As Tony Malkin, CEO of Empire

State Realty Trust Inc. states: "*...a lot of people originally thought of the shared office-space providers as bringing tenants...it's really much more about disrupting the relationship of tenants to landlords, of tenants to brokers, of brokers to landlords*". For example, to be able to capture more of the upside it brings to buildings through its ability to attract tenants, WeWork is now raising a separate real estate acquisition fund called ARK which puts it in competition with landlords. It is also starting to compete with brokers, collecting a fee from landlords from tenant referrals (yahoo.com). In addition, as evidence of its increasing focus on enterprise tenants, WeWork's enterprise membership share grew from 25% in Q2 to over 30%, and through its new initiatives such as Powered by We and HQ by We, combined with its upcoming strategic partnership with **American Express**, we expect WeWork will gain even more traction. We also expect niche co-working companies like The Wing will continue to gain traction. For example, The Wing, the female-co-working company that has grown to five locations with 6,000 members since it launched in 2015, has raised $75 million in a Series C round that includes strategic investors like WeWork and Airbnb. The Wing plans to use the proceeds to open new locations next year in West Hollywood, Chicago, Boston, Toronto, London and Paris (techcrunch.com).

The Community: January 16, 2019

WeWork plans for global domination as it re-brands to The We Company

As a result of market turbulence, **SoftBank** has decided to invest $2 billion in WeWork instead of the previously announced $16 billion. However, WeWork is not slowing down. As a signal of its intent to advance its total addressable market beyond office leasing, it is re-branding to The We Company, which as it states in its blog, "*bringing all of our business ambitions together to operate in service of how we work, how we live, and how we grow*" and its guiding mission will be "*to elevate the world's consciousness*" (wework.com/blog). As the ultimate evidence to our thesis that WeWork has always been more of a human capital play than a real estate play, the company just shared a slide from a pitch deck it put together back in 2009 titled, *The we brand companies* of which "*the we community social network is the backbone of all the we brand companies. By connecting members with diverse histories across geographic and socio-economic borders, we empower all of them to learn from each other, and to profit from each other's success*". As a testament to WeWork's plan for global domination, the we brand companies didn't just include we work and weLive, but also weSleep, weConnect and weBank (wework.com/blog).

WeWork makes a strategic investment in Laird Superfoods

WeWork Labs just led the $32 million venture round in Laird Superfoods, a health food company founded in 2015 which makes vegan and gluten-free non-dairy creamers, premium coffee and coconut water. The investment is strategic as WeWork plans to offer the products to its members and employees at select WeWork locations in NYC and sell them in its WeMRKT retail stores (fortune.com). Apparently, Adam Neumann, WeWork's CEO, broke his finger over the holidays in Hawaii when he was surfing with Laird Hamilton, the founder of Laird Superfoods and a famous big-wave surfer. Neumann's passion for surfing also played out back in mid-2016 when WeWork took a stake in Wavegarden, a maker of wave pools.

Jones Lang LaSalle embraces technology to improve tenant

experience

To compete with WeWork, real estate services firms are starting to ascend the customer and structural pyramids. For example, **Jones Lang LaSalle** is launching its JLL Curae Approach program. Through Curae, which translates to "*I care for*" in Latin, JLL hopes to help its landlords care better for their tenants by enabling them to offer experiential amenities for employees like yoga, wellness programs, social events and educational services. Landlords will also gain access to the HqO app, which will update and assist tenants on daily needs such as transportation alerts, smart building features and amenities. Interestingly, JLL is also launching JLL Marketplace for Tenants Program, an e-commerce site that enables tenants to take advantage of its buying power with **Office Depot**, who, along with JLL Spark, was a strategic investor in HqO's $6.6 million seed round in September (us.jll.com).

The Obsession: January 22, 2019

WeWork starts to show corporate governance red flags

A *WSJ* article exposing that WeWork's CEO, Adam Neumann, is buying properties and leasing them back to WeWork is raising corporate governance red flags at WeWork. To be fair, WeWork disclosed this conflict of interest in its debt offering prospectus back in April, stating: "*We have been since January 1, 2015, party to certain lease agreements with landlord entities in which Adam Neumann and certain of his immediate family members hold ownership interests.*" WeWork paid over $12 million in rent for these leases between 2016 and 2017 and future payments total over $110 million over the life of the leases. The other concern, also disclosed in the prospectus, is that Neumann controls over 65% of the total voting power for WeWork (wsj.com). WeWork faces increasing competition as Knotel is expanding its European presence through the acquisition of Deskeo, the largest co-working firm in Paris with 17 locations. This follows shortly after its acquisition of co-working firm Ahoy! Berlin last June. We note Knotel has raised $160 million since launching in NYC in 2015 and currently operates over 2 million square feet of co-working and flex office space in over 100 locations (techcrunch.com).

What If?: January 29, 2019

WeWork blurs lines between co-working and retail with launch of Made by We

WeWork is blurring the lines between co-working and retail with the launch of Made By We. The "town square"-like space at 902 Broadway in NYC's Flatiron District is open to the public and features a retail shop, coffee shop and co-working area. The retail shop is brilliant as it is an extension of the WeMRKT concept it debuted in June that leverages WeWork's customer capital by showcasing a select curation of products made by WeWork members. The co-working space offers 100 seats that you can book ahead of time (at a cost of $65 for the day) or on-demand (at a cost of $6 for the first 30 minutes and $0.20 per minute thereafter) and 6 conference rooms, costing $50–$125 per hour. WeWork will also use the space to host events focused on "*people who are shaping culture and influencing the modern workplace*" (curbed.com).

The Empowerment: February 13, 2019

Starbucks faces another disruptive new entrant in China: WeWork

Starbucks could soon come under attack on a second front — the experience front — as WeWork is flipping Starbucks' model in China — offering a third place — but with free coffee and paid space. Just a week after debuting on-demand office space booking at its new Made By We in NYC, WeWork is launching WeWork Go in China. Although I'm personally worried that opening up access to the public could take away from the sense of tribal belonging and community between members, it makes sense from a financial perspective. By providing pay-as-you-go access to its hot desks, WeWork will be able to increase the desk utilization rate at its existing locations, create a new free customer acquisition channel and expand its total addressable market. The new app operates via the WeChat mini program which enables people to check the occupancy rate of WeWork locations and then scan their QR code at the gate. During WeWork Go's pilot launch at its 18 locations in Shanghai the past three months, WeWork has received 50,000 registered visitors (techcrunch.com).

WeWork moves deeper into enterprise software and education

WeWork just acquired Euclid, a spatial analytics platform that tracks the identity and behaviour of people in the physical world. Although WeWork did not disclose the cost of the acquisition, we do not believe it is too material given Euclid had only raised a total of $44 million since it launched in 2010 in San Francisco, having last raised a $20 million Series C round three years ago. WeWork plans to test the platform internally and then integrate it into its "workplace insights" software analytics package to sell to enterprises. WeWork also continues to expand into the education space. Since the online graduate degree program provider **2U** partnered with WeWork last January, 10,000 of its students have signed up to gain access to WeWork. Now they are expanding the partnership to provide access to 2U's 2,000 faculty members and course administrators (fastcompany.com). We believe WeWork is going on the offense in China with its decision to open up its co-working locations to the public on a pay-as-you-go basis as a drought in VC funding and intense competition from deep-pocketed global giants like WeWork is leading to attrition in China. In China's first tier cities, co-working start-ups operate 520,000 desks, equating to 42 million square feet of office space. However, according to a report by the China Real Estate Chamber of Commerce, 40 start-ups in the shared-office sector vanished last year between January and October and 40% of co-working offices are more than half empty. For example, Kr Space, China's largest co-working firm with 3.2 million square feet of office space, hasn't been able to raise any capital since its $200 million venture round in May, so it is now being forced to cut staff and scale back its ambitious expansion plans to add 10,000 desks per month (scmp.com).

$USTAINABILITY: March 5, 2019

WeWork rival in China plans to IPO at $3 billion valuation

Ucommune, WeWork's main rival in China, plans to IPO on NASDAQ as early as Q3 at an expected $3 billion valuation. Since Ucommune launched in Beijing in 2015, it has raised $650 million and grown its operations to 200 locations in over 37 cities, mostly in China, but it also has an international presence in Hong Kong, NYC, Singapore and Taipei. Ucommune plans to accelerate its international expansion growth to 350 cities in 40 countries. Interestingly, by 2030, Ucommune expects co-working to comprise nearly 30% of office space (dealstreetasia.com).

The Scooters: March 13, 2019

Air Canada partners with WeWork

Air Canada is offering a complimentary WeWork Global Access membership to its +400,000 Business members, providing them with discounted access to WeWork's global network of over 600 co-working locations. The partnership makes sense as Air Canada flies to over 60 of the 100 cities around the world where WeWork has co-working offices (aircanada.mediaroom.com).

The Ubernomics Quake: March 19, 2019

WeWork launches food tech accelerator

WeWork is committing over $1 million to launch WeWork Food Labs, its new food tech accelerator open to early-stage start-ups focusing on the food tech ecosystem, ranging from AI to robotics to kitchen appliances to supply chain to ag tech. Beyond the normal WeWork amenities, the start-ups will have access to an R&D kitchen, pantry and storage, merchandising showcase and tasting table, event space, and even a podcast and photo studio. More importantly, they will gain access to a dedicated lab manager and WeWork's global member network (pymnts.com).

The Unicorns are Coming: March 26, 2019

The We Company is launching a "future cities" initiative

To advance its new aspirational mission to "*elevate the world's consciousness*", The We Company is launching a "future cities" initiative. It is being led by Di-Ann Eisnor, a former Google executive who spent over a decade as the Director of Growth at Waze. She will be in charge of leveraging the massive structural database that The We Company is building from the operations of its 600+ co-working locations in over 100 cities around the world (qz.com). Convene is transforming the retail space at Brookfield Place in lower Manhattan previously occupied by Saks Fifth Avenue (**Hudson's Bay Company**) into a hybrid office/hospitality space. Convene just signed a 10-year lease with plans to transform the 73,000 square feet into a space to host conferences, corporate meetings and cultural gatherings (bloomberg.com). Interestingly, **Brookfield Asset Management** was a strategic investor in Convene's $152 million Series D round in July.

The Two Flavours of Kool-Aid: April 2, 2019

WeWork's revenue doubled last year to $1.8 billion, but its losses also doubled, to $1.9 billion

WeWork's revenue doubled to $1.8 billion last year, but its exponential expansion led its losses to also double — to a staggering $1.9 billion. As new offices take 18 months to fill, it's not surprising that its occupancy rate fell to 84% from Q3 to 80% in Q4 as it opened a total of over 300 new locations in 2018. But with over $6 billion in cash sitting on its balance sheet, it doesn't look like WeWork is going to slow down anytime soon (wsj.com). And this looks even sweeter than my WeWork — the Belize Tourism Board is promoting the first over-the-water shared bungalow co-working space on a tiny island 10 miles off the coast of Belize (fastcompany.com).

Dr. Alexa: April 9, 2019

WeWork expands into office services

WeWork is expanding beyond office leasing to become the operating system for offices. WeWork is acquiring Managed by Q, the office services management platform that has raised $97 million since launching in NYC in 2013 (wsj.com). Although WeWork did not disclose what it paid, Managed by Q was valued at $249 million back in January when it raised a $25 million Series C round, of which **Oxford Properties Group** was a strategic investor. Managed by Q, which offers office services ranging from cleaning and maintenance to supply replenishment and wellness, will provide WeWork with valuable supplier capital for its own locations. More importantly, it will enable WeWork to expand its offering for its Powered by We office space-as-a-service division as well as its HQ by WeWork, a WeWork-lite offering for medium-sized companies.

A Different Species?: April 16, 2019

WeWork introducing co-branded WeWork Labs with Alibaba in China

WeWork is partnering with **Alibaba** Cloud in China to introduce eight co-branded WeWork Labs. WeWork Labs currently has over 50 locations in 32 cities in 15 countries (technode.com).

The Experience: May 2, 2019

The We Company confidentially files for IPO

The We Company (formerly known as WeWork) has confidentially filed for an IPO (techcrunch.com). The female co-working company, The Wing, is bringing its expertise in female-focused design sensibility and its brand to the corporate world, designing rooms for other companies (fastcompany.com).

The Rules: May 7, 2019

WeWork will soon be the largest office tenant in Chicago

Only four years after entering Chicago, WeWork is poised to become the city's largest office tenant. WeWork is planning to open two new locations, which will bring its footprint in Chicago to 13 locations with a total of 1.2 million square feet. It is already the biggest private office tenant in the cities of NYC, D.C. and London (therealdeal.com). In LA, WeWork is looking to "*democratize access to professional, high-end media and entertainment facilities for all creators*" with the opening of its new +45,000-square-foot hub in the Pacific Design Center. This WeWork is uniquely tailored for Hollywood, offering styling suites, casting rooms and four soundproof recording and editing rooms with state-of-the-art equipment (hollywoodreporter.com).

The Naked Unicorn: May 14, 2019

WeWork enters its first revenue-sharing agreement in the U.S.

WeWork has entered into its first revenue-sharing agreement in the U.S. WeWork is partnering with RXR Realty to manage

90,000 square feet of co-working space at 75 Rockefeller Plaza in NYC. Instead of leasing the space, WeWork will split the cost of renovations with RXR Realty and share the revenue. Apparently, one of WeWork's enterprise clients has agreed to lease the entire space, which is targeted to open this fall (crainsnewyork.com). It's interesting as RXR Realty just partnered with Airbnb to convert the top third of this office building into Airbnb units.

The Lines: May 22, 2019

Office and retail real estate becomes less bond-like as lease duration declines

According to MSCI, the average commercial real estate lease duration in the U.K. has declined by one-third since 2002, with the average lease duration declining for offices from 12.5 to 8.4 years and for retail from 14.8 to 9.4 years. This is leading to a reduction in the stability of cash flows, reducing the financial leverage capacity and changing the investment profile for commercial real estate from bond-like to equity-like risk/return characteristics (ft.com).

The We Company's revenue soars 113% in Q1 as it preps for IPO with launch of $2.9 billion ARK fund

The We Company's revenue soared 113% to $728 million in Q119, mainly driven by the 111% growth in its customer base to 466,000 members. However, it is still unprofitable as its net loss was $264 million (cnbc.com). Now The We Company is now directly in competition with landlords. The We Company is launching a $2.9 billion real estate investment fund called ARK to manage its growing real estate investment portfolio in partnership with Ivanhoe Cambridge, a real estate subsidiary of La Caisse de Depot, which is investing $1 billion in ARK.

ARK's real estate portfolio will comprise $1.8 billion portfolio of buildings owned by WeWork Property Advisors, which includes the iconic Lord & Taylor's century-old former flagship luxury department store on Fifth Avenue in NYC that WeWork acquired from **Hudson's Bay Company** for $850 million in October 2017. In addition, to resolve conflict of interest concerns prior to its IPO, The We Company's CEO, Adam Neumann, is selling ARK his property interests at cost. As the company disclosed in its debt offering prospectus a year ago: "*WeWork paid over $12 million in rent for these leases between 2016 and 2017 and future payments total over $110 million over the life of the leases*". To further resolve any conflicts of interest, ARK will be governed by an independent investment committee, co-led by Wendy Silverstein (former CEO of New York REIT) (therealdeal.com).

Equinox partners with Industrious, Accor enters co-working, Taco Bell opens pop-up hotel

We are seeing the increasing blurring of hospitality, leisure and office space with Equinox's new partnership with Industrious to offer co-working alongside its upscale fitness clubs. The first project is at Hudson Yards in NYC where Industrious will offer 44,000 feet of co-working space on two floors of the same 72-storey building hosting Equinox's new lifestyle hotel. The two plan to partner on projects in several other major cities (wsj.com). We note that Industrious, which operates 76 flex workspace locations in 42 cities across the U.S., has raised $142 million since launching in NYC in 2013. **Accor SA** is also expanding beyond hospitality, with the launch of its Wojo co-working brand. Accor will roll out 150 "Wojo Spots" across its hotels in Paris and Lyon this summer with the goal to reach 1,000 across Europe by 2022. The "Wojo Spots", which are essentially just secure Wi-Fi connections, will enable Accor to capitalize on its structural capital by offering a monthly subscription for people to work out of the bars, restaurants and lobbies of its hotels. It will also launch 100 dedicated "Wojo Corners" co-working spaces by 2022 across a broad range of its hotels as well as train stations, airports and shopping malls. And its last offering, "Wojo Sites", are standalone WeWork-like co-working locations, which it is developing in partnership with real estate developer Bouygues Immobilier (**Bouygues**). Accor, which currently operates 10 "Wojo Sites", plans to have 50 open by 2022 (businesstraveller.com). We are seeing further blurring in real estate as Taco Bell (**Yum! Brands**) is opening a "taco oasis" pop-up hotel in Palm Springs in August. "The Bell" will offer fans an immersive fun and flavourful brand experience with themed guest rooms, sauce packet floaties in the pool, a gift shop with exclusive Taco Bell-themed apparel and, of course, a Taco Bell restaurant (cnbc.com).

The Membership Economy: May 28, 2019

Life Time Village offers working out, living and co-working under one roof

Bahram Akradi, the founder of Life Time Fitness, is bringing to life his vision for Life Time Village as he looks to appeal to Millennials searching for apartments that offer a health club and co-working space under one roof. In Dallas, Life Time is opening a 390-unit Life Time Living health-focused residential experience that is attached to a 190,000-square-foot Life Time Fitness and a 50,000-square-foot Life Time Work space (bisnow.com). We note that The We Company is also blurring the real estate lines as it expands beyond WeWork (co-working) to WeLive (co-living) and WeRise (health club).

The Strategic Map: June 4, 2019

Knotel launches furniture subscription rental; WeWork looks to raise $2.75 billion in debt

Knotel, a flex space and office design company that has raised $160 million since launching in NYC in 2015, is launching a furniture subscription rental service. Knotel used to sell tenants its own pre-fab modular furniture line called Geometry as part of a package deal. Now, to offer its tenants a greater level of convenience and variety of choice, Knotel is renting them its Geometry furniture for a monthly fee (fastcompany.com). We're wondering if designing its own line of furniture to rent to its HQ by WeWork and Powered By We space-as-a-service enterprise clients could be a further option for The We Company to leverage its customer capital and expand its total addressable market. We note The We Company is apparently in talks with banks to raise $2.75 billion in debt ahead of its IPO (reuters.com).

About the Author

Barbara Gray is a former top-ranked sell-side Equity Analyst and the founder of Brady Capital Research Inc., a leading-edge investment research firm focused on structural disruption. Her two decades of sell-side equity research experience, combined with her creative ability to piece together emerging structural disruption trends, enables Barbara to come up with unique insights for her institutional investment and corporate clients.

She is recognized as a leading expert in structural disruption and was invited to be the keynote speaker at a number of events, including the 2018 annual conference for one of Canada's leading investment firms and the 2017 Investment Advisory Committee meeting for a top Canadian Crown corporation. Barbara is a Chartered Financial Analyst (CFA) and graduated from the University of British Columbia with a Bachelor of Commerce in Finance. She is also the author of *Secrets of the Amazon 2.0* (2018), *Secrets of the Amazon* (2017) and *Ubernomics* (2016).

Barbara lives in Vancouver, Canada with her husband and two sons. You can follow her on Twitter at @barbcfa, reach her on LinkedIn or email her at barb@bradycap.com.

Disclosure

I, Barbara Gray, certify that the views expressed in this book accurately reflect my personal views about the subject company (ies). I am confident in my investment analysis skills, and I may buy or already own shares in those companies under discussion. I also certify that I have not and will not be receiving direct or indirect compensation from the subject company(ies) in exchange for publishing this commentary.

The author holds a long position in Amazon (AMZN-NASDAQ), Facebook (FB-NASDAQ), Farfetch (FTCH-NYSE), lululemon athletica (LULU-NASDAQ), Spotify Technology (SPOT-NYSE), Stitch Fix (SFIX-NASDAQ), Tesla (TSLA-NASDAQ), Uber Technologies (UBER-NYSE) and Zillow Group (Z-NASDAQ) and a short position in Lyft (LYFT-NASDAQ).

This investment analysis excludes any target price, and is not a recommendation to buy or sell a stock. It is intended to provide a means for the author to share his experience and perspective exclusively for the benefit of the clients of Brady Capital Research Inc. The book may contain statements and projections that are forward-looking in nature, and therefore subject to numerous risks, uncertainties, and assumptions. The author does not assume any liability whatsoever for any direct or consequential loss arising from or relating to any use of the information contained in this note.

This information contained in this commentary has been

compiled from sources believed to be reliable but no representation or warranty, express or implied, is made by the author or any other person as to its fairness, accuracy, completeness or correctness.

This book does not constitute an offer or solicitation in any jurisdiction.

www.ingramcontent.com/pod-product-compliance
Lightning Source LLC
Chambersburg PA
CBHW022101210326
41518CB00039B/356

* 9 7 8 1 9 9 9 4 8 8 4 2 0 *